British Power Boat Company MTB

<small>DESIGNED BY BRITISH POWER BOAT COMPANY, POOLE, DORSET</small>

Displacement: 47 tons
Length Overall: 71 1/2'
Beam: 19 1/4'
Engines: Three Packard 1,250 hp (later 1,500 hp) and one Ford auxillary
Top Speed: 41 knots
Armament: Varied, but generally included two 18" torpedo tubes, two two-pound pom poms (later six-pound), twin 20mm Oerlikons, twin Vickers .303 machine guns

Fairmile 'D' MTB/MGB

<small>DESIGNED BY FAIRMILE MARINE COMPANY, COBHAM, SURREY</small>

Displacement: 95 tons (as MTB), 90 tons (as MGB), 105 tons (as combined MTB/MGB)
Length Overall: 115'
Beam: 21 1/4'
Engines: Four Packard 1,500 hp
Top Speed: 31 knots
Armament: Varied, but generally included four 18" torpedo tubes, two six-pound pom poms, one twin 20mm Oerlikon, two twin .5" Mk Vs, two twin .303" machine guns

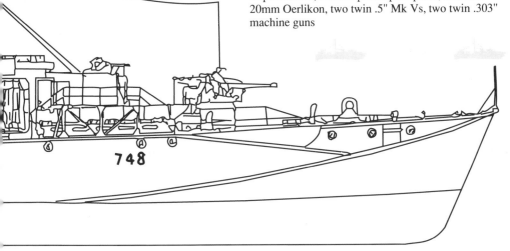

Champagne
NAVY

by the same authors

Brian Nolan
HERO: The Buzz Beurling Story
KING'S WAR: Mackenzie King and the Politics of War,
1939–1945

Brian Jeffrey Street
THE PARACHUTE WARD: A Canadian Surgeon's Wartime
Adventures in Yugoslavia

Champagne
NAVY
Canada's Small Boat Raiders of the Second World War

BRIAN NOLAN
BRIAN JEFFREY STREET

Random House
Toronto

Canadian Cataloguing in Publication Data

Nolan, Brian
    Champagne navy : Canada's small boat raiders of the Second World War

Includes bibliographical references.
ISBN 0-394-22141-9

1. World War, 1939-1945—Naval Operations, Canadian. I. Street, Brian Jeffrey,
1955-   . II. Title.

D779.C2N6 1991   940.54′5971   C91-093993-4

Jacket Design: Brant Cowie/ArtPlus Limited
Maps and Endpaper Illustrations: A.L. Stachiw/Trident Products

Printed and bound in Canada by John Deyell Company

To All Those Who Served in Small Boats

Contents

raid *n. & v.* **1.** Sudden attack made by military party, ship(s), or aircraft; predatory incursion in which surprise and rapidity are usu. relied upon, foray... **4.** Hence ~'ER[1] *n.*

The Concise Oxford Dictionary, Sixth Edition

Introduction

Motor torpedo boats and motor gunboats were the smallest fighting craft in the Royal Canadian Navy during the Second World War. To be accurate they should be referred to as ships, but the crews who manned them invariably called them boats. For example, the 71½-foot British Power Boat Company MTBs and MGBs were known as "shorts," or "short boats." The 115-foot Fairmile MTBs and MGBs designed by the Fairmile Marine Company were known as "Ds" or "Dog boats." The vernacular was not only used by the crews but also appeared regularly in official navy records and documents (nor was the practice exclusively British or Canadian: the Americans called their fast-attack craft Patrol Boats, or PTs). And, of course, they were designated as either His Majesty's Motor Torpedo *Boat* or Motor Gun *Boat* (italics added). Accordingly, we have chosen to use the description "boats" rather than ships more often than not. We hasten to add the authors do know the difference between a boat and a ship.

A word, too, about the German fast-attack craft. They were known as "E-boats," although the term is considered imprecise among academic historians. In fact, E-boat—a shortened version of "Enemy War Boat"—described a variety of little ships. The equivalent of the Canadian MTB was the *Schnellboot* (the plural of which is *Schnellboote*), called "S-boats" by their crews and numbered as such. These varied in length, from an 81-foot prototype built in 1930 to a 115-foot model mass produced in 1943 and

1944. In addition to S-boats were a number of larger craft known as *Räumboote*, or R-boats, which were similar to Allied motor launches (MLs). They were used during the war for such duties as coastal convoy protection, minelaying, minesweeping and air-sea rescue operations.

However, the Royal Navy and RCN (as well as the press and the public) evidently preferred the term "E-boat" when describing all enemy fast-attack craft. We have followed the practice except where it is felt more detailed descriptions will assist the reader's comprehension. There are several reasons for adopting the wartime custom. For one thing, among skippers and crews "E-boat" was generally intended to mean S-boats. In hindsight, the term has certain advantages. It was often relied upon when the distinction between S-boats and R-boats either could not be determined at the time of an engagement by one of its participants, or had been forgotten.

In describing battle action we have relied on official documents, including action reports (which were usually written within hours of an engagement), and the monthly reports of proceedings composed by flotilla commanders. For some of these actions we have sought the personal recollections of individuals who took part in them. All such sources have been checked for accuracy wherever possible.

Still, the events described happened nearly half a century ago, and so many of them were of the heart-stopping variety. Thus it is worth pointing out that our narrative includes a number of accounts which the modern-day reader may find too incredible, but which the participants assure us are true.

We would like to express our appreciation to the following: first of all, to Stephanie Chamberlain, for her diligent research on our behalf; to Cameron Graham and Douglas Steubing, for their timely assistance; and to Florence Smythe, whose watchful eye for detail proved itself again on several occasions.

The staffs of the National Defence Headquarters Library and Directorate of History in Ottawa (DHist) were particularly helpful despite many demands made of them. The same must be said of Janet Dimock of the Canadian Armed Forces Photographic Unit, and Diane Martineau and her colleagues with the Collections Consultation Unit, Documentary Art and Photography Division, National Archives of Canada, whose courtesy and zeal especially will not be forgotten.

We are indebted to Donald Graves of DHist, for his considered comments regarding a late draft of the manuscript.

Douglas Pepper, Executive Editor at Random House of Canada, was a continuing source of enthusiasm and encouragement.

Finally, we would like to express our gratitude to all the veterans of Coastal Forces, too numerous to mention, whose advice and co-operation made this book possible.

Brian Nolan   Brian Jeffrey Street
The Homestead, West Quebec   Ottawa, Ontario

"Then came the war, old sport. It was a great relief, and I tried very hard to die, but I seemed to bear an enchanted life."

F. Scott Fitzgerald, *The Great Gatsby*

Prologue

Life on the Ocean Wave

I N SEPTEMBER 1939, the British nation rose to defend its shores, finally recognizing that Adolf Hitler's intentions of conquest really did mean *"die ganze Welt"*—the whole world. In the early days of the war, a small part of that tentative defence lay in the hands of the Royal Navy's long-neglected Coastal Forces. Commanded by a handful of professional sailors, Coastal Forces' obsolete and sometimes leaky collection of motor boats and river launches were manned by groups of hastily assembled reservists who made their way to the tiny fishing ports and tidal estuaries of the English Channel. The only experience these citizen-sailors brought with them was the knowledge gained as weekend yachtsmen who madly believed Kenneth Grahame's dictum that there was absolutely nothing so marvellous as messing about in small boats. Their ineptness was sorrowful. Plagued by administrative chaos, poorly-maintained and obsolescent equipment and weaponry, Coastal Forces in those early months of the conflict deservedly, if regrettably, earned the disparaging description "Costly Farces."

Early wartime propaganda was put to use on film and in print by authorities in an attempt to counter the image, but the information merely served to heighten awareness of the amateurishness of the troubled force. If audiences and readers were to believe the propagandists' cant, these former Sunday sailors were all named Derek, Trevor or Roger, and they all owned Morgan roadsters, which took them from the docks at dawn to the arms of their women, invariably named Daphne, Cynthia or Penelope, peaches-and-cream creatures in smocks of printed flowers who waited in open doors of thatched cottages.

No matter. In those first months, heroic images and words were effective weapons to reassure a fearful and disconsolate population, no one word more deliciously delivered than Winston Churchill's ludicrous pronunciation of the Third Reich's National Socialists as "naw-zees." It struck the British as terribly funny, exactly what the fireplug war-horse had intended. Humour, too, could be a weapon in the race to buy time until these amateur Englishmen could shed their slapstick image of the British music hall. This they had done in time to carry out the miraculous evacuation of the British Expeditionary Force from the beaches of Dunkirk in late May and early June of 1940.

In time, Coastal Forces grew into a formidable fleet of motor torpedo and motor gunboats, menacing the enemy on the shores of the Channel, the Mediterranean and along the coasts of the Aegean and Adriatic seas. In southern Asia too, small boats ranged the Indian Ocean from Java to Sumatra, from Malaya to Burma. And from the very beginning, it was this hit-and-run navy and its unique brand of warring that attracted Canadian fighting sailors, most of whom served as Royal Canadian Navy Volunteer Reservists, the RCNVR, the "wavy-navy," so-called because of the undulating pipings of rank on their sleeves which differed from the "straight-stripes" of regulars in the RCN and Royal Navy. Canadians served in various RN flotillas until February 1944, at which time they formed two all-Canadian flotillas, the 29th and the 65th, to operate in the English Channel and commanded a third flotilla, the 56th, which roamed the Mediterranean, the Aegean and the Adriatic.

It was never entirely clear why small-boat warfare attracted so many Canadians. Malcolm "Mac" Knox, who skippered Motor Torpedo Boat *743* in the 65th Flotilla, suggested it was their empathy for "open spaces and the out-of-doors." That's partly true since all the gun crews operated on open decks and the officers conned the boats from exposed bridges. But the kind of fighting they did and the tactics they employed were characteristically un-Canadian. Victory in battle was almost always achieved by stealth, deception (flying false colours was common) and strict adherence to a primal instinct for survival reminiscent of the American wild West—shoot first and ask questions later, a principle that sometimes produced disastrous results. Because attacks were carried out at night and at high speed with only mere yards separating their boats from the enemy's, Canadian crews sometimes killed each other by mistake. This piratical way of life that was more akin to the buccaneers of the Spanish Main than it was to modern naval warfare attracted Canadians from every walk of life. There were labourers, tradesmen, middle-class citizens, sons of the rich mercantile families and bona fide bluebloods. In the vanguard were graduates of Canada's old-line universities of McGill, Queen's, the universities of Toronto and British Columbia, as well as members of the alumni of the private schools of Ontario's Little Big Four, Upper Canada College, Ridley, St. Andrew's and Trinity colleges. They were among the very first to enlist, a few shamelessly using family connections to pull strings to get into uniform. Alex Joy had no compunction calling on his family's old-boy network to pass his medical. Turned down twice, first for poor eyesight and later for what was thought to be a heart murmur, Joy arranged through his grandfather, the dean of the school of medicine at U. of T., to take a private medical, the results of which were sent to the doctor who originally turned Joy down. "Oh, hell," said the importuned doctor, "you're in!"

Membership in the once clannish RCYC, Toronto's Royal Canadian Yacht Club, didn't hurt Joy's chances, or others' either. The truth was that some recruits who were junior members of other exclusive yacht clubs across the country promoted the suggestion that since they were already gentlemen, they probably qualified to be officers, a position that nearly backfired for one eager recruit. This was Jack McClelland, who in post-war years earned the unique distinction of being both the *enfant terrible* and the doyen of Canadian publishing as the flamboyant head of McClelland and Stewart, the publishers. At his interview to see whether he would become a probationary sub-lieutenant, he was asked by an admiral on the panel, "Have you been sailing all your life?" McClelland replied, "No sir, just since I was about five years old."

Interestingly too, young Americans of the landed aristocracy were similarly attracted to the U.S. Navy's PT boat squadrons, the equivalent of Britain's and Canada's motor torpedo and motor gunboat flotillas. Young Jack Kennedy of Harvard and the youthful raconteur Alfred Vanderbilt were counted among the recruits who came from some of America's socially prominent families. But unlike the Canadians who got to train at cold, wind-swept ports along the Channel, many of the Ivy Leaguers trained either at Melville Island in Narragansett Bay close to their ancestral homesteads in Rhode Island and Massachusetts, or at Florida's Biscayne Bay near their families' wintering grounds at Palm Beach.

For both Canadians and Americans, part of the attraction of the small boats was a distinct likelihood of early command. By the end of 1943, hundreds of boats were being commissioned in dozens of boatyards in England and Scotland. It stood to reason they'd need skippers. That's what twenty-one-year-old Charles Chaffey reasoned. When he had tried enlisting in 1940 as a fighter pilot, Chaffey was told "they were all full up for the rest of the war." He volunteered for MTBs, which he believed offered him the chance to do "his own thing." Eventually he did, as commanding officer of MTB *465* in the 29th Flotilla.

Naturally the navy tried to discourage individual behaviour, as did the RAF and the RCAF brass in dealing with their fighter pilots, most notably so in the case of George "Buzz" Beurling, the brilliant loner in air combat. Authorities failed to harness the lanky Canadian ace, but they marginally succeeded in taming the exuberant skippers of the small boats. Teamwork, not individualism, was stressed in the wartime fleets.

Scott Young, the newspaperman who served as an information officer in the RCNVR, found his copy censored when he wrote that "the work of Coastal Forces gives infinitely more opportunities for individual thinking than any other single branch of the navy." Even if that sentiment was true, the navy was never willing to admit it. The sentence referring to individualism was excised from Young's battle-front report to the folks back home.

The fact was that survival in small-boat warfare demanded quick, decisive judgement and a full measure of courage and unfailing nerves. The old maxim of he who hesitates is lost was never truer than in the little ships. It separated the quick from the dead. Those who developed versatility in their thoughts and actions were the survivors. Although it seemed a contradiction that the colourful skippers operated differently than normal naval procedure dictated, teamwork in battle was the key factor in nearly every successful action.

It was fair to say, too, that these citizen-volunteers who made up the bulk of the fighting crews reflected a spirit of independence not always evident in the personalities of the regulars, especially at the staff level. It wasn't that the reservists so much defied authority but rather that they learned to live with the dreary "square-bashing," King's Regulations & Admiralty Instructions, and the confining regimentation of service life. Sanity had to be retained at any cost. Take the case of Al Morton, who was tactful enough to "dress ship" in leaving port to salute the commanding officer, but found irresistible the temptation to bid farewell by blasting a lively rendition of "Life on the Ocean Wave" by loudspeaker towards shore. The Canadians were cheeky. There was an air of irreverence about them, an air of the mischievous schoolboy. At the top of the class was the impish and irrepressible Cornelius "Corny" Burke, who became a legendary fighter in the famous 56th Flotilla in the Mediterranean and Adriatic. The son of the president of Boeing Aircraft in Canada, Burke was seldom restrained by regulations, even at the beginning of his career. Heading overseas as a newly minted sub-lieutenant, Burke decided to smuggle his recent bride aboard the troop-ship assigned to take him to England, a feat

Burke accomplished by bribing a transportation officer with a
bottle of Scotch. Later, when he had become a masterful tactician
in small-boat warfare, Burke demonstrated with humour his displeasure at having to attend lectures by less experienced officers
on the subject of attack manoeuvres. He'd produce the snake
charmer's flute he always carried and, sitting cross-legged in the
back of the room, monotonously tootle the following refrain:

> *They don't wear pants*
> *In the hootchie-kootchie dance*
> *They just wear tights*
> *And they take them off at nights.*

His antics involved the enemy as well. Once in a night attack on a
small German-held port on the west coast of Yugoslavia, Burke
momentarily broke off the action to flash a signal towards the
enemy. Slowly the Aldis lamp clicked out the letters:
   "H-E-I-L (pause) C-H-U-R-C-H-I-L-L!"
   The collective antics of the 56th, like its members, were celebrated ones in the Adriatic campaign, especially when it came to
an accounting of the captured spoils of war. Its prizes seized in
battle included a sumptuous villa, a magnificently engineered
Italian sports car, a full orchestra and two tons of goulash.
   Curiously, while the torpedo and gunboat warriors maintained a
no-holds-barred philosophy in matters of battle and booty, they
developed a more magnanimous attitude of *noblesse oblige* for the
enemy, sometimes stopping to rescue survivors of the very boats
they had blasted out of the water, on at least one occasion to the
startled apprehension of a rescued German sailor. Knox recalled
pulling a number of survivors from the English Channel following
a short, fierce engagement. The first German hauled aboard struggled to jump back in the water when he was confronted by Knox's
cook, who suddenly appeared on deck wielding a huge butcher
knife. The German reasoned his throat was going to be slit, or
worse. "Finally someone got the point across it [the knife] wasn't
going to be used on his throat or his balls," Knox laughed. The

cook had been ordered to cut off the Germans' uniforms because they were drenched in oil. Tom Fuller, a distinguished gunboat fighter, was equally unresentful when it came to the question of survivors. Fuller, a wealthy Ottawa construction magnate, had joined the navy at age thirty-two, becoming known as "Gramps" by his various crews since everyone was in his early to mid-twenties. Coming upon a German submarine that had foundered, Fuller discovered that among the survivors was the sub's cook.

"Through my torpedo officer we interviewed the cook," Fuller remembered. "He decided he'd rather join the Royal Navy than be a prisoner of war. So we signed him on as Able Seaman 'Jock MacPherson' and put him on the payroll."

The bond that developed between the Canadian and German sailors was nothing less than extraordinary. When the 29th and 65th Flotillas held a reunion at Toronto's Royal York Hotel in 1989, the Canadian Coastal Forces Veterans Association invited as one of its guest speakers Harro Garmsen, a former crew member of a *Schnellboot*, the German version of the torpedo boat. Garmsen, who was warmly received, told his former enemies that since emigrating to Canada he had been asked to join the Royal Canadian Naval Reserve in Halifax, with the same rank he had held in the Kreigsmarine, and that he was also a member of the mess of HMCS *Unicorn* in Saskatoon.

Garmsen greeted his former belligerents with the words, "So... you were the ones."

In truth, there were many similarities in both the Canadian and German fast-attack navies afloat or ashore, especially their partiality for strong drink. In both services, Canadian and German sailors were known to take more than a little sherry at Christmas. Hal Lawrence, a much decorated sea-dog who, carrying a sabre and wearing only undershorts once captured a U-boat, succinctly summed up the drinking habits of all navies and all sailors. Asked if he had ever drunk Devon cider, he replied, "I must have. I drank everything else." For Corny Burke this included one of the more esoteric concoctions called a Black Velvet, a potent mixture of Guinness stout and champagne.

No less exotic were some of the nicknames the Canadians invented for one another. "Guns," "Daddy Bones" and "The Brain" were just a few among many of the sobriquets that made them sound like characters from a 1940s cops-and-robbers radio drama, even more so when James Kirkpatrick, "The Brain," who commanded the 65th Flotilla, persisted in using the phrase "calling all cars, calling all cars," on the radio-telephone when rounding up his boats.

All these diversions, of course, were ways to balance constant fear and the threat of death. Mortality was never to be discussed. Anyone showing signs of cracking under the pressure was quietly moved to less dangerous duty without recrimination. Officers especially had to lead by example, even the padre. Knox recalled inviting two padres along on one operation. It was the first and last time. "As soon as anything like action was joined," Knox said, "this one gentleman was down on his knees with his prayer beads in his hands. It wasn't exactly setting the best example for some of the crew."

Death was simply the luck of the draw. "You have to be lucky, or a good Presbyterian and figure that your number hasn't been called, that life is pre-ordained," Knox said.

The ruddy-faced McClelland concurred. "You really couldn't be sure you would still be alive the next day, or even that night," he remembered. "Not a minute of your life was wasted. If you weren't out getting laid, you were scrounging food, or booze. You were always doing something."

It was doubtful that young Canadians on the eve of war had even the remotest understanding what catastrophic, boring or absurd experiences lay ahead when they volunteered. They were members of the swing generation who went to war in flannel bags, corrupted, said the puritans, by jive and the jitterbug; the generation who discovered that the mysticism of war was the ultimate journey, the ultimate trip so personally intense they've never been capable of forgetting it. They made the journey as members of what someone has called the greatest club in the world, the navies of Canada and Britain in their best vintage years, and which, like the very best champagne vintage of France, might be described as the champagne navy, a sentiment they would view with cynical humour, best summed up by Jack McClelland. Watching a documentary about the torpedo and gunboat war at that 1989 reunion, the rumpled tough-guy publisher-turned-literary agent growled in his best stage aside, "It's all unmitigated bullshit, you know!"

But it wasn't. The story of their deeds and actions, had there been no eyewitnesses, would sorely test the most credulous of listeners.

1

To the Narrow Seas

I T WAS THE FIRST great thrill of a night action, according to one veteran of small-boat warfare. "Suddenly there is a dark spot, half-seen, half-imagined. The binoculars sweep away from it and back again—yes, there it is—a ship—and another. Those are enemy ships."

Finding the enemy in the English Channel was not always a simple task, and as often as not it was unexpected. But when contact was made, short, explosive sea battles invariably followed, battles familiar to listeners of the BBC, which frequently opened its radio broadcasts with the phrase, "Last night our Light Coastal Forces..." In the long and bitter struggle to keep supply routes open and to deny the enemy use of the English Channel, the small-boat sailors were involved in hundreds of these fantastic shoot-ups—although few were as outrageous or spectacular as Tommy Fuller's one-man night action against an enemy convoy in the summer of 1942.

Fuller, a lieutenant in the RCNVR on loan to the Royal Navy, was commanding one of three motor gunboats in a unit based at Dover. According to Lt. M. Bray, RNVR, aboard the Senior Officer's boat that night, they had just completed a routine mine-laying operation off the coast of France when they saw the enemy. There, steaming northbound in two columns, was a convoy of some twenty-two vessels including flak trawlers and as many as eight E-boats.

Bray's account does not say as much but presumably the convoy was engaged before the unit made a hasty retreat, "chased by the usual assortment of whizzbangs, tracers and starshells." It was not an uncommon tactic to rush astern of a convoy and once there, far enough away from the umbrella of light, gather unseen before going in to resume an attack. But in the confusion, Fuller was left behind. Bray said it was likely engine trouble. "Over in the distance we saw a terrific concentration of fire," he added, "all of which seemed to be directed on one spot where we thought we could see a boat." There was only one conclusion. " 'Poor old Tom,' we said. 'He's had it. There won't be anything left by the time we get there.' " Moments later, the telegraphist interrupted with a signal from Fuller. "Having lots of fun," it read, "come and join us!"

Incredibly, Fuller's version of what happened that night gives no hint of engine trouble and, in fact, suggests he was left behind deliberately. It is difficult to accept this part of his story. For one thing, the unit's Senior Officer, Lt. G. D. K. Richards, DSC, was widely regarded as one of the most daring and courageous of skippers. Fuller also states that the unit was sent out from Dover to intercept this convoy, using co-ordinates provided by radar operators at Dover Castle, but he was speaking from personal recollection almost fifty years after the fact and without any supporting documentation such as an action report. Bray's account, on the other hand, was obtained during the war and seems the more reliable.

Whatever happened, either by accident or by choice, the fact remains Fuller found himself single-handedly engaging the convoy. Moreover, his signal to the Senior Officer's boat was typical of him. Instinctively piratical and brash to the point of insulting even his superiors, he had earned a reputation both at sea and on land as a maverick colonial, "definitely of the two-gun variety," according to one former naval officer, who admitted his fellow Canadian was amongst the most effective of the small-boat skippers.

The latter was certainly true on this night. Fuller did perhaps the last thing the enemy would have expected in the circumstances. He throttled open the MGB's huge Packard engines and charged headlong down the middle of the convoy, his gunners firing in both directions. If he'd had them, Fuller might have shouted, "Damn the torpedoes!" as he went, merely for its dramatic effect. Brandishing a sabre or cutlass might have been still more appropriate. There was no need for either. His attack was Hollywood enough already.

Soon the enemy guns were answering, but Fuller's boat was moving too fast. He pressed on, still firing, while behind him the sky was ablaze with crazy patterns of multi-coloured light. The enemy ships continued to blast away, but now that he was no longer in their midst, they were blindly hammering away at each other, with sufficiently lethal effect that Fuller—once he had cleared the end of the convoy—disengaged completely. "We'll let them shoot it out," he announced as he broke off the attack. It was a good night's hunting when the enemy did the rest of his job for him.

Fuller was awarded the Distinguished Service Cross for his "skill, bravery and resolution" in that night's action. Put another way, his attack was a combination of colossal arrogance, inexplicable fearlessness and outright insanity. That he survived was due largely to his "who dares, wins" attitude in life generally, and the unbelievable good luck that sometimes comes with the element of surprise. Even so, his own gunners chided him shortly after the battle: "Twenty-two to one—bit heavy in the way of odds, don't you think?"

Fuller's reply, if one was expected, is not known. But it was understood that regardless of the odds, it was their job to engage the enemy. "Only one thing redeemed the night's work, the resolution to attack," said Peter Dickens, a legendary MTB skipper who also wrote one of the half-dozen or so classic accounts of small-boat warfare. "There must be no shirking the issue since our flotilla existed for no other purpose." Son of a famous admiral (and grandson of the great British author), Dickens had the background to appreciate and accept this rough code. But others willingly accepted the "unrelieved, lip-biting, white-knuckled woe" of toiling in the Channel with only the thought of meeting E-boats to keep them going. Indeed, they were gleefully prepared to meet the enemy. "If ever a group of people were keen," remembered Cornelius Burke, "we were. We all wanted to fight!" He attributed this to the traditions of the Royal Navy, which somehow imbued men with an aggressive if not ruthless fighting spirit, "without actually saying very much." The fervour of Nelson and Drake was palpable in all they did, even if the navy brass sometimes had its doubts. To them the Coastal Forces spoke only of "flashy fast craft, piratical young officers and scruffy men, who dashed in small units at great speed all over the ocean and away from the restraining hand of authority, to indulge in who could tell what abhorrent deviations from the conventional norms of discipline," remembered Dickens, with transparent disdain. Sure, they felt a romantic pull to the navy's powerful narrow-hulled speedboats. And so what if discipline sometimes fell short of the Admiralty's expectations? "Bravest by far, I thought," said one scribe who accompanied the Canadians later in the war, "were these kids—they were all so young—to whom action in a form that held all the close combat risk of the aerial dogfight or the infantry assault was almost a daily diet." Their sole function, as one of them saw it, was to go out "looking for trouble" on the war's high seas. If, in the course of finding it, the result was casualties or boats so badly shot up they were often unrecognizable, so be it. "You realize what your duty is and it becomes unthinkable to do anything less," remembered Burke. That duty, he said, was to "engage the enemy and to close."

This determined confidence was not borne without some difficulty. Too often, it had to be admitted, especially in the earliest days of the war, men had "stood forth for mortal combat against the foe, with an ardent desire to get at him but with woolly thoughts on how to do so," as Peter Dickens discovered to his chagrin. The generation of skippers that fought in the Second World War were daring enough, and ingenious, which was just as well; and they certainly had a flair for attack. But they might have done better from the outset if they had had some hard-won experience to guide them. Instead, they were left to devise their own methods, starting from scratch. Tommy Fuller remembers that when he arrived in Dover he received "one typewritten sheet on how to fight MTBs and that was all." Tactics were worked out at sea by a painful process of trial and error. Not surprisingly, mishaps occurred. Some were tragic, a few were comical; but in the end all contributed to the rapid progress men made in learning their mercenary trade. They brought such vigour to this that by the end of 1942, many of the colourful young skippers in Coastal Forces were legendary—men like Hichens, Gould, Pumphrey, Dickens and Scott. So, too, were a handful of the spirited if not slightly unorthodox Canadian small-boat raiders who had been among the earliest to benefit from tactics pioneered by the leading British "sea aces." They in turn handed down what they had learned to the young skippers that followed.

But first they had to get there. This they accomplished with varying amounts of duplicity, deception, collusion, well-timed falsehoods and, occasionally, the truth—as though it mattered. The way Tommy Fuller tells it, he was practically blackmailed into joining the navy. The day Canada declared war, he marched into an Air Force Recruiting Office on Rideau Street in Ottawa and presented his log book and various flying club membership cards. For good measure, he added letters of introduction from various officers in the RCAF, including Air Vice Marshall G. M. Croil. He was told to fill out an application form, which proved his undoing. Fuller discovered he was in a reserved occupation.

"I went back to my partner, George Rich, and said: 'George, will you sign this letter, please?' The letter said: 'To whom it may concern: This is to certify that I have bought, for one dollar and other considerations, the shares of Mr. T. G. Fuller in the Fuller Construction Company, and have duly fired him.' I went back to 38 Rideau Street and walked upstairs. 'Oh,' they said. 'We couldn't possibly put you on the flying list, you are far too old. What about coming in as Works and Bricks?' I said, 'No dice,' and walked out."

Several days later Fuller received a telephone call from the recruiting officer. " 'I've got wonderful news for you, wonderful news. They'll take you straight in as a flight lieutenant.' And I said, 'Flying?' 'No, Works and Bricks!' I said, 'I can do Works and Bricks. I'm building airports now and getting goddamn well paid for it!' " The officer called again in a few days. " 'We'll take you in as a flight lieutenant and give you squadron leader's pay!' I said, 'I'm still not interested!' " That night Fuller ran into a friend at the local yacht club who suggested his future was not as a fighter pilot. Later he arranged an appointment with the Naval Secretary. "I went down to Queen Street and they said, 'This is very interesting. We can offer you a warrant officer's job in Works and Bricks.' I thought, 'Christ, I'm going downhill!' " Even Fuller admits this was becoming a bit surreal, a joke that was soon to reach its climax. "I was sitting in my office, minding my own business, when I got a phone call. 'Lieutenant Commander Robertson RCNR.' He said, 'Your name has been given to me as a person who might be interested in joining the navy.' I said, 'Who in the hell are you kidding?' I thought it was just someone from the yacht club pulling my leg or something. 'No, no,' he said, 'I'm serious, can you come around and see me?' So I went around, and three days later I was on the *Duchess of Richmond* going overseas."

Not everyone's experience enlisting was as predictably madcap as Tommy Fuller's. Nor were the reasons they volunteered all that difficult to fathom. Some undoubtedly went out of patriotism, although beneath that veneer were other motives. Charles Burk of Toronto remembers that a lot of ratings told him they had joined in 1933, during the depth of the Depression. "I said, 'Why 1933?' They said, 'Room and board, three square meals a day.' They stayed on as career sailors, loved it, but that's why they joined.' "*

---

*Readers should be alerted to the possibility in this account of confusing Charles Burk and Cornelius Burke. Both fought with distinction and were

Others, Burk noted, "joined to get away from their wives." Today he laughs at the thought. "But most people joined because everybody else did," he says. This was particularly true as the war progressed, although significant increases in enlistment occurred with the fall of France in June 1940, and again at the end of 1941, following the surprise Japanese attack on Pearl Harbor. That's when Tom Ritchie, a seventeen-year-old who had worked as a parcel boy, time keeper and sales clerk with Eaton's in Winnipeg, signed up. There were others who grew up as farm lads in western Canada and joined as so-called prairie sailors. More than a few left the railways or western oil patch. Peer pressure, a longing for adventure and the fact that the war dominated one's daily life yet remained an untried fascination all proved sufficient reasons to enlist. For some the decision was made unexpectedly. Leslie Bowerman of Pender Island, B.C., had been with the Canadian Coast Guard vessel *William J. Stewart* for several years when he signed up in 1942. "We were up the coast at the time and I thought it was time for me to quit the hydrographic survey and...get in the war."

The same impulsive urge affected Tom Ladner, Douglas Maitland and Cornelius Burke, all from Vancouver. "They made a trio of fascinating contrasts," remembered L. C. Reynolds, who served in Burke's boat in the Mediterranean, "and yet they were in many respects complementary one to another. Maitland, the senior, was outwardly hard-bitten and crisp of speech; Corny was rugged, forceful and decisive in all his actions; and Ladner possessed a penetrating brain, a serious nature and a far more sensitive personality. They all had enormous zest for life and a refreshing ability to

---

colourful characters in their own right. Not surprisingly, however, at least one amusing anecdote arose from the similarity in their surnames. In 1943, when Burke left the U.K. for the Mediterranean, the fruitcakes his mother despatched on a regular basis continued to arrive at Lowestoft, where prior to his departure he and Burk were based as part of the same gunboat flotilla. Burk, who stayed behind at Lowestoft, got them. Later he sent word to Corny in the Med, suggesting he write to his mother in Vancouver to express his (Burk's) appreciation!

throw off the weight of responsibility and to relax light-heartedly off duty, when their sense of humour was rarely dormant." Maitland (who, for reasons long forgotten, was known as "Wimpy") was sailing on Cowichan Bay with friends when he felt the call to arms. "We dropped out of our race, produced the orange juice and gin and had a good snort to His Majesty." Maitland went down to HMCS *Discovery* on Dead Man's Island next to Stanley Park and signed up with the RCNVR. "I didn't know, really, what was going on," he admits now. "Nobody did, in fact." He spent the next few months training five nights a week. Then in April 1940, he came across a copy of a signal from the Royal Navy requesting two hundred and fifty young men "who had boating experience." Maitland volunteered immediately and so was amongst the first group of twenty-five sent overseas. He left Halifax aboard a captured cargo ship re-christened *Sinbad*.

Tom Ladner was with Corny Burke on Paisley Island the day Britain declared war. They were sitting on the floor of a cottage, listening to a battery-powered radio, when they heard Neville Chamberlain's solemn announcement. Ladner went back to Toronto and Osgoode Hall, where he had to finish his bar exams, and enlisted with the RCNVR. He spent the winter of 1939–40 in training at HMCS *York*, returned briefly to Vancouver to see his family, and finally left for England in mid-June 1940, sailing from Halifax. Burke spent the same winter at HMCS *Discovery* under the stern and watchful eye of Lt. Jeffry Brock, RCNR. "He made it clear to us that unless we could comport ourselves as officers and gentlemen (even at that age he was very much of the old school), we would never be accepted as officers into the Royal Canadian Navy." The message was reinforced at the drill hall. "This was considered highly important," Burke says now with a hint of the anxiety he felt in front of Brock. "I can remember, living as I was with my bride of thirty days, putting a broomstick on her shoulder and marching her around our bed-sitting room on Robson Street. So frightened was I that I would not measure up as an officer and a gentleman and one capable of commanding men that I marched her around this flat!" Burke's natural leadership abilities, as witnessed later in both the English Channel and the Mediterranean, should have allayed any fears he or his commanding officer might have had—although it did seem he was somewhat intimidated by Brock. He once ordered a parade drill straight into a wall while a horrified Brock watched from a reviewing stand. "How you sorted that out and what command you gave deserted me completely," Burke recalls. His naval career had not "collapsed on the spot" as a result of the incident, as Burke imagined; on the contrary, he was on a train across Canada the following March destined for Halifax and active service overseas as a newly minted acting sub-lieutenant on loan to the Royal Navy. It sounded grand, and evidently Burke felt it was, too—so grand, in fact, that he decided his wife should share the adventure. He smuggled her aboard the *Duchess of Atholl* in Halifax and sailed that much more happily to England for it.

They might have wondered what they were getting into. Just off the Isle of Wight, Maitland's ship was dive-bombed by a Stuka. There was a lot of excitement, but the ship was unharmed. Still, it was a rude reception. "He really scared hell out of us," Maitland said afterwards. Ladner at least made it to London without incident; in fact, the crossing aboard HMS *Ettrick*, a troop-ship from India, had been rather pleasant. "We were virtually the only people on board except for a group of Newfoundland seamen or fishermen who were going over to run naval trawlers and things like that," he explained. But Ladner had the bad luck to land during one of the first daylight air raids on London. He was at Victoria Station when it happened. "It was quite interesting," he said. "Nobody really had any understanding of what they should be doing." Bombs were falling close by, yet there was little panic. "Then all officialdom arrived with all the tin hats and God-knows-what, and air-raid wardens. So everybody was marshalled into the air-raid shelter down in Victoria Station. That was really the last time I ever saw anybody in the U.K. ever bother to go to an air-raid shelter in a daylight raid."

If Ladner and Maitland thought they'd had a shock, it was nothing compared to one of Corny Burke's earliest escapades.

He'd barely arrived at HMS *King Alfred*, the Royal Navy's training establishment at Hove in Sussex, when a general state of alarm was sounded following the invasion of France and the Low Countries. "Suddenly I found myself volunteering—practically by command did I volunteer!—to join a demolition force. In the middle of the night, we went off to Dover and the next morning boarded a destroyer headed for Le Havre. There were five Canadians, as I recall, each in charge of a hundred men. Our orders were to blow up the locks and harbour installations in Le Havre and deny their use to the enemy." Burke says the operation was commanded by the legendary Captain (soon to be Admiral) Philip Vian, an energetic and tireless leader who had daringly rescued several hundred British prisoners from the *Altmark* in February of that year. Even so, it was to Burke, at least, a dangerous, ill-conceived mission for which he was untrained, particularly with regard to explosives. "I hardly knew one end of the fuse from the other and, furthermore, I was absolutely terrified. The Channel was still very much controlled by the Luftwaffe." This appalling thought occupied Burke as the demolition charges were loaded aboard a destroyer and they steamed towards the embattled coast of France. "We expected that the entry into Le Havre might be opposed by the enemy, and that they were already there. So little did we know."

In fact, it turned out to be a lovely spring day when they landed. "People were walking up and down the esplanade and it was all very peaceful." Burke, at this point professing to be the unlikeliest of commandos, bedded down in the Transatlantique dock along with his cohorts and "proceeded to lead a very pleasant life for three weeks." But even Burke admits in the end he had "a great deal to do." This included destroying a number of lock-gates, bridges and derricks at Le Havre and St. Valéry, work that became increasingly urgent as the Battle of France sped towards its tragic end. Then on June 12, an expeditionary force made up largely of elements from the 1st Canadian Division had landed at Brest in a desperate, last-ditch attempt to support what remained of the French Army. The operation quickly proved a fiasco, although it was not the 1st Division's fault. Poor planning and the prevailing chaos in France had doomed the expedition to a miserable fate from the outset. Burke remembers hearing that units of the British 52nd Highland Division that had accompanied the Canadians were trapped at St. Valéry, and that "suddenly everyone had to leave to...see if they could rescue these people." He and a fellow named Eric Blanchet of New Brunswick were left behind "to do some more demolition, with no crew, no men, just ourselves. And rather vaguely they said: 'We'll come and get you if we can!' "

Burke and Blanchet took refuge in a warehouse filled with sacks of flour. "Luftwaffe were pirouetting around in the sky up above and we made a little fire out of box wood and cooked a dinner of bacon and beans. I was so frightened that I wasn't really hungry." Shortly after this, Burke discovered that a small contingent of British soldiers had been left behind as well. They invited Burke and his party to lunch. "Several of us went and they did us very proud and served Black Velvets." According to Burke, he spent the next five days getting "monumentally drunk" on the stuff. "It also gave us the courage to go and shake our fists at the sky and shout imprecations in the general direction of the Luftwaffe." This went on until finally a despatch rider came into the old cobbled courtyard where Burke and his hosts were enjoying their Bacchanalian drinking bouts. "It could have been out of some grade-B movie," Burke recalls. "He was covered with dust and leapt off his bike with the wheels still spinning. He rushed into the mess and pointed dramatically up the road and said, 'Jerries!' At this point I performed the bravest act of my entire naval career. I went weaving out into the courtyard, gazed defiantly up the road and rasped in a booze-laden voice, 'Well let 'em come!' Fortunately, Jerry was late coming or I would have torn them all limb from limb I'm sure."

Not long after this, Burke and the others left Le Havre. "We were rescued just in the nick of time," he says. "A trawler came in, picked us up, and as we left the harbour the German tanks rolled into town." The episode had left Burke a bit shaken at times (when he wasn't plastered), but also impressed. "I'll never forget the bearing and the manner of the British troops that came down there. Their kit was in order and their ranks were decimated, but their shoulders were back and their heads were high and they were going to fight again. They made a great impression on me as to how men can react to adversity." No doubt he meant it, too. The episode, apart from all the larking-about it had offered, was a large part of Burke's introduction to the reality of war. From this evolved an ability to play hard and fight hard in equal measure. Beneath his seemingly irrepressible high spirits was a recognition of the mind-numbing swiftness with which death could be dealt. It had also taught him that soldiering—it could be applied equally to seafaring—was a profession in which some men took great pride.

Burke took his impressions of Le Havre back with him to England and to *King Alfred*, where he resumed his training (ratings went to such establishments as HMS *Raleigh* at Plymouth—in groups of twenty-five, "as many as a Nissen hut could accommodate"—where they spent ten weeks along with some ten thousand other ordinary seamen). "KA," as it was called, or simply "Alfred," was a converted old bath house with a gymnasium, situated on the coast. Tommy Fuller didn't care much for the shore billets he was given, so he and a fellow officer rented a flat overlooking the English Channel. "It belonged to a big-game hunter in Kenya, and there were stuffed heads all over the place. There was also an old hurdy-gurdy with it, with a big brass wheel. Every time you'd go out, you'd give the handle a crank, and as you were going to the elevator you'd hear *ta-da-dum* and the music would come out of it." One of Fuller's favourite haunts in nearby Brighton was the Kit Kat Club, "run by Josey, a Flora-Dora Girl some thirty or forty years before," he reported. "But she could still kick the chandelier!" By all accounts there was an informal atmosphere at *King Alfred*, too. Maitland remembers it well. "We'd show up in the morning, having had our breakfast, and on we'd go to whatever we were supposed to be doing." Forming fours and rifle drill took up a lot of unnecessary time, he thought. Later, Maitland was more forgiving. His initial criticisms tempered by experience, he said the Royal Navy's system was excellent. "It took me a couple of years to realize how much I'd learned—the *right* way."

Three months at KA was invariably followed by time spent aboard Armed Merchant Cruisers (AMCs) to further acquaint the Royal Navy's young officers with actual conditions in a war zone, ship routine and celestial navigation (ratings also served aboard AMCs and, if they were officer candidates, attended *King Alfred* afterwards). Alex Joy of Toronto remembers he drew an AMC uneventfully plying a route between Belfast and the south coast of Iceland. "We just sailed backwards and forwards," he said with disdain. His fellow Torontonian, Charles Burk, agreed the time aboard AMCs could be monotonous. One of the few highlights he remembers was returning to Plymouth from Halifax with a peg-legged captain—"a tough old bugger," Burk said of him—in command of an equally decrepit four-stacker obtained in the Lend-Lease deal with the United States. It was rare to find such inaction. Most had their first real baptism of fire on AMCs. Tom Ladner was aboard HMS *Forfar* when it was torpedoed off Iceland in early December 1940. This was towards the end of *die glückliche zeit*— "The Happy Time"—for U-boats in the North Atlantic. Ladner thinks it was the war's leading wolfpack ace, Kapitänleutnant Otto Kretschmer, whose deadly aim and "one torpedo, one ship" policy had wreaked havoc with Allied shipping, that sank the *Forfar*. If it was Kretschmer, he was not alone that night. Ladner was standing next to a lifeboat when a second torpedo hit (in all, he says, about nine were fired at the ship). "It was hanging in its davits and it blew up in my face," he remembers. "Another torpedo hit and it blew oil from the hold, right up the ventilating system. I don't know how it did it. I ended up being absolutely covered with oil, which turned out to be a blessing in disguise, really." Ladner was wearing a greatcoat under his life-jacket when he finally went over the side; the oil acted as additional insulation. He still can't recall how long he spent in the freezing Icelandic waters. "It really became a nightmare," he says now. Eventually he found sanctuary with fifty others aboard a lifeboat and waited until noon the next day when they were picked up. Ladner ended up convalescing in

Glasgow. "We were in pretty grim condition," he recalled. This was followed by a brief period of survivor's leave. Ladner went down to Fowey in Cornwall, where he spent Christmas with Corny Burke and his wife, Wendy.

But he didn't actually see much of Burke. The latter was rumoured to be somewhere in the English Channel with a unit of MGBs exploding acoustic mines by running their boats over them! In a way, this was due to Burke's part in the hare-brained assignment to Le Havre in the spring. He had come back something of a minor hero for it. "Because of this," Burke later explained, "I was offered practically any job I wanted. I immediately asked to get into Coastal Forces."

It is not clear what motivated him to do so. In the summer of 1940, little was known of the Royal Navy's ragtag fleet of armed motorboats; in fact, "Coastal Forces" as such did not yet exist, although recent events had suggested its likelihood. Prior to this, the Admiralty had to be persuaded that small ships had a legitimate role to play in the war at sea.

2

Harry Tate's Navy

I T WAS WILLIAM MANCHESTER who observed, "Not only is it easy to be wise after the event; it is, for military historians, almost irresistible." Still, it must be said that at some point in the Second World War, torpedo boats would likely attack, and, if they were lucky, sink something. That was, after all, what they were designed to do. That Britain seemed unable to comprehend that one of its own vessels might be the target was nothing short of ludicrous. But that is what happened on the night of May 9, 1940, when, for the first time in the war, a unit of E-boats attacked a small force of British warships in the English Channel. In the ensuing mêlée, Kapitänleutnant Opdenhoff, commanding *S31*, fired two torpedoes. They struck HMS *Kelly*, Lord Louis Mountbatten's flagship in the 5th Destroyer Flotilla, with devastating results. Later it was announced by Radio Berlin that the ship had been sunk; in fact, the 1,695-ton vessel was severely damaged and had to be towed back to Tyne for extensive repairs (it was eventually lost in action off Crete in May 1941 while still under the command of Lord Mountbatten). The incident shocked the British Admiralty, which previously had dismissed the E-boats as incapa-

ble of inflicting such damage. Equally alarming was that they had
ventured so boldly into the Straits of Dover.

The E-boats scored again during the evacuation from Dunkirk in
late May and early June, sinking the destroyers *Grafton* and
Wakeful, as well as two armed trawlers, the *Argyllshire* and *Stella
Dorado*. The SS *Abukir*, returning from Ostend with as many as
two hundred evacuees on board, was sunk as well. The cruiser
Calcutta was almost added to the grim litany of casualties; it was
barely missed by torpedoes fired from an E-boat. In an attempt to
thwart this new menace, the Royal Navy sent virtually every fast-
attack craft it had. This amounted to about a dozen MTBs and
Motor Anti-Submarine Boats, the latter known by their acronym
MA/SB as "Masbys." For the handful of regular officers who
commanded this pitifully small force, it was an opportunity to
demonstrate their worth. They made the most of it, too, wherever
they could and usually in hostile circumstances, by escorting ships
to the scene of this epic drama, ferrying troops from the beaches,
shuttling officers back and forth between vessels and, occasionally, battling with the E-boats. The gunners aboard one MTB even
brought down a twin-engine bomber. Throughout the so-called
miracle of Dunkirk, the boats of Coastal Forces performed
bravely, even if, as author Richard Collier said, they went about it
with "the grim gaiety of the gambler, staking all his chips on the
last spin of the wheel." Among the commanders present were
several who would become legends, including Stewart Gould,
Christopher Dreyer, Hillary Gamble and H. L. "Harpy" Lloyd, all
regular navy officers. Lt. W. G. Everitt, commanding MA/SB 6,
was responsible for bringing back Lord Gort, the Commander-in-
Chief of the British Expeditionary Force. MTBs and MA/SBs had
also safely delivered members of the Belgian Cabinet, Admiral
Keyes and General Alexander.

There was more than a touch of irony in the abundance of praise
from senior naval officers who had witnessed their exploits. For
years—ever since the end of the First World War, in fact—the
importance of small boats was routinely dismissed. Following the
armistice in 1918, most of Britain's impressive fleet of Coastal

Motor Boats (CMBs) and Motor Launches (MLs) were scrapped or sold. It was a hard fate, particularly in view of their enviable record of service during the First World War. With the Dover Patrol and in actions off the Belgian and Dutch coasts, the little ships had proved their worth in such tasks as chasing submarines, escorting convoys, mine sweeping and laying smokescreens during the many daylight raids across the English Channel. Among the more spectacular successes they achieved was a raid on Kronstadt in 1919 following the October Revolution, when they sank the cruiser *Oleg* and disabled two capital ships and two destroyers for the loss of only one CMB.

Nor was there a shortage of heroism amongst the crews, which included a number of Canadians, the most surprising of which was the distinguished historian Arthur Lower. Born to English parents in Canada in 1889—Sir John A. Macdonald was still prime minister!—Lower was raised in the small Ontario town of Barrie, just north of Toronto. He was twenty-eight when he went overseas in 1916, having volunteered despite little experience in yachts or motorboats. Prior to this, he had put himself through the University of Toronto by working summers as a fire ranger in the north Ontario bush. Yet he fit in perfectly with the little ships. There is a photograph of Lower in his autobiography, *My First Seventy-Five Years* (published, appropriately enough for this ardent nationalist, during Canada's centennial), standing on the bridge of a motor launch in late 1916, glaring menacingly into the camera, one hand resting impatiently on his hip as though only moments before he'd discovered his revolver was missing. He has the look of a dangerous man, and perhaps he was. More accurately, he seems the archetypal outdoorsman, an athletic adventurer who had merely changed into the uniform of a lieutenant in the RNVR as patriotism dictated he must.

Others did the same. Lower says there were at least "a half-dozen" Canadians attached to the famous Dover Patrol, although he mentions only Colimer Calvin of Kingston, Ontario. For the most part, they served aboard U.S.-built seventy-foot launches powered by two petrol engines that, in the words of Admiral Sir

Reginald Bacon, who commanded the patrol for several years, were noisy enough to "frighten a submarine miles off." Worse, the engine ventilators discharged noxious fumes into the cockpit, enveloping the captain and cox. The boats were poorly armed, if at all. Equipped originally with an old thirteen-pound Horse Artillery gun widely regarded as "a satanic piece of ironmongery" and "a nasty Yankee box of tricks," such armaments as they had were removed and given to merchant ships, leaving the MLs virtually defenceless. There were "mishaps," too, so many, in fact, that Lower remembers that the Dover Patrol was dubbed "Harry Tate's Navy," after the renowned English music-hall comedian, "who secured his effects by getting himself snarled up in crazy collections of crazier 'gadgets.'"

Lower says his contribution to the war effort was "microscopic," but in fact he saw plenty of action. He spent the brutal winter of 1916–17 as a substitute officer on MLs with the Dover Patrol, watching for U-boats attempting to pass through the Straits. There were numerous hit-and-run actions off the Belgian coast. Lower remembered that with the coming of spring in 1917 the sea was covered with debris from sunken ships. Then in the autumn, Lower was transferred. His new skipper was Lt. Rowland Bourke, an English-born Irishman from British Columbia whose gallant action during a raid at Ostend and Zeebrugge won him the Victoria Cross. The man positively lived for action, it seemed. Lower remembered that sometime later, during a raid on Dunkirk, Bourke strode along the quay, rubbing his hands gleefully as shells crashed around them, and shouted, "This is splendid, this is war!"

Such were a few of the First World War's small-boat fraternity, a hardy breed and reservists, mostly—young men who had signed up on the eve of the conflict expressing the wish "to be useful if war should come." It did, and so did a handful of Canadians, even if the Royal Navy wasn't always comfortable with these amateur yachtsmen. Lower admits that despite his education he was unaccustomed to saying "sir." Looking back on it all from the vantage point of a brilliant academic career that had included Harvard, United College in Winnipeg, and Queen's University in Kingston,

Lower admitted his "intimate acquaintance with the sea" had a lasting impact. "The blue water, the foam-flecked ocean, the bounding little ship, here were values to which something deep in my nature responded."

Sadly, though, the Admiralty was much less moved at the war's end. The little ships were abandoned with astonishing alacrity, the navy's brass intent on maintaining intact its Grand Fleet mentality and its casual mistrust—it bordered on contempt, really—of amateur sailors.

It wasn't until 1935 that the Admiralty ordered its first modern MTBs, as the inheritors of the First World War CMBs and MLs were called. These were sixty-foot craft designed by Hubert Scott-Paine's British Power Boat Company (BPBC) based at Poole, Dorset. They were armed with two eighteen-inch torpedoes and .303 machine guns, fore and aft. Powered by three 500-horse-power Napier Sea Lion petrol engines, they had a top speed of 33 knots. The Admiralty purchased six. These were formed into the 1st MTB Flotilla led by Lt. Cdr. G. B. Sayer, RN, and sent to Malta in 1937. That same year the Admiralty ordered twelve of the BPBC's sixty-six-foot MTBs. Six of these were sent to Hong Kong, where they were formed into the 2nd MTB Flotilla. The others were intended for duty in Singapore, but as they had only reached the Mediterranean by the summer of 1939, when war seemed imminent, it was decided they should remain at Malta so as to bring the 1st Flotilla to strength. This was virtually the entire complement of MTBs available to the Royal Navy when war was declared in September—an appalling state of affairs in light of the enormous burden the little ships were expected to carry within just a few months. "This was not due to lack of foresight on the part of individuals in the country," remembers Peter Ayling, a former BPBC employee who now owns and operates a marina in Merrick-ville, Ontario, on the Rideau Canal. "Individuals were constantly experimenting with planes, engines, small high-speed boats, arma-ments, rockets, electronics, and so on."

Ayling started at the British Power Boat Company in 1937 at age sixteen, eight years after the yard had been purchased by Hubert

Scott-Paine. Prior to this, he had worked as a sort of "Fuller Brush man" in London. But Ayling had always been interested in boats and boat building; it was, in his words, "in the blood," even though his father, a chartered accountant, never owned a boat in his life. Ayling's great-grandfather, on the other hand, was an inventor who had built an early amphibious vehicle.

Scott-Paine, too, was something of a visionary when it came to boat-building. His original plan when purchasing the BPBC was to apply his prefabricating methods to the mass production of high-speed runabouts such as Chris Craft was making in the United States. But soon his attention was turned to other possibilities. Incredibly, it was Lawrence of Arabia, who had left behind the intrigue of the desert war for the anonymity of life as "Aircrafts-man Shaw" in the Royal Air Force, who gave added impetus to this change of plan.

In the 1920s, T. E. Lawrence (as Shaw) wrote an eighty-page manual on handling the new approach to boat construction pioneered by Scott-Paine. This evolved into an unlikely, if not incongruous, partnership. In one photograph, the enigmatic Lawrence—square-jawed, with the rugged good looks of an actor in an early silent movie—is standing next to the rotund Scott-Paine, who bears some resemblance to a latter-day Peter Lorre. Lawrence's reputation was that of a tormented but influential messiah, a man of painfully clandestine dreams and ambitions who died in a mysterious motorcycle accident in 1935. Scott-Paine, on the other hand, was perhaps no less mercurial—Ayling remembers him as "a genius and an oddball and a bit of a hustler"—but he confined his adventuring to the world of high-speed boat racing and the development of suitable navy versions of such craft. Indeed, he still held the World Salt Water Speed Record when he died in Connecticut in 1954. His impact during the pre-war years—along with that of Cdr. Peter du Cane of Vospers—was profound. Here at least were men with the foresight to understand that small high-speed craft would play a meaningful role in the years ahead.

Meanwhile other British yards began competing for orders. The firms J. I. Thornycroft, Nicholson and Camper, and J. S. White built MTBs as private ventures, and eventually a contract was awarded to Cdr. du Cane's Vosper yard, which produced a series of high-speed craft that became the basis for most of the "short" boats used by the Royal Navy during the Second World War. Initially, they were powered by Italian-made Isotta Fraschini petrol engines, which by all accounts were among the best available. These were gradually replaced by supercharged Hall Scott engines following Italy's entry in the war in June 1940, which made supplies of the Isotta Fraschini difficult to obtain, until the Packard "Liberty" engines, so ably demonstrated in U.S. racing specialist Commodore Gar Wood's *Miss America*, became available and were made the standard.

However, Scott-Paine's BPBC was not completely out of the picture. In 1939, he sold one of his boats to the U.S. Navy and arranged to have others built under licence. Unlike their British counterparts, the navy brass hats in Washington had seen little need for such boats in the First World War and had subsequently confined their interest to the purchase in 1920 of two Thornycroft motor launches to be used for "experimental purposes." Unofficially, an important appreciation of the high-speed craft came from rum-runners who used old British-built CMBs to smuggle Prohibition booze from Canada to the eastern seaboard of the United States. "They were constantly trying to improve the performance of the craft in order to elude the Customs patrol boats," noted Bryan Cooper, author of several books examining the lore of the MTBs, "and their experiments, which included the adaptation of the Liberty engine to marine use, provided valuable information at the beginning of the war when the U.S. Navy first began to build motor torpedo boats." It wasn't until 1937 that the United States broadened its outlook. Franklin Delano Roosevelt, while Assistant Secretary of the Navy during the First World War, had been among the few to appreciate the value of small boats. Now, as president, FDR sponsored the appropriation of $15 million for the development of U.S.-made boats, commonly known as Patrol Boats, or PTs. There were three main builders: the Huckins Yacht Corporation of Jacksonville, Florida; the Higgins Boat Company (or

Higgins Industries) of New Orleans; and the Electric Boat Company—also known as Elco—of Bayonne, New Jersey. These were the same companies that had fashioned offshore weekend cruisers and yachts in the Depression years. Huckins's pre-war boats were described by *Time* as "the Deusenburgs of the small yacht class." Frank Pembroke Huckins loved power and speed, a sentiment reflected in his sales pitch to the rich: "Breakfast at Marblehead, lunch off Monhega, dinner in Northeast Harbor!"

Building PTs, on the other hand, presented a formidable challenge to the tough-minded company presidents who had retooled their boatyards for war, although Elco at least had an advantage inasmuch as it had sold hundreds of MLs to the Royal Navy during the First World War. Frank Huckins confessed he was daunted by the prospect of designing a seventy- to eighty-foot boat constructed of diagonally planked mahogany or laminated plywood that could perform at 40 knots for one hour under a full military load of fuel and ordnance out of all proportion to any other naval vessel. But they threw themselves into the task anyway, ever mindful of potentially lucrative navy contracts. The race to design PTs culminated in a series of Navy Board of Inspection trials known as the "Plywood Derby" convened off New London, Connecticut, in July 1941. "Nobody who was in it will ever forget it," Frank Huckins said. "Whatever you have to say about the navy, they are thorough. If there was anything that can be done to a PT boat that they didn't do that week, I don't know what it is—and I have been trying to unwind the twists in my spine that I got those days ever since." Huckins might have had good reason to complain, but as a result of the Plywood Derby contracts were awarded and the push to develop an indigenous PT building program was significantly advanced.

Canada, too, had begun to consider the need for high-speed attack craft. The last part of an ambitious three-year building plan promulgated in the aftermath of the Munich Crisis in September 1938 anticipated the construction of thirty-two MTBs with a proposed rate of replacement of sixteen a year for two years. In August 1939, the Chief of the Naval Staff, Rear Admiral Percy W.

Nelles, defended the program in a brief to the Honorary Naval Advisory Committee, which needed to be convinced of the value such vessels offered. Nelles wrote:

> With regard to Motor Torpedo Boats there are many firms equipped to produce boats of varying degrees of efficiency at the present time. These boats, as you know, have a very strong "Bite" for small cost, when it is definitely established that the vessel to be attacked is an enemy and deserves sinking. Their effect is obtained, however, by the use of speed and a small target to place their torpedoes in the water close to the enemy. When stopped in the vicinity of any ship, exercising the right of visit and search to establish whether or not the ship is subject to sinking, the M.T.B. does not retain the authority which 4.7″ guns give to a destroyer, but lies at the mercy of anyone who wishes to open fire with a machine gun. In other words M.T.B.'s are excellent weapons in offence but lose value when being used in defence as they would be used in the RCN. Considerable progress is being made with a lightly constructed, high speed diesel engine which would minimize the risk of fire and expense of upkeep of M.T.B.'s. For this reason the Naval Staff is not pressing for early purchase of this type of vessel. They can be procured at shorter notice than larger vessels in time of emergency and any delay will add to the efficiency when they are purchased.

The powers-that-be might well have procrastinated even longer except that in May 1940 the peripatetic Hubert Scott-Paine arrived and founded the Canadian Power Boat Company in Montreal. He offered to build his seventy-one-and-a-half-foot MTBs, employing hundreds of skilled workers in the process. It was too good an opportunity to miss. Accordingly a contract with the government was formally signed in July. The young Peter Ayling had arrived by then and was placed in charge of production at the new plant built on Montreal's Old Lachine Canal. In the first year and a half, dozens of boats built under licence from the parent company were handed over to the Royal Canadian Navy, RCAF and even the U.S. Navy. But the real reason the plant was built, according to Ayling, was to ensure that the boats, now considered vital to the Allied war effort, could continue to be supplied if the parent plant on the south coast of England was destroyed by enemy bombing—or, worse, captured in the event England was invaded. This never happened, of course, and so eventually the plant scaled down its boat-building operation to produce some 250 Mosquito bombers, which were also made of wood.

In addition to the Scott-Paine boats, more than a hundred Fairmile MLs were built at yards across the country. The standard price for each vessel was $85,000 except in British Columbia, where it was $76,000. This was the only ship-building program during the war that saw west-coast prices lower than those in the east—or, to be more precise, Ontario, where most of the MLs were built at such yards as Greavette Boats Ltd. of Gravenhurst, Grew Boats Ltd. in Penetanguishene, Hunter Boats Ltd. in Orillia, MacCraft Corporation in Sarnia, and J. J. Taylor and Sons in Toronto. Such names evoked the unpretentious, almost homespun atmosphere that still surrounded many of the country's small ship-building companies as the war progressed.

For its part, Germany, too, had pursued an interest in small boats, but not with any of the vigour so characteristic of its advances in other fields. Indeed, one of the major incentives of such a program was that it was a way to get around a few of the restrictions regarding size and armament of vessels the Reich was permitted under the terms of the Treaty of Versailles. This scheme was promoted in 1928 when the Reichsmarine obtained the plans to a luxury motor cruiser being built privately for an American customer. Powered by three Maybach engines, it could reach a top speed of 30 knots. "It was from this basic design," according to Bryan Cooper, "that the *Schnellboot* was later developed." The first of these, *S1*, was built in 1930. Its most important divergence from the original design was the incorporation of three 1,000-horsepower Daimler-Benz diesel engines. Built with impeccable workmanship, more powerful and certainly much less hazardous to operate than the high-octane petrol models used by Allied boats, the diesel engines were a clear-cut advantage from the outset.

But they didn't exploit it sufficiently. Only five more boats were built by 1932, enough to create a flotilla, and that was it. Following sea trials that had revealed a number of flaws, modifications were made and plans were redrawn, increasing the vessel's length to 106 feet by the time eight more were built in 1934. The length was again increased, partly to accommodate more powerful engines. Now at 114 feet and bristling with weapons, including 21-inch torpedoes, they took on a sinister look. But only nineteen were built in 1939. Even this relatively prodigious output left the Kriegsmarine with a total complement of only twenty-four serviceable E-boats at the war's outset (the prototype, *S1*, had been scrapped).

For reasons of its own, the Royal Navy had done little better than its adversary. There were perhaps as few as twenty-two MTBs dispersed among several flotillas. The 1st MTB Flotilla, which had been recalled from Malta in 1939, had by the end of January 1940 taken up its duties at Felixstowe on the east coast of England, but it was used primarily for such mundane tasks as escorting convoys, air-sea rescue and ferrying messages or supplies to and from ships of the Home Fleet. This was not the sort of action their crews secretly craved. Worse, they came under the authority of individual commanders-in-chief, some of whom were evidently inclined to treat any MTB as a glorified admiral's barge. The E-boats, on the other hand, came under the general command of Konteradmiral Bütow, the Kriegsmarine's "Führer der Torpedoboote" (FdT). Later, a distinct *Schnellboote* command, FdS, would be established, with Rudolph Peterson—who, as a younger Kapitänleutnant, had led the attack in which the *Kelly* was damaged—as its Kommodore. But this was a few years ahead. Throughout the winter of 1939–40, the seven E-boats of Kapitänleutnant Peterson's *2. Schnellbootflottille* had carried out uneventful patrols off the north coast of Germany, staying relatively close to Wilhelmshaven where they were based. In the spring of 1940, the E-boats had so far participated in only one meaningful event, the invasion of Norway in April. Then, following a brief overhaul at Wilhelmshaven at the end of the month, they were sent out into the English Channel with orders to attack British shipping. Few of the E-boat commanders knew what to expect of this mission. The return trip was roughly four hundred miles. They had never operated so far from base.

In fact, the E-boats were low on fuel when, at 2200 on the night of May 9, they unexpectedly met the enemy and seriously damaged HMS *Kelly*. With the fall of France only weeks later, in June, the E-boats moved to new ports established at Boulogne, Cherbourg, Le Havre, Ijmuiden, Ostend and Rotterdam. In one stroke, they had eliminated the long haul from their old base at Wilhelmshaven. Now they could harass British shipping in the English Channel as they pleased.

It was at this point that the Admiralty finally decided it would need greater numbers of such craft to meet the enemy on its own terms. It was also evident that the requirements of quick expansion would mean diluting the "regular navy" character of Coastal Forces with the addition of reserve and so-called Hostilities Only officers and ratings, a notion that was greeted by some amongst the navy's brass with almost apoplectic dread.

These new realities, however uncomfortable to the establishment, were soon greeted by a handful of young Canadians with an enthusiasm that was positively shocking. Burke was one of the first to join, although Tommy Fuller couldn't have been far behind. Maitland and Ladner were in by January. And there were others. Following a brief spell of training at the Royal Navy's establishment at Fort William in Scotland and working-up at HMS *Bee* at Holyhead, the newest recruits to Coastal Forces were considered ready.

They might have disagreed; indeed, events would prove they had a lot to learn yet. But now, like the Stephen Leacock character who got on his horse and promptly rode off in all directions, the first of Canada's small-boat raiders were sent out to meet the enemy—wherever and however they could find him.

3

"Oh, I say—madly war, isn't it?"

THE ROYAL NAVY HAD a number of ways to express its disdain for the little ships. Peter Dickens remembered one officer's parting words after issuing orders sending his flotilla to some far-flung destination, "Take your flying bedpans up there and stand by." To this Dickens could only reply, "Curse the man! His description was only too apt."

Such remarks betrayed the navy's own prejudices as much as the shortcomings that were undoubtedly a part of Coastal Forces early in the war. This attitude prevailed with some vigour, too, until the end of 1941 when the so-called Costly Farces redeemed itself with several successful actions. Even then resentment lingered, as another exchange reported by Dickens reveals. He was once sent out on a mission with the tart command, evidently meant to convey a low opinion of the flotilla's scruffy-looking crews, "Off you go and do your worst; Ali Baba and the forty garage proprietors!"

The Canadians were to know similar insults. But in all fairness it must be said they had contributed as much, if not a disproportionate share, to the many calamities that befell the fledgling Coastal

Forces, which in turn gave rise to its sometimes lamentable reputation. Not surprisingly it was Corny Burke who led the way again. Just about the first thing he did was his "worst."

He blew up his skipper's boat.

It happened in the early part of 1941, not long after Burke had joined the crew of MGB *42*, one of six boats in a unit operating out of Fowey, a romantic little town in the middle of Daphne du Maurier country on the Cornish coast (according to Burke the famous author lived just across the river). His commanding officer aboard *42* was a straight-striped "two-and-a-half" named Fitzroy Talbot. Translated, it meant Talbot was a regular officer in the Royal Navy, and a Lieutenant Commander at that. In several weeks of operations out of Fowey, they had not yet seen any real action. Most of the time they were involved in air-sea rescue patrols, as they were again on this fateful day.

"We left Fowey and went around the Lizard and around Land's End into the Bristol Channel looking for some airmen," Burke recalled, the geography sometimes as intimidating and arcane as the language they used about each other. "We couldn't find them and we were coming back. It was rather a long haul. For some reason the Skipper said, 'Give me a course into Penzance.' We had to get fuel or something like that." Burke gave his commanding officer the course. "Unfortunately there were some chart corrections which had come out just before we left Fowey, which I hadn't quite got around to putting on the chart; and the course I laid off was right over an acoustic mine which was lying in Penzance Harbour. It blew the whole rear of the boat to smithereens."

Somehow they still had one "wheel" (screw, or propeller) working—Burke was amazed—and so they were able to beach the MGB before it sank. By yet another miracle, no one was killed in this unfortunate incident. As for Burke's fate, it was now in the hands of the Senior Naval Officer at Penzance Harbour, who had witnessed the explosion. He turned out to be "a delightful old barnacle" only recently dragged out of retirement. There was a glint in the old man's eye as he took Burke aside afterwards and said, "Subbie, I know full well that you were right on top of a mine, the existence of which had been promulgated. But let us say nothing, Subbie, with respect to your future career in the navy. There is no harm done. The boat is gone. There were no casualties. You were just, shall we say, two cables to the east."

Incredibly, Burke was given command of his next boat, MGB *90*. It was one of the many Scott-Paine boats manufactured by Elco in the United States (which had substituted Packard engines for the original Rolls-Royce versions) and shipped back to England on the decks of merchant ships as part of the Lend-Lease agreement. Burke picked it up at Liverpool and took it down to Weymouth with another boat, MGB *92*. Together they completed the sea trials and various exercises that were referred to collectively as "working-up." Burke was confident, if not cocky, as he came alongside one day.

"Well, I guess I've got things nicely wrapped up," he announced. "The crew's trained. I've got all my paperwork done. The books are starting to get in shape. I'm rather proud and I'm delighted I have this wonderful boat. Now let's get cracking!"

Burke was ready to take up his new duties with a flotilla based at Lowestoft. Later he recalled how everything seemed to fall apart in split seconds.

"My standing orders were all properly posted and one of the standing orders was, of course, that all guns were to be unloaded before entering harbour. The boats were lying alongside each other. I was sitting in my cabin getting the last of the paperwork done. There was a rating on the bridge cleaning, if you please, a Lewis gun. There was one round in the chamber and he pulled the trigger to make sure it was working and he fired the .303 shell. It hit a box of Oerlikon ammunition which was sitting on the deck of the boat alongside, which immediately exploded. Both boats were masses of flames with shells exploding all over the bloody place. The wheel house, the bridge, everything was blown to smithereens."

How Burke or anyone else survived this conflagration is not known. "I remember pouring foam into open fuel tanks— 100-octane petrol," he recalled. "It was just hopeless. The boats were burned to the waterline." There ended Burke's first command, and the third of His Majesty's motor gunboats with which he'd had a connection. And he hadn't even met the enemy yet!

Such losses were galling, particularly in view of the small number of boats at the Royal Navy's disposal early in the war. But they were not without some benefit. Having survived his calamitous experience aboard MGB *42*, Burke escaped the displeasure of their lordships by the good graces of an old sea-dog who understood that some lessons had to be learned the hard way. In the first year and a half of duty as neophytes, the Canadians were to find no end to proof of this wisdom.

They started out eagerly enough. Maitland and Ladner had followed Burke's example and by the spring of 1941 had passed through HMS *St. Christopher* on Loch Linnhe at Fort William in the north of Scotland. Maitland said it was "a very fine practical training ground" for officers assigned to MLs, MTBs and MGBs. Not surprisingly, Tommy Fuller left with a much different view of the place. "Scotland's a godforsaken country," he complained. "It rains...and on Sunday you've got to walk five miles to get a drink!" Most of all he disliked the establishment's commanding officer, Lt. Cdr. A. E. P. Welman, a much-decorated veteran of Coastal Motor Boats in the First World War. "It seemed for the rest of the war Welman and I never saw eye to eye," he said. Part of this was due to Welman's penchant for crack-of-dawn marches and jogtrots into the rugged Scottish glens. Fuller preferred to slip unseen into a nearby pub. It was a lot more inviting than "all this silliness of climbing up a mountain and back again," Fuller said. "I'd have some nice cold milk and some cheese and fresh bread, and then I could just join in on the way back. Not to come in first, you know, but somewhere along the middle. Just to make sure that you got enough warm water for your shower."

It's hard sometimes not to view Fuller as a conceited, self-absorbed prima donna who evidently felt he was doing the Royal Navy a favour by providing his services (especially in view of how much he could have done for Works and Bricks!). His antics were occasionally schoolboyish, as he demonstrated in Scotland. Indeed, much of what he did was redeemed only by his subsequent record in fighting with the enemy, particularly when he arrived in the Mediterranean and the Adriatic. Modesty was never one of his virtues, although more often than not he knew his business and could prove it, which he enjoyed doing at every opportunity, regardless of who got in the way.

By his own account, Fuller's temperament was on display throughout his brief period of training in Scotland. Not everyone caroused as much as he did, although a few shared his general impressions of the surroundings. Ladner, especially, was unforgiving. "I went all through this area and can't remember any of the names," he said. "It's just dreadful." Among the few landmarks he recalled at Fort William was an aluminum plant. It, at least, was a source of some amusement. Ladner said that every Friday at three o'clock an enemy aircraft would fly over and drop a bomb on it.

Part of the problem, of course, was that the would-be skippers were all impatient to draw assignments at sea, preferably within range of the enemy. Fuller says he was infuriated when he was posted as Second Lieutenant on a Harbour Defence Motor Launch in Belfast, and spoke to Welman about it. "I went in and said: 'I gave up a job that was paying me fifty thousand dollars a year to come over here to fight a war, not to sit on any goddamn harbour defence craft in Belfast...I came over to get into a scrap!' I will say one thing," Fuller recalled, "he acted very quickly. He took down the telephone right away and phoned the Second Sea Lord's office. He said: 'Is that Miss Dalrymple?' (I immediately put that name in the back of my mind, and that was a very, very astute thing to do.) He said: 'I've got an officer here who wants to fight. Yes, yes, yes—49, you say—yes, yes.'" Welman rang off and told Fuller henceforth he could be as scrappy as he wished. He'd been given command of a motor gunboat and was to report forthwith to "Hell Fire Corner."

"Where in the hell is Hell Fire Corner?" Fuller asked.

Welman exploded. "Dover, you damn fool—Dover!"

For once, Fuller did as he was told. He arrived at Dover and took over MGB *49*, a converted MA/SB. He says he went out on his first operational mission that night. Five miles off Cap Blanc Nez, the boat developed serious engine trouble. It limped back to Dover without having met the enemy, Fuller's initiation to little-ship action no worse off for it.

Ladner was equally determined to be posted, but his instincts told him there was a better way to go about it. "So what we decided we'd better do was really blast our way through the exams," he explained. "We should be better than anybody else. As a result we each got appointed to a command (if you can believe it) never having been to sea. It was really quite a joke." Ladner was assigned to MGB *19*, which as it turned out was still being built. In the meantime, he reported to the Camper & Nicholson yard in Southampton to pick up an air-sea rescue yacht, assembled "a motley pick-up crew" from a depot in Portsmouth, and joined a convoy on its way to the Thames Estuary. Ladner said the journey was nightmarish. "I didn't know damn-all about anything. There were minefields on either side, stuff in the air around you. But anyway, we finally got this yacht delivered to wherever she was supposed to go. We went back and I picked up MGB *19* and there I had the wonderful experience of being a Canadian RCNVR sub-lieutenant in command of a sixty-three-foot motor gunboat with an entire Royal Navy permanent force crew."

That was Ladner's good fortune in the spring of 1941. Of the Vancouver connection of Burke, Maitland and himself, he was the only one to start out with a command. "My first trip with this RN crew," he said, "was very pusser, with white sweaters; it was really quite an episode." He spent about a month working-up out of Portsmouth. Maitland finished up his training by mid-February, went down to London briefly while the brass hats decided what to do with him, and was finally sent to Greenock, back in Scotland, as First Lieutenant aboard MGB *69*. This was to be the Senior Officer's boat in a flotilla based at Lowestoft. By late April, Maitland had delivered *69*, not to Lowestoft—it was closed off as a result of enemy mine-laying—but up the Humber River some twenty miles to an old coal dock facility at Immingham. Not long after this, the flotilla set out on what should have been its first patrol in the English Channel, leaving just after dark. They'd barely cleared the mouth of the Humber when MGB *69* struck a mine. It blew the stern off. Maitland and the SO, Lt. Allan Seymour Hayden, RN, along with most of the crew, were unhurt, but several ratings aft were killed. The boat, of course, was a write-off.

That Maitland and Burke were able to recover so quickly from such episodes was an indication of their determination, if not zeal. From this would spring the murderous intent they brought to bear in subsequent actions with the enemy. But before they could do that, they had to find him, and this proved a much more difficult task than they imagined.

For one thing, the boats weren't up to it. Following the disasters in France in May and June of 1940, a large-scale building program was implemented, but it would be some time before it produced results (as an indication of this, between late June 1940 and January 1, 1941, only fifty-six MLs and six HDMLs were built, while as many as thirty MA/SBs were converted to MGBs; in the next six months, only three MTBs were completed, although another thirty-seven MA/SBs were added to strength as MGBs: abysmally small numbers given that many were needed in training as well as operational duties). And so the early commanders had to live with mainly pre-war models, which were not always the best in a rough sea or were plagued by inefficient engines. Even as the building program got underway, it ran into difficulties. This was noted in an historical summary of Coastal Forces prepared at the war's end. "There were no suitable high-powered British engines available in quantity and their design and production were already pre-empted by the R.A.F.," the report's author observed. Peter Dickens said the engines broke down at sea largely because "they were too hastily designed and thrown together; but that was much less the fault of those who built them than the Navy's own." Peter du Cane of Vospers, he said, had designed his boat around one of the best engines available, the Italian Isotta Fraschini, going to great trouble to negotiate a licence to build it in England. He was not allowed to go ahead because the Admiralty said Britain might find itself at war with Italy, in which case Vospers could always use Rolls-Royce Merlins. "It may be imagined that the RAF had few of those to spare after the Battle of Britain," said Dickens. Eventually, a relatively successful substitute was found in the U.S.-built marine Packard, but it was not the engine for which the boats were designed. "Such makeshifts were far from satisfactory as was to be expected," Dickens noted, "for in a high-performance craft the hull and engines must be married for love and not convenience." The result, he said, was "yet another incompatible union." This was an understatement, judging by the impassioned prose Dickens used to describe the recalcitrant mistresses they took to sea. "The beautiful engine lay on the wrong-sized bed at an uncomfortable angle, uncertain, coy and hard to please despite passionate titillation—the pouting cause of intolerable frustration."

There were also problems related to organization and administration of the small boats. The need for a co-ordinating "head" was keenly felt as new bases were established along the southern and eastern coasts of England, including Portsmouth (HMS *Hornet*), Felixstowe (HMS *Beehive*), Weymouth (HMS *Bee*) for working-up—it was moved later in the war, when the coast became too crowded—and Dover (HMS *Wasp*). By the end of the year, additional bases would be established—at Lowestoft and Fowey, for example; throughout the war others appeared as required. The administrative chaos threatened by this quick expansion was largely controlled in October 1940 when Rear-Admiral Piers K. Kekewich, RN, formerly with the staff of the Vice-Admiral Northern Patrol, was appointed Rear-Admiral, Coastal Forces (RACF), initially with headquarters at Fort William and shortly thereafter at HMS *Attack* in Portland.

By all accounts, Kekewich was forthright and earnest in his desire to elevate Coastal Forces to the lofty heights of achievement he felt was its due. "But he wasn't the lord and master type at all," according to Maitland. "He didn't summon you to his office where you had to salute him and stand at attention in front of his desk." This was the best of praise amongst the unruly Canadians, whose reckless disregard—some might say contempt—when it came to authority, particularly that which took itself too seriously, was widely recognized. Kekewich, on the other hand, was admired. He had an easy way about him and demonstrated a genuine interest in the welfare of the small boats and their crews. "He would come out and visit our port, come aboard our boats... 'Well, Maitland, how are all of you and your crew?'...He was magnificent!"

Kekewich also brought an informed mind on the subject of small-boat warfare. In addition to his own background with the Northern Patrol, his Chief-of-Staff was Captain A. W. S. Agar, VC, DSO, RN, whose Victoria Cross was awarded as a result of his action in the 1919 raid at Kronstadt, in which the cruiser *Oleg* was sunk. There was also a Canadian connection at Kekewich's headquarters in Captain Henry Bell-Irving of the well-to-do Vancouver family (a son, also named Henry, who had enjoyed a brilliant war record of his own, was lieutenant-governor of British Columbia from 1978 to 1983). "He had served in the First World War in small boats and here he was (the old fool, at sixty) just having a ball," Maitland remembered. "Super fellow!"

But even such friendly relations as they enjoyed with Kekewich and his staff could not overcome the fact that Coastal Forces, of which they were now employees, was not the ideal arrangement. Historian and author Bryan Cooper observed that Kekewich in fact "worked under continual frustration in dealing with Commanders-in-Chief who were reluctant to give up any of the autonomy of their commands, and from Admiralty departments who hesitated to encroach on the established preserves of these Commanders." In the summer of 1941 a section of the Operations Division of the Naval Staff at the Admiralty was created as a means of keeping a hand in the running of Coastal Forces, a process that, with the implicit assurance of expanding given to all bureaucracies, led to the virtual annexation of Coastal Forces by the Admiralty's own department in 1943. This wrangling over jurisdiction and control, typical of large organizations no less in war than in peace (except that in war it is probably carried out with greater urgency, and occasionally more disastrous consequences) naturally had an effect on the MTB crews. There was some confusion regarding their mandate, which was both good and bad: it allowed a freedom of action not experienced by others in the Royal Navy but was also demoralizing at times, particularly as they struggled to obtain a measure of credibility as a fighting force.

The latter was carried out with an enthusiasm that was truly inspired—and seldom successful. In the six months between the end of June 1940 and January 1, 1941, Coastal Forces reported only ten actions in the English Channel, of which three were brushes with E-Boats. MTBs only were involved. On the night of September 8, 1940, they attacked a convoy anchored off Ostend, sinking an ammunition ship and possibly a supply vessel. There was some doubt afterwards regarding the number of enemy ships hit by torpedoes fired by the MTBs given that the RAF was carrying out its own bombing raid on the convoy. Offensive patrols (as well as mine-laying operations) continued into March 1941. They were uneventful mostly, although several small ships were sunk or damaged. In the same period, three MTBs were destroyed in an air raid, another was sunk in an accident and one MGB was damaged by "stress of weather," according to an official report.

And so it went, with little action to speak of and almost as many boats lost as sunk, as both Burke and Maitland were painfully aware. Nor was it because the enemy had gone into hiding. By the late summer of 1941, E-Boats based along the coasts of France and the Low Countries began attacking British convoys with a vengeance and, perhaps more dangerously, laying mines off the east coast and in the swept channels off the south coast of England. Coastal Forces tried to prevent such operations by positioning their craft at fixed positions known as "Z-points." Both sides operated mainly at night to avoid each other's aircraft and shore batteries, but the MTBs—lightly armed and under-powered— were no match for the faster and better-equipped E-boats. This, in fact, was the reason MGBs were developed, initially by removing an asdic dome on the hull of MA/SBs to boost their speed while cramming the decks of such craft with Oerlikon and Lewis machine guns to obtain greater firepower. It was stop-gap at best; at its worst it was somehow reminiscent of Arthur Lower's description of "Harry Tate's Navy" in the First World War. Engines continued to be a problem; indeed, they were so rebellious they made completing an operational sortie a doubtful event. The truth was that even when they encountered enemy shipping, a few of the early crews were too poorly trained to mount a convincing attack, or were guilty of being overly cautious, sometimes firing their torpedoes at ranges of up to four thousand yards—almost two miles away! Such ill-conceived notions had little chance of success. As a result, the advantage clearly went to the E-boats throughout most of 1941. Operating mainly against the east coast of England and especially the approaches to the Thames Estuary, they sank a total of thirteen ships. In the same period, the British small-boat raiders had yet to score again. This continued into autumn, no doubt greatly frustrating their commanding officers. In fact it was not until September 8, 1941—a full year after the attack at Ostend—that they reached a turning point. That night a unit of the 6th MTB Flotilla based at Dover was sent to intercept a convoy leaving Boulogne and moving northward, attempting to pass through the Straits of Dover. Three boats—all that was available, and these had been at sea for five nights in a row—charged towards Cap Blanc Nez in the hope of cutting the enemy off. Lt. Cdr. E. N. Pumphrey, RN, a veteran of MTB actions at Dunkirk in 1940, was in command of this small force. Following the SO's lead aboard MTB *35* were Lt. P. E. Danielson, RNorN (one of many Norwegians in Coastal Forces), aboard MTB *54*, and Lt. C. E. "Chuck" Bonnell, RCNVR, in command of MTB *218*. Little is known about Bonnell, which is both baffling and regrettable in view of the fact that he was likely the first Canadian small-boat raider to actually engage the enemy. He was also an eyewitness to at least part of that night's stirring action, the first great victory achieved by Coastal Forces.

According to fellow MTB skipper Peter Scott, who gave an early account of the action based on his interviews with its participants, the crews were enjoying the local "leg show" at

Dover when they received word to return to their boats. These were usually tied up at the ferry dock, out of harm's way from the armada of grey-painted destroyers and various other ships, all bristling with guns, that jammed the harbour. Within minutes they were at sea, planing at high speed to meet the enemy.

Arriving off Cap Blanc Nez about two miles from the planned intercept, Pumphrey cut his wing engines, signalling the others to do the same. There were a few anxious moments waiting, especially after the head-pounding din of the boats, but by 2330 the enemy convoy was spotted. First came two merchant ships of about three thousand tons—fully loaded, too, Pumphrey judged—followed by several trawlers and perhaps as many as eight E-boats. Later, Pumphrey remembered the mounting exhilaration he felt.

> It was a flat calm night, moonless but not very dark. We saw them at 4,000 yards and ran in unseen almost on their beam. It was desperately exciting, creeping in the dark, still unseen and getting nearer and nearer. There had never been a serious MTB attack from Dover before, and the escort was half asleep. We got right in, passing between two of the screening E-boats, about 1,000 yards from the rear ship. As we passed the E-boats we rung on wing engines in a crash-start, a noise to wake the dead, and the balloon was up!

Immediately the enemy ships began firing at the MTBs. Pumphrey said the tracer came at him in "green rivers, but it was badly aimed, mostly too high." He ran *35* in to eight hundred yards and then pulled the firing levers to both torpedoes—"a promising salvo," he thought—before turning hard astarboard, his gunners pouring rounds of flaming red tracer in the direction of the convoy as he sped away. Then a great flash leapt from Pumphrey's target. The Dover flotilla had its first victory.

Incredibly, the E-boats made no attempt at pursuit. Five minutes passed before Pumphrey cut his engines and inspected his boat. He discovered his starboard torpedo had misfired and was still in the tube!

It was shortly past midnight. By now the convoy was well out of sight, but Pumphrey decided to resume the chase. He sent a radio message to Dover Castle, requesting the most up-to-date radar plot before setting out again to intercept. Meanwhile, a couple of MGBs that had been operating in the area that night were converging on the convoy. These were MGB *43*, under the command of Lt. Stewart Gould, another veteran of the fighting at Dunkirk, and MGB *52*, Lt. Barry Leith's boat. It was Gould, in fact, who first spotted the convoy. He signalled Pumphrey and then shadowed the enemy, waiting until the MTBs appeared going in to attack. Moments later, he heard several craft approaching astern of the convoy. "Thinking they might be our MTBs," Gould said afterwards, "I challenged. This was answered by heavy and accurate fire from shell-firing machine guns. I then saw that they were German E-boats, four of them, in line abreast." The enemy's gunfire raked across Gould's boat, gravely wounding two of his gunners and knocking out one engine. Undeterred by this, Gould increased his speed so that he crossed the bows of the leading E-boats and dropped a depth charge that destroyed one of the enemy craft. The others were blasted with Oerlikon and Lewis gunfire until they were able to slip away. Gould immediately set upon the convoy, which was firing wildly in all directions, including that in which the E-boats were making a hasty retreat.

All this proved a perfect opportunity for the MTBs now fast approaching but unseen. As Gould and Keith were busily engaging the convoy from its port side, the MTBs came up on the starboard beam. From about twelve hundred yards Danielson, on MTB *54*, fired both torpedoes. He then made smoke and disengaged to port. Pumphrey was on his tail. "We ran on through the smoke," he said, "and emerged to find four E-boats converging on the starboard bow. However, our blood was now well up and we were going to make certain of it. At six hundred yards the merchantman was sitting across the sights like a row of houses and the E-boats were far too close and hitting us hard and often. The time had come to fire—and as I pulled the levers I saw the target obliterated by a great black column of water and wreckage. *54*'s torpedo had hit square amidships and mine was wasted."

In fact, Pumphrey's boat got almost as much as it gave in this engagement. He turned hard aport only to meet a trawler at one hundred yards. In the withering gunfire, first his engines were shot up completely, and finally a three-inch shell took half the stern away. Pumphrey himself was wounded, as were two of his crew. But one of *54*'s gunners had kept up with his own barrage and had succeeded in putting the trawler out of action.

Not long after this, the E-boats vanished from the scene. Pumphrey decided to call it a night, steering his half-demolished boat in an erratic course for home. So ended the first great action in the English Channel, a combined operation in which MTBs and MGBs had been used effectively to obtain the element of surprise and, most importantly, achieve devastating results. In view of this, it was not surprising that Pumphrey, Gould and Danielson were each awarded the Distinguished Service Cross. There were also plenty of Distinguished Service Medals and Mentions-in-Dispatches to go around amongst the crew members afterwards.

Of course the reader might wonder what happened to Lt. Chuck Bonnell, the lone Canadian who had gone along on this operation. He was virtually the only individual who did not receive a commendation for the night's work, although he was probably not upset by this. In fact, he was probably slapping his forehead for a long time after he returned, for he had been the victim of bad luck and a cruel lesson in small-boat warfare. He, too, had closed to attack the convoy when it was spotted off Blanc Nez and had withstood the torrent of green tracer coming from the enemy ships. Later he chased after an "M" Class minesweeper moving up astern of the convoy. In the account Pumphrey gave to Peter Scott, MTB *218* closed on this vessel and fired both torpedoes, but the ship, "either by chance or design," had altered its course at just the right moment to avoid being hit. Bonnell was soon hotly pursued by a couple of E-boats with which he had a running battle until he disappeared from view. The details of what happened after this are sketchy, but it seems Bonnell, having fired both his torpedoes, assumed both Pumphrey and Danielson had done so as well—it was, after all, standard procedure, and not even Pumphrey knew as yet he had one "fish" that had misfired or that Danielson still had both torpedoes. And so Bonnell had made his escape from the fulminating contest with the E-boats, racing full out at 30 knots to an agreed rendezvous point, where he waited. Half an hour passed without any sign of Pumphrey or Danielson. Bonnell concluded they had returned home and set course himself to meet them there. Why he failed or was unable to contact Dover, in which case he would have learned his Senior Officer was still in pursuit of the convoy, remains a mystery. In all likelihood, though, he found out soon enough. Word of the battle in the English Channel had spread throughout Dover Castle, where reports of its progress were received with the rapt attention ordinarily given to, say, a rugby match. It must have been one of Bonnell's worst moments, that he was part of such an important action—and had missed most of it!*

Two months later, Pumphrey and Gould struck again (without Bonnell, although his boat, MTB *218*, was involved in the action; according to Peter Scott it was commanded by Lt. H. P. Granlund, RNVR). On the night of November 3, Pumphrey's flotilla sank a five-thousand-ton vessel and got away unscathed chiefly because of the spirited work of Gould's MGBs, which had stayed behind to shoot up the enemy convoy and engage its obstructive E-boats. Their teamwork proved a tremendous influence on the subsequent development of tactics used by Coastal Forces. Henceforth it would become almost a standard practice to use MTBs and MGBs in tandem, the smaller craft used in a noisy diversionary role allowing the torpedo boats to approach with some stealth from an opposite direction before firing—at least until the enemy expected

---

*Evidently Bonnell recovered from whatever disappointment he might have felt. He was awarded a DSC in 1942 after sinking a merchant ship off Boulogne. But author Gordon Holman offers this sad note in his book, *The Little Ships*, published in October of the following year. "He was reported missing a few months ago, after engaging in a particularly hazardous operation, the details of which will probably not be revealed until after the war." The author was too optimistic.

this, in which case variations of the feint-and-attack had to be worked out. Most of all, experience had shown that successful engagements were fought at close quarters, hundreds of yards at the most and often much less than that. This took a horrendous toll in men and boats, of which MGBs particularly bore the brunt.

But success was like an opiate; others grew increasingly impatient to enjoy the euphoria of victory, while the cumulative effect was to increase the likelihood of doing so. An early indication of this occurred on the night of November 19, when the 6th MGB Flotilla based at Felixstowe enjoyed its first decisive victory against the E-boats, which had lately begun to play havoc with Allied shipping in the North Sea and off the coast of Holland. Leading this action was Lt. Cdr. Robert Peverell Hichens, RNVR, "the modern Drake," as he was sometimes called. Hichens and another MGB skipper surged into the midst of an E-boat patrol off the Hook of Holland, raking the enemy with gunfire from as close as fifty yards. They were outnumbered five to two, but Hichens had the element of surprise and a determination to make the most of his opportunity after a year or so of searching for the enemy. The E-boats suffered as a result.

Later that night, Hichens came across one of the enemy boats abandoned off the Dutch coast. He wanted desperately to tow it back to Felixstowe, but it had been so badly shot up it sank before they could get underway. He had to settle for a captured Black Swastika flying under his White Ensign when he returned to port. The symbolism was fitting. Hichens had proved that with aggressive leadership, MGBs could beat even the heavily armed, diesel-powered E-boats in a straight fight. This had a direct impact on the handful of Canadians with Coastal Forces, including the Vancouver trio of Burke, Maitland and Ladner, as well as Tommy Fuller and several whose names have yet to surface in this account. In the winter of 1941–42, when they were sent more often to defend the coastal convoy route through an area that became known as "E-boat Alley" (roughly speaking, off Norfolk and Suffolk)—an unhealthy spot, as the MGB crews discovered—they brought a confidence to their task that was based on proven tactics, many of which came from the brilliant mind of Hichens.

He had spent his youth sailing small boats along the rugged Cornish coasts and among the Channel Islands. Later he had developed a passion for motor racing. Educated at Marlborough and Magdalen College, Oxford, he was returning to his native Falmouth in Cornwall to practise law when he decided to join the Royal Navy, entering through the Supplementary Yachting Reserve. Hichens was thirty-one when he found himself serving aboard a minesweeper during the evacuation from Dunkirk, where he won his first DSC. He transferred to Coastal Forces in November 1940 and was sent to the 6th MGB Flotilla at Fowey (it is more than likely that he and Corny Burke served together briefly, although Burke has not offered his impressions of any actions in which they operated jointly).

In March 1941, Hichens moved to Felixstowe and took part in the summer's few inconclusive brushes with E-boats. He grew frustrated, but was devising methods he felt were more appropriate to small-boat warfare. The following August, he was promoted to Acting Lieutenant Commander when he took over the flotilla—the first VR officer to receive such a command. He used it to great advantage, too. He lobbied to equip the MGBs with more Oerlikon guns, which paid huge dividends when he finally met the enemy, and he was partly responsible for persuading the Admiralty to replace converted MA/SBs with British Power Boat Company MGBs specifically designed as such.

But it was action that Hichens really craved. For a year, he had toiled in the English Channel without success. Having met the enemy and achieved a decisive victory in November's battle, Hichens craved it even more. His stamina was incredible. In his unfinished memoir published during the war, he said he had often spent as many as sixteen or eighteen hours on end and in the cramped quarters of his MGB while being tossed about in the English Channel, "much of the time in the dark where an instant's inattention or lapse of judgement might mean disaster sudden and

devastating." It was the greatest physical and mental strain to
which a serving officer could be subjected as a matter of normal
routine, he suggested. Many among the small-boat fighters,
including the Canadians, would find similar ways to describe the
sea's fury and their endless toil in little ships, while Hichens
merely added that he had raced repeatedly in the twenty-four Le
Mans "and not found it so exhausting as a bad night in a gunboat."

By all accounts he was equally fearless. Others might be ap-
palled to watch him bring his boat to less than a few hundred yards
of his chosen target—so close, in fact, that the enemy couldn't
depress his guns enough to fire at him—before he dropped a depth
charge, except that his example soon meant they did it, too.

This image of a ruthless professional waging a private, if not
obsessive, war with the E-boats seemed at odds with his reputation
as a loving husband and father, a man who went to sea with small
candies his son had carefully wrapped for him tucked in his
pocket. But his instincts were like those of his colleagues "to
engage the enemy and to close," which he did with greater success
than most. In the best fraternal spirit, he shared his methods and in
turn heeded observations proffered by his fellow skippers during
regular briefing sessions (the latter usually enlivened by jars of
gin). Among the tactics he advocated were the slow approach,
putting along on auxiliary engines or even waiting until the last
seconds before crash starting and shooting out first the bridge of
the enemy's vessel. Tom Ladner, who served with Hichens in
1942, remembers it became their practice to load the Oerlikons
with a high percentage of incendiary bullets so they could merci-
lessly hammer E-boats around the bridge—and elsewhere—creating in his words "alarm and despondency which was excessive."
It often proved decisive in winning the battle.

For obvious reasons, it was to Ladner's great advantage that he
served with Hichens, even if much of what he learned was not used
to its fullest until he reached the Mediterranean the following year.
He joined the 6th MGB Flotilla based at Felixstowe midway
through 1942. Prior to this, Ladner had spent a few seemingly idle
months covering Allied shipping off the east coast or running

across the English Channel to stop the E-boats from breaking out. Somehow he lost MGB *19*—possibly because of engine troubles; they were constantly breaking down, enough that "How will we *ever* win this war?" was a common lament—and as a result he was ordered to pick up a new seventy-one-and-a-half-foot British Power Boat Company boat at Hythe.

But before he could do this, he found himself involved in one of the greatest foul-ups of the war, a bungled British attempt to intercept the German warships *Scharnhörst*, *Prinz Eugen* and *Gneisenau* in the English Channel. Ladner had taken over a C-class gunboat at Grimsby when its commanding officer became ill. Off he went, blasting over to the Dutch coast in broad daylight while overhead the sky was alive with enemy aircraft. They were too busy with the RAF to notice a small flotilla of six MGBs. "We got about twenty-five miles off the coast and by this time it was dark," Ladner recalled. "So the flotilla leader decided we would just sort of circle." They spent the night doing this while listening to reports on the radio. "Finally, about five o'clock in the morning all the action reports had stopped. I signalled up to the SO and I said: 'Why don't we ask somebody to tell us what to do?'" Ladner had spent the night wondering what sort of "burnt offering" he and the others represented in the navy's grand scheme. Now it was obvious they had been completely forgotten! "The whole thing was a real fiasco," he said afterwards. Nor would it have diminished his ire had he known that two of Canada's small-boat raiders, Tony Law and J. R. H. Kirkpatrick, had at least got to within shooting distance of the enemy warships (of which more will be said) while he had wasted a night off the Dutch coast.

In the aftermath of this absurd exercise, Ladner was sent to Portsmouth again to work up an MTB until his own boat was finished. It was useful, getting to know something of the fastidious nature of torpedoes. Finally, though, he took command of MGB *75*. So began his real education as a fast-attack skipper based at Felixstowe with "the immortal Hichens."

It was an eventful summer. In July the E-boats, which had met enough resistance from MGBs in the North Sea, suddenly moved south. Two *Schnellboot* flotillas operating out of Cherbourg began to inflict heavy damage on British coastal convoys, sinking as many as six ships on the night of July 7. To meet this threat, Hichens and his new 8th MGB Flotilla—including Ladner, Lt. R. A. "Bussy" Carr, Lt. L. G. R. "Boffin" Campbell (both RNVR) and another Canadian, Lt. G. F. "George" Duncan, RCNVR, of Montreal—were shifted to Dartmouth. Within hours of their arrival, they were at sea. The following night, July 14, they also had their first success, surprisingly not against the enemy's own fast-attack craft but a tanker, which they sank off Alderney with a spirited depth-charge attack. Two weeks later, they finally met some E-boats.

It was a special operation for which Hichens and his boats were selected. On the night of August 1, in a thick fog, they lay in wait outside the harbour at Cherbourg until a unit of E-boats appeared. Their diesel engines made a growling noise that reminded Hichens of the last dying echo of a thunderclap. Fittingly, it was the Allied MGBs that descended on the E-boats with the swiftness of lightning.

"Crash start! Steer towards, full speed!"

The frenzied battle that followed was typical of so many the small-boat attackers experienced. Shore batteries illuminated the scene with a barrage of starshell and other pyrotechnics, some of which would have been deadly had they found their targets. But the MGBs got away. This was Ladner's initiation to small-boat warfare, and it had been bloody. But that was the way of gunboats, as Hichens had insisted. "If we were to have success, we must fight for it," he said to his officers. "I told them plainly that we intended to seek out and engage the enemy; that unless their guns continued to fire and fire straight, it would be they who would be killed and not the enemy. The alternatives were success or death. They must be efficient."

They were, too—but just picture it. It was mayhem once battle was joined. Boats churned the sea at high speed, guns blazed at close quarters—it was almost too much. How they functioned in the midst of this, manning their guns with iron resolve while all kinds of shot and shell whirled murderously around them, the stench of cordite and smoke and death everywhere, took more than simply adrenalin; it required a faith in immortality, or, failing that, the conviction that death could be put off a while yet.

Sometimes the gunboats worked alongside the MTBs of Peter Dickens's 7th Flotilla, which had also come to Dartmouth that autumn to meet the latest threat in the English Channel. Among the flotilla's young officers was twenty-four-year-old Lt. Charles D. Chaffey, RCNVR, of Vancouver, serving aboard MTB *232*. He remembers vividly the confusion that quickly followed the start of most actions. "I challenge anybody to know what the hell is going on or see anything when it happens," he said almost resentfully. "Everything is lit up with starshells, everybody is making smoke, gunfire is going on and everything's in a great big mist—you don't really know where the heck you are!"

Chaffey had learned this almost the first time he went out on his MTB. On the night of August 7, 1942, he was involved in what has since become known as the Second Battle of Barfleur, so named for its proximity to Cap Barfleur on the Cherbourg Peninsula (the first was fought by Admirals Russell and Tourville in May 1692 during the War of the English Succession, resulting in ex-King James II being permanently thwarted from invading England). "Euphoria is often short-lived when in the presence of the enemy," said Peter Dickens, the Senior Officer of the flotilla. His wisdom proved itself again at Barfleur. In the deadly free-for-all that ensued, Chaffey's skipper was gravely wounded. Chaffey took command—boldly, too—and saved his boat; yet afterwards he had difficulty remembering details of this extraordinary action. It had been simply too confused. So, not surprisingly, what Chaffey remembered most vividly was the emotional impact of such actions. Later he said of his wartime experiences in small boats, "Ninety-eight per cent of the time it was boring and the other two per cent you had enough excitement to last you for a lifetime."

In all likelihood, Chaffey's next action fell into that narrow margin. On August 19, he went to Dieppe as a spare CO aboard

ML *309*. He was one of the fortunate, inasmuch as he got back to England in one piece to serve again—in his case, aboard MTBs with one of two all-Canadian flotillas established in 1943. But "excitement" wasn't the word to be used about Dieppe. Like many who survived the disastrous raid, Chaffey speaks of it reverently, in measured terms. Pressed to give at least a brief description of what he saw, Chaffey answered, "Mostly blood."

That men like Chaffey went out to sea again—willingly, too—after being a part of such bloody initiations was truly extraordinary. Ladner, for example, recalls he was often dashing across the Channel to mix it up with E-boats or patrolling off Guernsey while the legendary Dunstan Curtis rescued downed pilots. Invariably, according to Ladner, "something happened."*

Waiting outside the enemy's ports on the French coast continued to be successful. Ladner recalls approaching Le Havre one night. From the amount of light flooding the harbour, Hichens surmised something was going to happen. "So we crept in there...and we waited; and sure enough the gate opened and out came this lovely convoy." If this wasn't good enough, another convoy steamed into view. Now they had to decide whether to attack the convoy coming out or the one going in. They settled on the one coming out, shooting it up with such fury that the harbour was in chaos for days afterwards while the enemy cleared the wreckage.

Not long after this, the E-boats resumed their operations off the Dutch coast, partly in response to the effectiveness of the small-boat flotillas. Like a flying squad with Scotland Yard, the 8th Flotilla returned at once to Felixstowe. September was a profitable

---

* Lt. D. M. C. Curtis, RNVR, had played a leading role in an attack by MGBs, MTBs and MLs on the port at St. Nazaire in March 1942, hailed as "the greatest raid of all." As far as can be determined, only one Canadian was involved. This was Lt. Graham Baker, RCNVR, of Toronto, commanding one of the MLs, who displayed "unshaken devotion" to controlling his guns in the action. Killed while leaping to a jetty to make fast several other launches despite the enemy's murderous crossfire, Baker's courage was recorded in a posthumous Mention-in-Dispatches.

month in their encounters with the enemy off the Dutch coast. Then on the night of October 2, 1942, disaster struck. Based on Ladner's recollections and an account of the action Hichens provided in his memoirs, this is what happened.

They had set out to lie in wait for E-boats off the Hook of Holland. This much was fairly routine by now, although Hichens was troubled somewhat by the brilliant moonlight. They all preferred the cover of darkness. Sighting the enemy ships, he realized he might have the advantage after all. "So far so good," he said. "We were in a perfect position. The enemy approaching slowly, on a course to pass us a few cables to starboard. They were in line abreast doing about four knots.... Here was a chance to try out our oft-discussed plans."

Time was short now. Hichens had to decide which of his boats should lead the attack. He knew that Lt. Duncan, the other Canadian in his flotilla, had been pining for an opportunity.

"Would you like to carry out the attack, George?" Hichens shouted.

"Yes, I would!" came the reply, eagerly. It was settled. And thus, as Hichens wrote, "A very brave man was started on the short run to swift death."

Two cables off, they were challenged by the trawlers. Buzzers sounded on the MGBs and all at once a dazzling torrent of red tracer hit the enemy boats, almost certainly inflicting heavy damage before the gunfire was returned. The MGBs increased speed and began circling in the blinding light, guns still firing with lethal intensity at the quarry they'd surrounded.

Then, confusion.

According to Hichens, they somehow lost contact with Duncan. "We sped shorewards, searching for him, but found nothing." Ladner says several other enemy ships had appeared out of nowhere, scattering the MGBs. It is agreed they ended up perilously close to the great shoaling sands of the Dutch coast, but Ladner suggests Duncan was still with them at this point and even tried to charge through the enemy boats. He didn't make it. In an attempt to disengage, he ran aground and so was a sitting target. Duncan's boat was shot to pieces by the enemy's guns.*

Ladner, too, tried to slip out; in all likelihood he owed his success to the fact that Duncan had momentarily drawn the enemy's fire. But even Ladner's boat suffered horribly. In the tumult, he made for the only protection he could find, a buoy large enough to screen his battered gunboat. "I decided if I hung behind that buoy, in the dark, I couldn't be seen," he explained. "I turned out to be right and I ended up finding my way back to Felixstowe. I had a big hole in the bow. The boat was a mess, badly shaken up. We had a lot of casualties on board. That was the end of 75," he said. "It was a terrible night."

Hichens, too, felt the pain of losing a fellow officer who was also his friend. As the flotilla's Senior Officer, he knew also the bitter self-reproach that came with not having led the attack, although it seems unlikely Duncan's fate had been determined by this alone. Nor was Duncan inexperienced. He had earned a DSC and several Mentions-in-Dispatches for his "leadership, coolness and skill" during actions in the English Channel. Accordingly, he was known among his fellow officers as "Fearless and Resolute George."

In his memoirs, Hichens remembered the Canadian skipper with great affection and sadness. "George had been straight and simple and brave. So full of life, so keen on his job. Of all people that I knew Conrad's praise of the Anglo-Saxon male seemed most applicable to him. 'A man of courage, initiative and hardihood, yet so little stained by the excesses of many virtues.' "

That was October 1942. It is difficult to know precisely how

---

*Ladner's version of what happened to Duncan differs considerably from the account given by Hichens, who says he continued searching for his officer that night and gave up only after he'd exhausted the possibilities of finding him. Ladner, on the other hand, has a vivid recollection of witnessing the destruction of Duncan's boat and its entire crew. It is difficult to reconcile such conflicting testimony, and so in many respects what happened to Duncan remains a mystery.

much Duncan's death affected Ladner in the coming weeks or months, although he did go straight to London afterwards for a bit of rest. There he went to see several officials, explaining that as he was once again "between boats" it might be a good idea if he had leave to return to Canada. His request granted, Ladner was back in Vancouver in time for Christmas, 1942.

Meanwhile his friends, Burke and Maitland, had observed the war's progress from a rather different perspective. Following his disaster with MGB *69*, Maitland says he went to Poole to get one of the new seventy-one-and-a-half-foot BPBC craft, which even today provokes in him almost a doting admiration. "They were beautiful, the British design." Three huge Packard engines powered this latest version. It was a glorified speedboat crammed with guns.

Burke was at Poole, also. So were a number of Canadians attached to a Motor Launch flotilla. The so-called Empire Gang included men from Australia and New Zealand, much to the horror of the Base Commander who evidently detested all colonials. "We were a little 'informal,' if you want to put it that way," said Maitland. This informality was on display around the yacht club at Poole, which Maitland recalls was "excellent," and at a local billiard hall. No doubt the brass hats, peevish at the best of times, concluded that what the young skippers needed to curb their impetuous behaviour was to get back into the war, and soon. This was, after all, what they were being paid for—at inflated Canadian rates, too!

It turned out they were just as eager to resume fighting, which they did in the spring of 1942. Maitland and Burke took their new boats to Lowestoft to join the 20th MGB Flotilla, which spent the next few months assigned to "E-boat Alley" and off the Hook of Holland. Maitland said they saw "a fair bit of action," although one of his most vivid recollections of that summer in 1942 concerns another Canadian skipper, Lt. Peter Thompson, RCNVR, who was with the 7th Flotilla at Lowestoft in command of MGB *91*. Thompson, he says, along with another skipper captured an E-boat one night. "They were towing her home, which would have been a great prize because the boat was virtually intact... And by God, they got two-thirds of the way back when the Germans sent out a dozen fighter planes and sunk it and also badly chewed up our two boats.''*

Maitland shakes his head—an uneasy chuckle coming to him. Those were dangerous times. So far, they had defied the odds against them, but they always knew death still was possible. The thing was to avoid discussing it, even when they had tempted fate more than was perhaps necessary.

It's hard to see how they did it, especially when Burke was around. His predicaments in the English Channel were legendary. The night he lost his "wheels" off the Dutch coast was a perfect example of this. Here is the way Burke explained it:

> The drill was that we would lie cut and stay joined with heaving lines, which we proceeded to do. We saw nothing during the night. By five o'clock in the morning Maitland said, "Start up. We'd better get out of here." The idea was to be halfway across the North Sea by first light because of the Luftwaffe. These boats were very vulnerable to fighter attack. I signalled all three engines slow ahead and all I got was a screaming noise. I got the motor mechanic on the bridge and I said, "What the hell's wrong with your clutches?" He said, "The clutches are working, sir." I started to get very frightened indeed. I didn't want to jump into the North Sea at five o'clock in the morning on a blustery March day and so I ordered the First Lieutenant to go over the side and look. He came up with a look of incredulity on his face and he said, "There aren't any wheels!" I said, "Don't be ridiculous, man. Look again. How did we ever get here?" He went down again and he said, "I've touched the ends of all three shafts

---

* Maitland also neglected to mention that while Thompson had indeed lost the E-boat, he did manage to bring back its entire crew as prisoners. The native of Oakville, Ontario, was awarded a DSC for this gallant action. It is not certain that the Luftwaffe in fact had "a dozen" night fighters to spare for such an operation in the summer of 1942. Perhaps Maitland is fuzzy on this point.

and there are no propellers." What had happened was I'd put the boat up on the ways the afternoon before we left and had three new wheels put on; and the dockyard matey, being sloppy, hadn't properly tightened them. The thrust of the propellers was such that we got over there all right because they'd stayed on by themselves, but lying cut all night, first of all the boss-nuts simply unturned on the threads and then the wheels just twirled off and we had no propellers! You can imagine if a convoy had come along what would have happened to us that night. Maitland had to tow me all the way home, which wasn't really a labour of love on his part, I can tell you!

The episode demonstrated yet again that they were lucky—as lucky as they were wild, although not all of them had the aplomb of one shore-based engineering officer who accompanied his flotilla one night as an observer and, upon finding himself unexpectedly in the middle of a battle, proclaimed with more glee than was perhaps appropriate in the circumstances: "Oh, I say—madly war, isn't it?"

If they laughed, it was because they recognized the essential truth behind such madness. As one among them later wrote: "War has been said to breed but one virtue; a spirit of comradeship and community rarely seen in saner times."

By the end of 1942, this spirit had emerged and was flourishing amongst most of the small-boat commanders, although in many respects the Vancouver trio of Ladner, Burke and Maitland had an advantage in having known each other for so long. Others, like Peter Thompson, had made a great impression on the fraternity and would continue to be a part of it. Burke said, "We didn't have any great triumphs, but we did have some actions which at least blooded us." Maitland concurred. "We didn't really start to make any scores until we got to the Mediterranean."

Perhaps the only exception was Tommy Fuller. He'd lost several of his own boats in numerous actions, told a gunnery instructor at Weymouth advocating old-school shooting methods he was "all balls"—which he subsequently proved in front of the Base Commander with a demonstration of his preferred technique—and earned a reputation as a mean son-of-a-bitch both at sea and on land.

"I might say that I was the roughest commanding officer of anybody," he once confessed, "and you might say a perfectionist."

Later, in the Mediterranean and the Adriatic, he said he refused to board his own ship at night without hailing the Officer of the Watch. "I figured that if I went down by myself with no officer as a witness, the crew would have thrown me overboard, they hated my guts so much."

Loyalty was a different matter, even if it was given grudgingly. When one of Fuller's boats was written off in the Med, he was surprised when the entire crew asked to be transferred with him to his new boat. Finally one of the ratings offered an explanation.

"Well, sir," he said, "we might be badly damaged, but you *always* bring us back to port, and that's what we want to serve on, a ship that always comes back."

It was a miracle they did, no less in the English Channel than Homer's "wine dark" sea—their next destination.

4

Dogs in the Med

W INSTON CHURCHILL, in a speech to the Lord Mayor's Day Luncheon in London at the end of November 1942, referred to the "deadly grapple" that had recently occupied the British in North Africa. There, he said, glowering over his half-moon spectacles with an artful composure, the enemy had "received back again that measure of fire and steel which they have so often meted out to others."

Modern audiences made cynical by politicians' cant might roll their eyes at such a declaration, but in its day the wartime leader's statement resonated with defiance. His remarks also had the virtue of being close enough to the truth. The campaign that had ranged back and forth across the desert sands, seemingly as great as any in heroic legend, had clearly reached a turning point with the victory at El Alamein and the Allied landings in French North Africa. This, in fact, was the prime minister's message when he sagely informed his audience, "Now this is not the end. It is not even the beginning of the end. But it is, perhaps, the end of the beginning."

So, if the world's attention was at all riveted to Allied fortunes in North Africa, it was justified. But no less momentous were the sea battles waged in the Mediterranean, Adriatic and Aegean—as the

men of Coastal Forces discovered. Here in the cradle of civiliza-
tion, the scene of countless crusades well before the time of Christ,
in seas that Minoans, Greeks and Trojans had once plied, the motor
torpedo boats and gunboats played a significant role in protecting
vital British interests and supporting land campaigns against the
Axis. Their part in the drama did not begin in earnest until 1942,
and it was not until late 1943 that they came into conflict with the
enemy. Then their fate was intimately connected with the pendu-
lum of activity in North Africa, the siege of Malta and the
invasions of Sicily and Italy; yet—if it was possible—they
enjoyed much greater freedom of action than was the case in the
restricted waters of the English Channel and the North Sea.

They had much in their favour, not the least of which was
Britain's dominance in the region. This had less to do with
numbers of ships—and they were much fewer in June 1940, when
the British under Admiral Cunningham destroyed the French Fleet
at Oran to prevent its falling into enemy hands—than a determination to win the Battle of the Mediterranean at all costs. Starting
with only a ragtag fleet of outdated battleships, a few cruisers and
several destroyers, the British faced the enormous task of guarding
both the western and eastern Mediterranean from bases at Gibraltar, Malta and Alexandria. The Axis, on the other hand, controlled
the entire coast from France to the Balkans, including Greece and
Crete, and the southern coastline from Algeria to the eastern
border of Cyrenaica, now Libya. Meanwhile Hitler's admirals had
urged him to exclude the British from the Mediterranean as part of
a grand, co-ordinated plan for the region. This vaguely recalled
Napoleon's ambitions almost a century and a half before, of which
he had written to Talleyrand: "The time is not far off when to
destroy England we shall be forced to occupy Egypt." But even
Napoleon had learned ultimately of Britain's unyielding attitude in
the Mediterranean, when Admiral Nelson smashed the future
emperor's fleet at Aboukir Bay in the great Battle of the Nile in
1798. Hitler, an admirer of Napoleon with similar plans for
conquest, understood the region's strategic importance but he, too,
underestimated the use of sea power. Worse, he left it to Mussolini

to carry out the job of eliminating their adversary. Il Duce was no visionary. He regarded the Mediterranean as an Italian lake. To defend it (and likely no more than that), he had built a well-balanced fleet of fast, modern warships—including an impressive number of torpedo boats.

Indeed, of all the wartime powers, Italy had the greatest advantage in small craft. The country boasted some 500 *Motoscafi Armato Silurante* (torpedo-armed motorboats), or MAS boats, at the war's outset—as many as all the other naval countries combined. They suited the Italian temperament and aesthetic tastes, from the sweeping, sculptured hull to the enormously powerful Isotta Fraschini engines—the best of all. In the First World War, too, Italy had promoted small-boat warfare and had carried out a number of successful raids against Austrian ships. To one Italian officer, Luigi Rizzo, went credit for sinking a dreadnought at sea, one of the few times such a feat was achieved. Between the wars Italy continued to improve its boats, with an obvious preference for speed over armament, which resulted in a fifty-foot craft powered by two Isotta Fraschini petrol engines capable of 42 knots, armed with only one 13.2-mm machine gun, two 17.7-inch torpedoes and six depth charges to be used in anti-submarine warfare. This became the basic design used in the construction of MAS boats produced until 1941.

But Italy never fully exploited its numerical superiority in fast-attack craft, either as a "fleet in being" or during the few engagements with Allied skippers. Most accounts suggest they fought largely a defensive war, even to the point of refusing contact with the Royal Navy on occasion. From 1940 to 1943, when Italy surrendered, the MAS flotillas based at Taranto, Naples, Sicily, Sardinia, Tripoli and the tiny island of Pantalleria carried out only a few successful attacks against Malta-bound convoys. This was odd, to say the least, given that the Italian small-boat navy had taken as its motto *memento audere semper*: "Remember always to dare."

Mostly, the Italians seemed preoccupied with their image. Gordon Stead of Vancouver, a young RCNVR lieutenant on loan to the

Royal Navy who commanded an ML with the Third Flotilla based at Malta, said the Italian boats never, *never* flew ensigns that were not immaculate. He reported also that the caps of Italian officers were said to be trimmed with gold braid. But as a fighting force, the Italians were seldom taken seriously. Even one of their most imaginative operations might have seemed farcical if not for the loss of life involved. This was an incredibly brave, and ultimately foolhardy, attempt by several MAS boats to penetrate Grand Harbour at Malta in July 1941. Major Teseo Tesei, one of Italy's most vocal proponents of small-boat warfare and the use of manned torpedoes, led this ill-fated raid. The Italian boats were spotted as they made their approach and were promptly blown to smithereens by Malta's coastal artillery.

Against this formidable but as yet untested fleet of MAS boats the British in 1940 could muster only nine of the old fifty-five foot Thornycroft MTBS, built originally for export but now hastily pressed into service with a newly formed 10th MTB Flotilla based at Alexandria. Alex Joy of Toronto, who had used his family connections and his membership in the Royal Canadian Yacht Club to enlist in the RCNVR in 1939, was among the officers who made the journey around the Cape of Good Hope and up the Red Sea to the Suez Canal. Shortly after their arrival, five of the boats, sent out to help with the defence of Crete, were lost during an air raid on Suda Bay in May 1941, leaving only four MTBs to patrol the harbours at Alexandria and Haifa. Joy, a twenty-three-year-old sub-lieutenant, was soon given command of MTB *215*. Later he said it was rather pleasant being such a young captain piped aboard when visiting battleships.

For a while Joy and the remnants of the 10th MTB Flotilla operated out of Mersa Matruh, patrolling westward on alternate nights along the coast of Egypt. Later they moved to the garrison at Tobruk. Little action was found during these early days. More than the uneventful sorties Joy remembers the difficulties he had with his boat. The clutches, which were complicated and caused more trouble than they were worth, were eventually replaced by a piece of railway axle. There was no way to idle. "So when you started an engine," said Joy, "you went!" This led to a disastrous incident one "rather rough and nasty night" on patrol, when Joy's boat was lying alongside the Senior Officer's and they both started up on opposite wing engines. The two boats slammed into each other. Joy's survived relatively unscathed, but the SO was left with a gaping hole in the hull of his boat. "We got him under tow but unfortunately the water got in too fast and eventually the boat sank," Joy recalled. According to Joy, his Senior Officer was "unfairly" reprimanded by a Court of Inquiry as a result of this small catastrophe.

There were other incidents, too. Joy says the hulls of their boats got so filthy their effective speed was reduced to 23 knots. In due course, a signal was sent advising the Commander-in-Chief in the Mediterranean of this lamentable development, which elicited only the tart acknowledgement: "MTBs are to be considered operational at 23 knots." Joy and his cohorts were not exactly pleased with the reply, but they understood the reasoning behind it. The lack of MTBs and other small craft in the Mediterranean was desperate. Even the prime minister knew of this, demanding in one of his missives to the foreign secretary as early as September 1940, "What is being done about getting our 20 motor torpedo-boats…?" He concluded with the adage, "Beg while the iron is hot."

Meanwhile the C-in-C Med was pleading with the Admiralty. This resulted in a signal to the Chief of Naval Staff in Ottawa, requesting assistance. The Canadian government offered to provide twelve of the British Power Boat Company boats under construction at the new plant outside Montreal. Later, two flotillas of ten Elco-built boats each were obtained from the United States. Meanwhile, the rapid building program underway in Britain made it possible to send a number of MTBs, MGBs and MLs along with trained crews. By August 1941, the Admiralty could report that as many as sixty MTBs and a number of other boats were being sent to the Mediterranean. The process would continue, with increasing urgency, well into 1942.

Invariably, they arrived "just in time," too. The war in the desert had taken an ominous turn in February 1941 with the arrival in Libya of Erwin Rommel, the "Desert Fox," with the vanguard of his Afrika Korps. In a matter of weeks he launched his first offensive. In the next eighteen months he ranged across Tripolitania, Cyrenaica, and deep into Egypt, coming at one point to within two days' march of Alexandria. It was soon apparent that Rommel's lines of supply would have to be attacked. Overnight, Malta became the base of operations for RAF bombers ranging far into the Mediterranean to intercept merchant ships carrying precious fuel and supplies to the Afrika Korps. To counter this, Hitler reluctantly ordered Field Marshal Kesselring's Luftflotte II from Russia to Italy—a massive armada of some six hundred front-line aircraft, including a new version of the ME 109. These were assigned the task of reducing the ancient island of Malta into dusty stone and rubble, assisted by the Regia Aeronautica. The epic siege of Malta was on.*

E-boats, too, were sent against the island fortress as part of a determined marine blockade. The first arrived with the 3rd E-boat Flotilla under Korvettenkapitän F. Kemnade in early 1942, following a secret journey through the Rhine-Rhône Canal down past Lyon and Avignon to the Ligurian Sea, during which they were disguised as fishing boats. They were based initially at Augusta, Sicily. For months, while the Luftwaffe battled the RAF and U-boats attempted to thwart Allied shipping to Malta, E-boats worked together with Italian MAS boats to string a necklace of acoustic mines across the route to the island. Naturally this had to be cleared.

In fact, mine-sweeping was one of the main tasks given to the Motor Launches stationed at Malta, including ML *126* commanded by the young Gordon Stead of Vancouver. In March 1942,

---

* The skies over Malta were soon hotly contested. But of all the fighter aces to emerge from the conflict, the most famous was George "Buzz" Beurling, a gangling twenty-one-year-old from Verdun, Quebec, whose twenty-seven "kills" in fourteen days made this inscrutable, supremely gifted pilot a national (if reluctant) hero in Canada.

they had run the gauntlet of enemy ships in the Mediterranean and had reached Malta—the tiny island reminded Stead of a "leaf upon the sea," a phrase he used again in 1988 as the title of his memoirs—owing to their superb navigational skills, careful conservation of fuel, and prudent avoidance of any contact deemed potentially unfriendly, the latter aided considerably by their flying the Italian ensign for much of their journey.*

By early 1943 Coastal Forces in the Mediterranean consisted of four flotillas of MTBs, seven of MLs and eight of HDMLs. The MTBs were soon amalgamated into two main flotillas, based at Malta. Four boats of this small force achieved the first major success of Coastal Forces in the Med on the night of January 19, 1943. Joy, now a Lieutenant commanding MTB 267, was among those who left the island at midday, headed towards Tripoli. Eight hours into the journey, 267 developed engine trouble and Joy had to turn back. The other boats pressed on. Waiting outside the enemy harbour, they spotted several tugs towing a submarine. In the furious battle that ensued, the MTBs took almost as much as they gave, but two days later when Tripoli was occupied by the British it was the Italian submarine, *Santorre Santorosa*, that was found abandoned with severe torpedo damage on the shoals outside the port. Joy, experiencing the bad luck that often befell the torpedo boat flotillas, had missed the action completely.

Of course, the war in the Mediterranean was far from finished, even if the Afrika Korps had begun its long retreat in the desert. Preparations were underway already for the invasions of Sicily and Italy. For this the MTBs would be needed to run diversionary operations in addition to their more customary interdiction of coastal convoys and search-and-destroy missions against the enemy's small boats. Then, if nothing else, MTB sailors would

---

* Stead, who once entertained Winston Churchill aboard his ML during a brief visit to the island by the Prime Minister, was awarded the Distinguished Service Cross in recognition of his outstanding conduct in various mine-sweeping operations.

prove themselves more worthy practitioners of the Italian creed, remembering "always to dare" regardless of the circumstances.

It was, arguably, the handful of Canadians who had served their apprenticeship in the English Channel who best exemplified this spirit—Ladner, Maitland, and Burke, soon to be known as "The Three Musketeers," and Tommy Fuller, who would be better known as the "Pirate of the Adriatic" when he moved to that theatre towards the end of 1943, but was no less a formidable figure in the Med.

The idea of joining Coastal Forces in the Mediterranean, when it was put to him, appealed instantly to Maitland. Here was an opportunity, as he put it, to "get off on another lark."

Maitland had returned to Canada in the autumn of 1942, spending eight weeks in Vancouver before returning to England shortly before Christmas. His closest friends, Ladner and Burke, had gone home as well. Ladner had returned on a French freighter from Madagascar, a dreadful ship that was infested with enormous cockroaches. Landing in New York, he went straight to the Barbazon Plaza Hotel, mesmerized by all the lights as he rode luxuriously—by wartime London standards—in the wide expanse of a warm city cab. Even more impressive, he remembers, was Bing Crosby crooning his soon-to-be-immortal hit, "I'm Dreaming of a White Christmas," on the cab's radio. Arriving at the hotel, Ladner went straight to the main dining room and ordered a quart of milk, two fried eggs and some bacon. This ambrosial repast somehow confirmed his arrival in North America.

Burke's adventures are not recorded, but no doubt he, like Ladner, made the most of his leave in Vancouver before returning to active duty in the U.K. Almost the moment they landed, Maitland was upon them with news of the proposed "junket," as it would be called, to the Med. They all volunteered.

Surprisingly, Tommy Fuller claims he was ordered to join them. He was greatly disappointed when informed of the decision. "I said, 'Christ, I know the English Channel like the back of my hands, so why send me to the Med?' But that was the way they wanted it."

Fuller *liked* England. He enjoyed the nightclubs, Josey the Flora-Dora girl—and, by his own account, a few other girls. It was true, also, that he knew the English Channel.

Perhaps the brass at Dover felt it was a good way to see the end of this obdurate maverick. In any event he, too, was slated to leave for the Mediterranean as commanding officer aboard one of the new Fairmile "D"s, 115-foot MTBs and MGBs known by all as Dog boats, that would sail as an armada in the spring of 1943.

For the Vancouver trio, their most important concern was assembling the best possible crew to accompany them. Ladner was especially pleased when his former cox, a chap named Nichol, was again assigned to him. Among his many sterling qualities, according to Ladner, Nichol possessed a colourful background. Raised as a "Barnardo Boy" in some far-flung corner of the world, Nichol had joined the Royal Navy at an early age (still in his young teens, in fact) and had served briefly as a servant to Lord Louis Mountbatten on Malta. Nichol evidently did not appreciate his master's "lordy ways." In fact, the only individual who drew more reproach from Ladner's young cox was Mountbatten's wife.

Ladner also had a young English First Lieutenant named Syrett aboard his new MGB, *663*, which they collected at Littlehampton. Indeed, they were all young. Ladner remembers the day his new Navigating Officer came aboard. He guessed the fellow was, at the most, nineteen. "I looked at this guy and I thought: 'My God! Is *that* supposed to navigate me from Milford Haven to Gibraltar?' Unbelievable!"

To their credit, the young British crews that went with the Canadian skippers to the Med performed admirably when tested, although there were some doubtful moments on the journey. Two-thirds of them were raw recruits. Most had never even been to sea!

It is also more than possible these callow ratings were somewhat apprehensive of their commanding officers, whose colourful reputations had become a kind of currency. Lt. L. C. Reynolds, RNVR, who joined Burke's MTB *658* as a nineteen-year-old Navigating

Officer in March, was informed of this by a Wren officer as she handed him his travel warrant before setting out.

"Oh, by the way," she said, with parting good humour, "your CO's name is Burke—Cornelius Burke—and the Number One is Pickard. Both of them are lieutenants, and they're both from Canada. Burke's a tough egg from the wild and woolly west—I hope he doesn't eat you! Cheerio!"*

Reynolds found his new skipper at Weymouth, in a gunnery shed, to be precise, making a hands-on inspection of a stripped-down pom-pom along with his First Officer, Herb Pickard of Winnipeg. Reynolds presented himself self-consciously and was immediately disarmed by Burke's easy-going nature. "Pleased to have you here, Pilot!" he said, flashing a wide grin while extending an oily hand. "There was strength, sincerity and friendliness apparent even in those few seconds' greeting," Reynolds recalled. "The skipper wiped his hands on a grubby piece of cotton waste and suggested that a drink was indicated."

They went to a nearby pub, where in the course of a leisurely hour or two Burke outlined their prospects in the Med. According to Reynolds, his skipper's greatest concern was that they would arrive too late to see any action.

"You see, Len, I reckon the big squeeze is bound to start in Tunisia in the next few weeks, and things will warm up at sea if Rommel's mob are going to be kicked out of Africa. When that happens, I want *658* to be there!"

Reynolds says it was March 2, 1943, when this conversation occurred. The war in the desert was temporarily at a stalemate, but sooner, rather than later, they expected the combined weight of various Allied armies would be hurled against the enemy, chasing him out of the desert before the Dog boats could play a role in their defeat.

It was further apparent during this drinking bout that Burke and

---

* The remark is found in Reynolds's excellent book recalling his experiences with Burke and the others in the Med, entitled *Gunboat 658*. Now a rare edition, it is highly recommended if a copy can be found.

Pickard, known as "Pick," were close friends. Reynolds formed a good impression of both men, as he did of the Canadians generally. As a rule they were more considerate of their subordinates. Lacking a sense of distinction based on class, and naturally gregarious if not occasionally reckless with their enthusiasms, they also provided an inexhaustible source of amusement— although Reynolds may have exaggerated their "cowboy" idiom.

In Weymouth, too, was another friend of Burke's commanding MGB *665*. This was Peter Thompson, whose exploits in the English Channel had almost included the capture of an E-boat. Following their working-up at HMS *Bee*, the two boats left for Milford Haven, a magnificent natural harbour on the southwestern tip of Wales. There they were reunited with Ladner and Maitland, commanding MGBs *663* and *657* respectively. Pembroke Dock, a few miles upriver from Milford Haven but still surrounded by evidence of the area's original Flemish settlers as well as Quakers who had left for this area from Nantucket Island, Massachusetts, in 1793, would be the staging area for the boats assigned to the Med.

Burke was unusually restrained throughout the journey, his mind evidently very much on developments in North Africa. Listening to the BBC one o'clock news back at Weymouth and hearing of the British breakthrough at the Mareth Line that had sent the Afrika Korps retreating through Tunisia, he openly despaired of reaching their destination before the war in the desert was finished. Tilting his glass, recalled Reynolds, he murmured reflectively, "We'll have to get a move on, or we'll be too late, y'know!"

But not even this could dampen Burke's spirits for long, especially now that he was with Ladner and Maitland again. Between the frequent gun drills and exercises that occupied their days, they spent a sufficient amount of time aboard an appointed "duty drinking barge," discussing matters while consuming jars of gin. It was at one of these sessions that a radio was switched on to monitor any fresh developments in North Africa. In the hubbub that resumed shortly, Ladner suddenly snarled, "Quiet!"—and everyone's attention was immediately arrested. Reynolds, who recalled the incident in his memoirs, said, "The voice of the announcer seemed to be personally addressing us rather than a vast unseen audience, and there was that sort of breathless, tensed silence in the wardroom which was rare—and the more memorable for being so."

The news fell hard as they listened.

> ...*The following communiqué was issued by the Admiralty today:*
> *On each of the last two nights, light coastal forces have had short, sharp engagements with enemy patrol craft close to the Dutch coast.*
> *As a result of these engagements, considerable damage has been caused to the enemy craft and many casualties must have been inflicted on their personnel.*
> *During the course of last night's engagement, it is regretted that Lt. Cdr. Robert Peverell Hichens, DSO, DSC, RNVR, was killed. The other casualties sustained...*

Ladner stared bleakly into his gin, feeling the weight of this solemn, incomprehensible moment. The "immortal Hichens," with whom Ladner had served a large part of his apprenticeship, the figure who epitomized small-boat warfare and a man who had earned the admiration and respect of skippers and ratings alike, was killed by a stray bullet after breaking off an engagement with the enemy. The date was April 13, 1943.

Shortly before they left Milford Haven, Peter Scott, son of Scott of the Antarctic and himself a distinguished fast-attack skipper, paid tribute to the legendary Hichens in a broadcast on the BBC. It could not have failed to move all who heard it, not least of all Ladner or his cohorts, who well understood the deadly nature of their business.

There was one more grim bulletin to come. Two days prior to their sailing, Stewart Gould, another larger-than-life MTB skipper, was killed during an action off the coast of Tunisia. Having felt the Battle of the Narrow Seas (Scott's phrase describing action in the

English Channel and North Sea) close behind them with the loss of Hichens, the Canadians might have seen in the death of Gould a foreshadowing of the danger that lay ahead.

Perhaps such incidents merely hardened their resolve as they received confirmed orders to sail. They set out at 1600 hours on April 30, seventeen little ships accompanied by two ancient trawlers passing one by one through the narrow channel at Milford Haven and into the stormy Atlantic.

Few who made the journey would forget it. "We sailed into one of the worst days you ever saw," said Maitland. It was so bad, in fact, that they had delayed their departure, advising the C-in-C Med: "Weather atrocious. Still doing work-up trials." Within twenty minutes, a signal came back: "Send me the boats forthwith. I will work them up!" And so they had sailed on the thirtieth, to do battle first with gale-force winds and a huge following sea that catapulted them towards the Bay of Biscay. If they survived this, meeting the enemy would be a very tame affair in comparison.

To conserve fuel, they travelled at 8 knots on one engine. They would need every drop for the 1,600-mile journey to Gibraltar, even with the extra 8,000 gallons in special tanks welded to the decks of their boats. For as long as the weather permitted, they sailed in four columns, two lines of MLs between the four MGBs to port, Maitland aboard *657* leading Burke on *658* and Ladner on *663*—with four MTBs to starboard, Lt. Cdr. R. R. W. Ashby, a hero of MTB actions off Hong Kong in 1941, in the lead. Tommy Fuller, aboard MTB *655*, was in this column.

Not long after setting out, they realized they were being fol-lowed—not by a ship, but a Focke-Wolfe Condor. It made a few desultory attacks. The pilot of this aircraft was bold enough to exchange signals with the little ships, at one point offering the opinion, "pretty good shooting. Not good enough, though." There was something ominous in its pursuit.

Mostly, the journey was a constant duel with the elements. Many of the ratings were seasick. The waves were so high that boats disappeared in front of one another, making it difficult to stay in formation. Burke, following Maitland, asked for a stern light to use as a reference. Throughout the night, as visibility grew worse, Burke asked to have this light turned up.

Fighting the wind and the ships' wheels in such conditions soon left the men exhausted. Maitland went below to rest, a seemingly improbable exercise. Nevertheless he says he was awakened an hour later, at midnight, by an unexpected noise—the sound of gunfire. "I thought: dammit, that's one of our gunners," he reported afterwards. Maitland's instincts told him one of the ratings had fallen asleep in a gun turret, accidentally triggering the machine guns. Then he realized bits of wood were flying around inside the cubbyhole that served as his sleeping quarters. "I was up on that bridge—tchwhooooo! There was the helmsman lying on the deck yelling his head off. Christ, his ankle had a hole right through it."

In the midst of such a storm, the last thing they had expected was the enemy, but not far off in the gale Maitland spotted a Nazi U-boat, reloading its Oerlikons. Maitland ducked, grabbed the wheel, and counted as the next twelve rounds—in four lots, including armour-piercing and high-explosive—were poured into his boat. "Two of them hit solid," he said later, "right through the bridge." Even more alarming was that one of the extra fuel tanks on the deck of his boat had been hit. This was every skipper's worst nightmare. Now, to his horror, Maitland watched as flames leapt fifty feet or more into the night sky. Instinct again seized him. He jammed the four engine throttle levers full ahead and spun the wheel hard astarboard, catapulting his boat headlong into the rising sea. The waves crashed over his boat, washing the flaming petrol off the deck and into the ocean before *657* had suffered any serious damage. It was a brilliant manoeuvre, which of course Maitland dismissed when asked by semaphore early in the morning if he was still in one piece. "All right now," he signalled, "slight casualties only, one petrol tank burned out and considerable experience gained in fire fighting!"

It had looked much worse to the other boats. Tommy Fuller said to Maitland afterwards, "Christ, I saw this thing—a human torch—going by the other way and I didn't know it was your boat!''

Fuller had his own share of adventure that night. It had been decided already that the Focke-Wolfe shadowing their journey probably tipped off the U-boat to the convoy's presence. Then, in the mêlée resulting in damage to 657, a second U-boat surfaced, colliding with the first. Fuller and another MTB from the starboard column of the convoy spent part of the evening collecting survivors, including the cook from one U-boat who was promptly drafted into service aboard 654 as Fuller's personal chef. This was Able Seaman "Jock MacPherson.'' In his casual way, Fuller added his own signal to Maitland the next morning: "Everything OK? Having a marvellous breakfast, scrambled eggs!''

So it was that when they arrived at Gibraltar on May 7, the convoy of little ships was granted something of a hero's welcome. It was relief enough to be basking for a change in the semi-tropical climate and enjoying the abundant luxuries of this legendary outpost. Indeed, to quote the distinguished British traveller and author Peter Fleming, "the raptures of arrival were unqualified,'' although Burke remained glumly preoccupied with developments in North Africa. This was apparent the moment he landed and was greeted airily by a young sub-lieutenant. Their exchange was reported by Reynolds.

"Good morning, sir. Welcome to the Mediterranean. What sort of trip have you had?''

"Bloody awful,'' Burke snapped. He complained of not being able to listen to the BBC. "What's been happening out here?''

"I thought you would want to know that, so I brought out today's paper,'' the subbie replied. Burke stared at the front page and immediately felt more dejected as he read the headline:

BIG RETREAT BEGINS
AFRIKA KORPS PREPARES TO EVACUATE TUNISIA

"We looked at each other,'' Reynolds said, the question now on everyone's mind: Were they too late?

It appeared to be so. Still, they made the most of their short layover at Gibraltar. Over the next few days Burke adopted a more stoical outlook.

Maitland attended to his damaged boat. To his dismay, he'd discovered that during the engagement with the U-boat his rum locker had been hit, resulting in the loss of four jars. He spoke to his Chief Petty Officer about it. Maitland wanted the rum replaced and the locker mended.

"Once the shipwright...," he started.

"Oh no, sir," the fellow whispered. "We'd better not get the shipwright."

"What the hell?"

"Oh no, sir," he continued with calm reassurance. There was also a gently conspiratorial tone to the fellow's voice, which was only beginning to dawn on Maitland. "Let's leave it the way it is. When we're in action, we'll get hit in that rum locker every time."

Maitland understood at once. The rum was sealed and, if damaged, the jars had to be produced with the seal intact before more could be issued. Henceforth they would "decant" their rum ration (smashing the jars while carefully and convincingly preserving the seals) and point to the holed locker as "proof" of the circumstances in which the official ration was lost. It was a delightful scam—worthy of Fuller, come to think of it. Maitland's boat never did run out of rum as a result.

Four days later, early on the morning of May 11, they left Gibraltar on the next leg of their voyage. This would take the convoy to Algiers, a mere four hundred and fifty miles away. For a change they sailed in perfect weather. By now the crew of each Dog boat had earned its sea-legs and was becoming a cohesive fighting unit—if only the war would wait long enough to prove it.

Arriving off Algiers, they found themselves in the middle of an air raid. Here, at least, was reason to be hopeful they were not too late. Smoke engulfed the harbour; Ladner said it was so thick he could hardly breathe. He pushed his way in to tie up somewhere and found himself alongside a corvette. Ladner was hailed by a disembodied voice with a Canadian accent, demanding, "What the hell would you be bothered to come here for?"

Of course there was no simple way to reply.

That afternoon a signal was rushed to the boats indicating they should be refuelled and ready to sail again by 0600 the next morning. Their destination turned out to be Bône on the northern coast of Tunisia. It was to be only a brief stop-over point, although Fuller and Lt. Ashby found enough time to round up a motorcycle on which they roared off to party with some American nurses working at a nearby hospital.

By June 1, they had received sailing orders again and were underway. Their destination: Malta. They arrived off the island's low, tawny coast the next day and carefully picked their way through the swept channels beyond which even now, six months after the epic siege had been lifted, the waters were still dangerous with mines. Then, while gliding into Marxamaxett Harbour at Valetta, the Canadians finally felt they had joined the Mediterranean theatre.

They were ready to go to war again.

Within days they received their first orders, to patrol the Sicilian coast from Cape Passero northward to Cape Murro di Porco (such exotic place names would take some getting used to). Little happened during this first outing—or the next one. In the new parlance they adopted in the Med, such uneventful assignments became known contemptuously as "Zizz Patrols." It meant everyone not on watch could sleep peacefully without fear of being disturbed. Their only value, in fact, was that they served as a working-up in this new environment. Not only did they need to acquaint themselves with the geography; they also had to adjust to the different realities of working pretty much on their own. In England, the small-boat crews enjoyed privileged lives by comparison. They would return from nightly sorties to find shore ratings waiting to clean, re-arm and refuel their boats. The latter especially was taken for granted. But in the Med, the crews did most if not all of their own servicing. Nor did they have any of the special fuelling equipment to which they were accustomed—no pipelines, no hoses fitted with filters and equipment to prevent sparks. Boats were refuelled by hand from forty-four-gallon drums, or petrol lorries. Often the high-octane petrol was dirty or contaminated with water and had to be filtered using a piece of chamois. It was arduous work. Sometimes even the Zizz Patrols were a welcome relief from it.

There was also comfort to be drawn from the happy circumstances that had resulted in Ladner, Maitland and Burke being together for the first time in the same flotilla. Reynolds, whose observations of the Vancouver trio possess the virtues of being both inspired and wonderfully recorded, naturally held the greatest admiration for Burke as his commanding officer, but he was equally a student of Ladner and Maitland and so was able to draw a number of insights into their characters—as in this passage from his book:

> Tommy Ladner was a remarkable man. Often very quiet, he would become very excited if his point of view demanded it, and his lawyer's mind and tongue were a formidable combination. He was thoughtful, too, and paid more attention to detail than Corny or Doug. Whereas Corny would demand a high standard, and leave its achievement to Pick or myself, only checking that all was well when next the matter was raised, Tommy would persist and remind his officers frequently and see personally that his wishes were being carried out. Both methods worked, but Tommy expended far more nervous energy his way!

Part of this "nervous energy" may have been caused by Ladner's appointment as acting Senior Officer of the flotilla, a position he held until the end of June when the regular SO arrived at Malta. Then, eerily repeating an experience they had had with one of their senior officers in the English Channel, the Canadian skippers found themselves at odds with their new leader, a "South African-English type" whom they felt wasn't aggressive enough. Several times, Ladner claims, they came across enemy patrols, in perfect attack position up moon, and yet he failed to close. "So that raised a hell of a row amongst all of us," Ladner said. One night Burke, out of boredom perhaps or to blow off steam, shot up a sleepy seaside resort at Avola on the coast of Sicily. He was severely reprimanded as a result of this episode, the Vice-Admiral at Malta personally taking the trouble to inform him: "Burke, in the Royal Navy we leave the killing of women and civilians to the RAF." From young Reynolds's perspective, however, it had been a useful exercise. They had baptized 658's guns—and besides, there was no evidence anyone had been injured let alone killed.

Several days after this episode, Reynolds met his skipper returning from HMS *Gregale*, the Coastal Forces Base housed in various hotels and villas on the other side of Marxamaxett harbour at Malta. Burke asked him to find Pick and to meet him in his cabin.

"And bring in a bottle and three glasses while you're about it, too!" he added. Something was afoot.

There was barely room enough for them in the small wardroom. But they crowded in anyway, drawn as much by Burke's sudden intensity as the promise of drinks. The moment made a great impression on Reynolds. "When we each had a full glass in our hands, Corny said quietly: 'It's going to be Sicily, fellers—in a few days from now. And it's going to be the biggest invasion fleet in history.'"

This was it, Burke thought. Their big chance.

Operation Husky, as the invasion was called, *was* a monumental and unprecedented feat of planning. Thousands of landing craft and transport ships had assembled around Malta in anticipation of the attack. Some 3,700 aircraft were assigned to duel with the Luftwaffe and Regia Aeronautica, provide covering support or to bomb strategic points on the island. Eventually almost half a million soldiers—including a significant number of Canadians— would be committed to the battle. Such a force, staggering in scale, was too great to hide for long, and so a risky but ultimately brilliant deception operation was mounted to persuade Hitler the real Allied target was Sardinia. The plan worked. Hitler reacted accordingly. Incredibly, Mussolini called the Allies' bluff but was too timid to ask for help defending Sicily.

According to Reynolds, on the eve of their departure a wild party broke out at Monico's, the most popular nightclub ashore. There the upper bar was crowded with officers of the 51st Highland Division, all extremely cocky. This did not sit well with a number of the Canadians—a notoriously pugilistic lot—also present that night, especially when the Scots began dancing to their favourite "tunes of glory" on the tables. Ladner said merely that "ruderies" were passed back and forth between the Canadians and the Scots—an ominous sign, usually the sort that led to fisticuffs.

But it was Maitland who stole the show. One of the Scots, finishing a particularly acrobatic jig on top of Maitland's table, demanded breathlessly, "Aye, bet ya canna do that!"

"Well, no," Maitland replied. "But I wonder if you can do this?"

He ordered a sherry in a long-stemmed glass from the barman, downed the drink—and proceeded calmly to eat the bowl of the glass! The large crowd of spectators that had gathered was stunned into awed silence. Maitland put down the stem and passed it to the Highland officer before offering his *coup de grâce*—as reported by Reynolds:

"Now, sir, I've left the greatest delicacy for you. How about it?"

Shortly after this, the party erupted into an open brawl in the guise of a rugby match on the floor of Monico's, which ended—as such incidents generally did—with the arrival of the Military Police. No doubt diligent research into the subject would produce an impressive list of similar small-scale riots between servicemen on the eve of battle, each in all likelihood prompted by some challenge to the manliness of one side or the other. It is a ritual as old as the strutting of peacocks and the reasons why men go to war in the first place. On this particular night, men who had never heard of Sicily let alone thought of conquering it were quietly considering its possible relationship to their own mortality.

In its broad form, the plan for Operation Husky anticipated huge numbers of Allied troops landing simultaneously at 0200 on July 10. These would be divided roughly into two main areas: the Americans to the southwest, the British and Canadians on the southeast coast of Sicily. The boats of the 20th MGB Flotilla, of which Ladner, Maitland and Burke were a part, were assigned to patrol off Syracuse and Augusta before moving in the early hours of the morning to cover the landings by Canadians at a beach called "Acid North," situated between Cape Murro di Porco and Avola, areas with which they had some familiarity.

TYRRHENIAN SEA

IONIAN SEA

OPERATION "HUSKY" AREA

A.L. Stachiw/Trident Products

They left, as their journey to Malta had begun, sailing into a tempest. This made it difficult maintaining a speed of 18 knots. Fortunately, nothing stirred off Syracuse or Augusta. "It seemed incredible that the Luftwaffe could have missed sighting our convoys that afternoon and evening, steaming steadily towards the beaches." Providence seemed much in the Allies' favour that night. By 0200, when the landing craft were due to go ashore, the wind miraculously dropped.

"We ploughed quietly southward towards Murro di Porco, wondering what we would see when we reached 'Acid North,' " said Reynolds. The spectacle they came upon took everyone by surprise. An armada of ships crowded the horizon, the landing transports with their davits hanging empty, signifying the men had left already.

"Wreckage on the port bow, sir!" one of the lookouts hailed. The officers levelled their binoculars and stared, aghast.

"Good God!" said Burke. "It's a glider—with American markings!"

They motored towards the scene, now clearly littered with floating debris. Nearby they found two more gliders half-submerged in the water, and the full horror of what had happened became apparent. The gliders, carrying paratroopers from the 82nd Airborne Division that were to lead an assault on Sicily prior to the main invasion force, had crashed in the gusting winds. The men inside had drowned. "It was just awful—*awful*," said Maitland, who came upon the disaster shortly after Burke and helped to bring out a few of the dead.

In the midst of this mournful scene, they quickly attracted the attention of a shore battery, which began lobbing shells at them, some as close as fifty yards astern. The Senior Officer ordered the boats away to a safe distance. And while the fighting on Sicily raged, they were told to get some sleep while they could. Instead, they watched the dogfights not far off the coast. With a worrisome predictability, the air battles began to drift towards the Dog boats, until they were in the target area and the spectacle was somewhat less enthralling. Soon they were fighting for their lives, all guns blazing in the direction of the Luftwaffe overhead. "The sky seemed full of them," said Reynolds, who was himself manning one of the pom-poms, the gun kicking madly in his hands. "A stick of bombs from a high-flying aircraft screamed down and straddled right across our line. We saw 657's stern lift and she suddenly disappeared in a great spout of water which seemed to rise beneath her. Breathlessly we watched the water cascade down again, and there, to our relief, was 657 still moving along."

Burke immediately hurried over to see if Maitland was all right. "Too close to be healthy, wasn't it?" he replied laconically. In fact, several ratings who were aft when the bombs hit were injured.

Later that night, they were ordered to return to the beaches off Acid North to watch for U-boats. By then their engines had been running almost continuously for thirty-six hours and they needed to refuel, which they did with the help of a nearby tanker. For several hours after this laborious procedure, they rested. Forming up again to resume their patrol off Murro di Porco, they spotted a number of Focke-Wolfe 190s streaking towards their tiny armada. Pickard bellowed over his loudhailer, "All guns select targets independently. Open fire!" Immediately 658's small battery was loosed upon one of the attacking fighters. It banked to avoid the hail of gunfire, but was caught already and took a lethal burst along its fuselage from the twin Oerlikons. The aircraft seemed to disintegrate as it dived into a hillside on the coast and exploded. 658 had its first kill.

Ironically, the E-boats had yet to make an appearance. Late on the evening of July 12—now D+2—they received an intelligence report that twenty to thirty of the enemy's torpedo craft had been sighted proceeding through the Straits of Messina, but when the Dog boats went out in search of them they were greeted by so much enemy starshell that they couldn't get through. Ladner said it was so bright in the straits he felt as if he were strolling along Broadway. Thereafter he referred to the episode, with its potential for disaster, as "Operation Burnt Offering."

The next morning, however, brought compensation in the form of orders to proceed to Augusta. It remained in enemy hands, but the harbour could be entered. With its vast facilities, Augusta would be an enormous prize to the Allied operations in the Med. They arrived unchallenged, but later that day the Focke-Wolfes returned. Burke's most proficient gunner, Able Seaman "Happy" Day, who earlier had brought down one of the FWs, claimed a second victim during an engagement with the aircraft.

Meanwhile the port was rapidly filling with supply ships unloading men and materiel. Soon a Mobile Coastal Forces Base was established, the first of several that would follow Allied progress in the Med. These would provide badly needed mainte-nance and repair shops as well as support staff. At Augusta, the base was situated "in an excellent part of the harbour, with a long, comfortable stretch of jetty," Reynolds said. Even so, Burke and the others preferred to tie up alongside a buoy closer to the pleasant vineyards, berthing only when in need of ammunition stores or to collect signals.

The new base at Augusta was ideally positioned to allow the Dog boats to secure control of the Straits of Messina. It was vital to prevent the enemy getting supplies through to Italy and, eventu-ally, to stop him from evacuating Sicily. Consequently, in the next few weeks, the pace of activity increased, resulting in several engagements with the enemy's small boats.

Tommy Fuller, to his credit, was among the first to see action against E-boats in the Med.

On the night of July 14, Fuller took *655* into the Straits. With him were Alex Joy aboard *633* and a British-led MTB. At twenty minutes to midnight, they sighted two E-boats. They attacked and destroyed both the enemy boats "after the expenditure of a considerable amount of ammunition," according to one report. Seven MAS boats were also sighted that night, but they escaped before the MTBs could close on them.

Word of Fuller's success in the straits was likely the subject of much discussion amongst the other small-boat captains, who so far had been frustrated in their attempts to meet the enemy. Four days after the invasion of Sicily, Burke had spent so many hours at sea on patrol or hunting for E-boats that he was virtually out of food.

The situation was so desperate that Burke came alongside a Royal Navy warship and with a megaphone shouted up to a rather prim-looking officer glaring at him from the rail, "I'll trade you gin for bread!" He explained that of course he had planned well enough with respect to wines and spirits for the wardroom, but "alas, not too well for the commissariat." Burke got his bread, but not before the officer demanded from above in a thick, Gilbert and Sullivan voice, "What *brrrrr and* of gin?"

Their other efforts had not gone unnoticed, however. In the course of an otherwise irksome recall to Malta for extensive and long-overdue maintenance routines on the *658*'s engines, Burke received an official "Memorandum" issued by the Captain, Coastal Forces, in effect a special commendation for his boat's outstanding record in the past few weeks.

Within a fortnight, *658* was back at Augusta and settling in to a routine that saw the Dog boats on patrol every other night, primarily in the Straits of Messina but also close to the toe of Italy. Maitland says the patrols were dull. To relieve the tedium, they rafted their boats together alongside a buoy one night and had "one hell of a party." By midnight they were sufficiently juiced that when Maitland wagered fifty dollars that he could put a torpedo through the harbour gates, his challenge was accepted. Unfortunately, he lost the bet. "It hit a corner wall," said Maitland, making "one hell of crash." This resulted in several U.S. warships at Augusta opening fire: their crews received extra pay whenever their guns were discharged, and so they had filled the air with shells. Maitland was severely reprimanded the next morning. He apologized, and, incredibly, escaped any formal disciplinary action. In fact, the brass at Augusta told him to quit larking about and "get out there and get after those Jerries."

Trouble was, Jerry couldn't be found—at least, there were no E-boats. So the object of the raiders' attention became the electric hospital trains being used by the enemy to carry troops along the coast of Sicily. Such a tactic, contrary to the conventions of war, revealed the enemy's mounting desperation as the Sicilian campaign progressed. Maitland, who felt the practice was despicable, seemed especially remorseless about shooting them up. One night he found himself perfectly situated to attack. "So I ran the boats in to about five hundred feet. They didn't know we were there. I put the boats in line astern, and with our six-pounders and two-pounders we just hit that train. Swhoosh! We blew it right off the tracks. It was confirmed later. It was a troop train."

These train-busting operations along the coasts of Sicily and the south shore of the mainland soon evolved into a macabre sport between the Dog boats and the Italian shore batteries lying in wait for them. "It was narrow and sometimes you'd get a little optimistic and go too far up. They'd let you come in, but as soon as you stopped—bang! On would go the searchlights and they had some pretty fair-sized 'rifles' there, you know—six-inch stuff."

According to Maitland, another of the Canadians with the flotilla, Sub-Lieutenant Peter Thompson aboard 665, went too close to the shore one night and paid dearly for it. His boat received a direct hit in the engine room, setting it ablaze until 665 sank beneath him. Most of his crew was lost as well, in addition to a Canadian press relations officer who was aboard that night, Lt. Cdr. (S) E. N. "Bart" Bartlett. Thompson was captured and spent the rest of the war in a PoW camp, where he was interrogated endlessly in the vain hope of learning more about the Allies' Dog boats.

The Canadian skippers were as interested in acquiring information regarding the E-boats, not least of all their whereabouts. Reports of sightings more often than not led to empty stretches of the sea, although ironically Thompson's boat had engaged several of the enemy's torpedo craft only a few hours prior to his mishap off the coast of Italy, sinking two of them. The MAS boats, on the other hand, were so seldom reported as to be virtually non-existent.

But all that would change soon enough. The fall of Sicily in mid-August left the Allies well poised to strike across the Straits of Messina and into the boot of Italy itself. Then the pace of activity would accelerate, bringing the Canadians into direct conflict with the enemy's coastal convoys, the protection of which was given largely to E-boats.

In the autumn of 1943, the Dogs in the Med were about to embark on their most productive hunting season yet.

5

The Importance of
Spectacle

EARLY IN SEPTEMBER Burke's boat was unexpectedly ordered to Malta again for repairs. Languishing in the island's "odorous" heat, despite the amenities available, did not sit well with the skipper of *658*. He was certain events were boiling to a climax in the theatre he had left behind and that he would "miss out on something."

Events proved Burke's instincts were right. There had been only a brief respite for Coastal Forces in the Med, as they were soon patrolling along the south and west coasts of Italy and elsewhere in anticipation of an invasion of Italy. This began with a naval bombardment near Reggio on September 2, followed the next day by artillery fire across the Straits of Messina and a dawn landing by units of the British Eighth Army, which was virtually unopposed. Italy capitulated that same day, ordering its troops and ships to cease operations at once. The news was not made public until the eighth, at which point the main body of the Italian Battle Fleet sailed to Malta—escorted, in part, by British MTBs—where they were surrendered to the Allies.

A.L. Stachiw/Trident Products

Landings were also carried out between Catona and Reggio, but the main effort was reserved for Operation "Avalanche," the Allied assault at Salerno which began on September 9. Partly as a diversionary tactic, the overall planning at this stage called for the capture of Sardinia and several small islands west of Naples.

Sardinia was thought also to be where Mussolini was hiding. Taking these islands was the task now given to the little ships of Coastal Forces. Sardinia fell on September 18 to the grand force of two MGBs, although they missed capturing the deposed Italian dictator by a matter of hours. The surrender of the smaller islands—Capri, Prochida and Ischia among them—was equally bloodless, if not downright hilarious. There was an element of danger in each operation, to be sure, but it was uncertain afterwards whether this came more from several of the protagonists involved or the possibility of meeting the enemy. The truth was the assignment to capture the islands proved to be an artfully engineered sideshow in which several of the small-boat skippers concluded they had been rated expendable for the sake of proving, for dubious purposes, what amounted to the importance of spectacle in the war's conduct.

According to Reynolds, who would have heard of it afterwards, while the crew of *658* was "propping up the dockyard wall in Malta," Ladner and Maitland had sailed first from Algiers to accept the surrender of the Galita Islands, midway between Bône and Bizerta. From there they had moved on to Salerno. Fuller was with them at least part of the time. So, too, was Alex Joy, who says he was sitting aboard his boat off Salerno one day, enjoying a pre-lunch drink, when several Italian dignitaries accompanied by the Senior Officer of an E-boat Flotilla arrived to surrender the Isle of Capri. This was on September 12. Already, various MTBs and MGBs had moved in on the idyllic island resort in the Gulf of Naples, site of the Villa Iovis of the Roman Emperor Tiberius and today still famous for its olive oil, wine and multitude of tourist attractions. Never has an island seemed more eager to surrender, in fact. Maitland remembers arriving off the isle in the early morning, a tin hat on his head while he peered over the bridge with his binoculars. "Not a goddamn thing happened," he recalled. "Nothing!" Ladner said, "We just went in the harbour and all we did was go ashore." The local population was waiting for them, he added.

Surely they weren't disappointed. For one thing, Capri's natural beauty remained largely unspoiled. And with such friendly inhabitants, they could make the most of their occupation. Anyway, that's what Maitland did. He got hold of an Italian petty officer who spoke some English and named him "Bill Venchenzo."

"The first thing we're going to need tomorrow morning," he told Bill, "is a good car." According to Maitland there were only nine cars on the island, but Bill nevertheless appeared the next day with a magnificent Lancia.

"The next thing we need is a villa," said Maitland. Bill drove them into the mountains. "So we go up there," Maitland recalled, "and take over Count Ciano's villa—Mussolini's son-in-law. My God! I'd never seen anything like it. They had swimming pools. It was the first time I'd ever sat on a toilet with a mink stole on it. We lived pretty well up there. Oh, we had a great time. Then we got our own orchestra together."

While on Capri Maitland says they went out on a few uneventful patrols. They also liberated the island of Prochida—another farcical episode. Tommy Fuller remembers when they arrived the harbour was graced by an enormous banner that read:

**EVERY WOMAN ON THIS ISLAND
HAS VENEREAL DISEASE!**

Prochida fell on the fifteenth. Then Maitland, who was nominally in command of the Canadians (excluding Burke, who remained at Malta), received word that an American destroyer, USS *Knight*, was coming in. This had a direct bearing on their operations as they had been temporarily assigned to an American unit known as Task Force 80.4. "It was in the evening and so I reported...to Captain Andrews who apprised me of the situation, that they had this Special Force aboard for special duties. I said: 'Well, what do you what me to do, sir?' " He suggested a meeting at ten the next morning. "So I reported at ten o'clock the next morning into the wardroom of the *Knight* and there I met this Special Force, comprised of Douglas Fairbanks, Jr., Lieutenant Commander Henry North (whose family were the controlling interest in Ringling Brothers Circus) and two of the most famous (at that time) war correspondents, Joseph Knickerbocker and John Steinbeck.''

Fairbanks, a Lieutenant Commander, was in charge. But as Maitland also discovered, the movie star's son evidently still lived by the relaxed rules of Hollywood. Still in his dressing gown at ten o'clock, Fairbanks was lounging on a divan in the wardroom. "His eyes were pink and he had a steward up there with his suitcase, getting out a couple dozen pairs of silk stockings!" Fairbanks, who may or may not have been nursing a hangover, informed Maitland, "Well, we haven't really got any plans yet regarding operations, so we'll just take a day to sort of settle in and so maybe come back at ten o'clock tomorrow morning." This went on for two or three days. There was nothing Maitland could do. He took his orders from this Special Force.

In fact, there *was* something Maitland could do. He went quail shooting. Finally, though, Fairbanks announced, "We're going to capture the Isle of Ischia!"

Maitland, now highly sceptical of the operation's likelihood of success, nevertheless called together the other skippers and gave them "the big picture."

> "So what we're going to do is, we're going to head out to sea just at dusk. This is a formidable show." At the last minute the USN says, "No, the USS *Knight* isn't going to participate in this. The waters are too enclosed and we can't endanger the vessel." So, I said: "Fine."

Fairbanks suggested they run the operation off Maitland's boat instead. Maitland agreed. They sailed at dusk.

> We made a great fuss about leaving harbour and heading out to sea as though we were doing somewhere. That was the whole idea. Obviously there were still some Krauts on the island or someone who would send a message that the boats have gone. That was good thinking. And then we were going to circle around after dark and come in on the south side of Ischia. Then go up around into the east side of it where there was a nice little bay with a long, an ordinary long dock as we

would call it, a wooden dock. And one o'clock in the morning was H hour or D hour or whatever the hell.

Maitland says he had ten Rangers on the deck of *657*, five each side with all their "guffle and stuff," in addition to Fairbanks, his bosun's mate and R/T operators. "But the funniest part of all was Knickerbocker. He was up ahead of the bridge, behind our forward gun."

> It was a *beautiful* night. It was dark, thank God! You don't want to be out in the full moon. This was a perfect night. There was no moon. It was still and clear down there. Just a lovely night to go yachting. So we're struggling along and we have a little chart table just off the bridge in there, with a little light on it so you can see. I carefully looked at the chart before we left but you don't remember all the little things. By now I had traded in some of our rum and store goods and I'd gotten an American surface radar that I had mounted on my boat. They were beautiful things. They'd pick up anything or everything. So we were going along and my fellow, Horely, down below, there was a little *tweet* on the voice pipe and he said, "Captain, sir, a fairly strong echo about twenty-eight hundred yards fine on the port bow," about three hundred and fifty degrees. He could tell, for example, if a thing was wooden, his echo was a little bit fuzzy. If it was steel the echo was sharp. He said, "Sir, I think it would appear to be something like an armed trawler, about a hundred-and-fifty or two-hundred-foot armed trawler. It's a very sharp echo."
> "Is it moving?"
> "No, it's not moving, sir."

Maitland reduced his speed to 8 knots and immediately called the other boats on his R/T, informing them he had an object ahead. Still not sure what it was, he had decided to stay on their present course. All that remained was to pass along his gunnery instructions.

> The gunners had earphones, an electric thing which was not always working too satisfactorily....And so we mounted loudhailers right behind the number one gun and on back,

behind the aftermost gun—plain, ordinary loudhailers. You know, when you put it on you go, "Phew, phew!" to clear it. It sort of spits a bit. I went, "Phew, phew," and right away the gun's crew know I'm going to pass them a message. Little Knickerbocker, who was down in front, pops his head up and said: "Would you do that again, Captain? Would you do that again, please?" Here I am, looking at an enemy and wondering what to do and all these people are about! I'm flabbergasted! Do what sort of thing? So I gave it another "phew" to clear it and then I hear him talking into this machine of his.

"And here we are. There's an enemy battleship on our port bow, but the Captain has decided to continue and will attack the enemy before..."

You see, these fellows, Knickerbocker and Steinbeck, that's the kind of stuff they write! But this was all going to the New York papers: DOUGLAS FAIRBANKS AT SEA! Holy shit! Then I said to the guns crews, the forward ones particularly: "There's something wrong about this, it just doesn't seem right. There's something wrong, but nevertheless the target is there." So I just alerted the gunners and then we carried on. As soon as I did that, [with] the loudhailer:

"Here we are facing the enemy who are ahead of us and you can hear the gunfire...."

What a lot of bullshit!

Maitland says his radar operator called him just as Knickerbocker was recording events for posterity.

"There's something about that, sir. It's becoming fuzzy."

Now Maitland's instincts were alerted. "It suddenly dawned on me and I said: 'Hey Steve, take a look at the goddamn chart.'" Steve Rendell was Maitland's First Lieutenant, or "Number One." He came from a well-to-do family in Vancouver, where his father had owned the prosperous Rendell Equipment Company.

"Yeah," said Rendell, "it's a rock. It's a rock off the point. It shows on the chart."

"Thank Christ!" said Maitland, who neglected to add what Knickerbocker made of this extraordinary development. Later, when the Canadian skippers were accompanied by PT boats in the Med, there would be other incidents in which landmarks were mistakenly identified as enemy targets. The equipment, as good as it was, was not foolproof. But one episode in particular, known henceforth as the Battle of Bottle Rock, revealed that with the proper amount of gullibility and a misplaced faith in technology, some folks could be convinced of anything. Then, Maitland and Ladner had just determined that their "target" was in fact another rock, as high as a smokestack actually. Ladner, on the R/T, said, "God, there must be an awful pile of seagulls on that!" Just then the PT in the lead called to say he had fired his torpedoes from a mile and a half off. "I called him and told him what I thought we had and got no reply," Maitland recalled. "So we just carried on slowly and got in a little closer. I can assure you those torpedoes hit. The first ones hit on the land there and you could hear the seagulls for miles. Christ, what a noise! So that was another of our Task Force 80.4 operations. It really got a little disheartening."

But that was later. Having made their passage without any serious mishaps, Ischia lay dead ahead. They motored in to the harbour and there found a crowd waiting for them, singing. Maitland was furious. "We went alongside...and off jumps Fairbanks and his gang and up they go. This was all pre-arranged!"

Thus, Ischia was captured in true Hollywood fashion—with a cast of hundreds at least, cheerfully waving and applauding from the dockside. *Ischia was free!* All that was missing from this scene was a director in his ascot and beret, shouting from behind the cameras as actor David Niven's favourite did, "Bring on the empty horses!"—or something equally preposterous. As it was, there were still photographers clambering all over the conquering heroes. "There were pictures of Fairbanks accepting the surrender from the mayor, I know that," says Maitland. The Canadians were infuriated by the entire episode.

Not even the celebration that followed their arrival could dim the Canadians' anger at having been dragged along into this. Maitland got the boats cranked up and pointed out to sea instantly, fearful they might have been lured into a trap. Eventually, though, he turned his boat over to Steve Rendell and went in search of Fairbanks.

"Look, we've got five boats and a lot of men and a lot of equipment, and the longer we hang around here, the greater the exposure. I'm getting off here and taking my boats *now*, in ten minutes. If you want to come, fine. If you don't, stay here."

Fairbanks was the perfect stage gentleman.

"You're absolutely right," he said.

With this, Fairbanks ordered his gang to the boats and they waved a fond adieu to Ischia. On the way back to Capri, the swashbuckling hero drank most of Maitland's fine Scotch whisky, enough anyway that when he got off the boat Maitland said he was "absolutely plastered." By chance, a bosun from the USS *Knight* witnessed this and later approached Maitland's boat.

"May I have a word with you, Captain?"

The bosun snapped to attention.

"Sir, I regret the activities of my officers. There's nothing I can do about it but I tender my own personal apology."

As Maitland said afterwards, obviously impressed, "This was a *professional* sailor talking."

Still, the entire episode with Fairbanks and his cohorts had left the Canadians that much more eager to return to some real fighting. They hoped also that Capri would remain their base of operations, but in the aftermath of the Allied breakthrough at Salerno it was realized the small boats would have to be based farther north. With the fall of Sardinia, the ancient island kingdom's harbour at Maddalena, a former Italian naval base, became available. This was where Burke finally rejoined the flotilla, after an arduous journey from Malta in late September. The atmosphere at Maddalena proved to be as congenial as that of Capri, with a few frills. Tied up at the jetty in the mornings, while refuelling or washing down the decks, the crews waited impatiently until the local belles paraded by for them in their horse-drawn landaus.

For all the action Burke missed, once he returned his boat was involved in one of the most spectacular engagements in the history of Coastal Forces. It occurred on the night of October 14, 1943, in the Piombino Channel between Elba and the Italian mainland. He sailed at 1500, Lt. Cdr. E. T. Greene-Kelly as the Senior Officer aboard Alex Joy's boat, *633*, and Lt. F. A. "Freddie" Warner commanding *636*. En route, Joy again had the bad luck to encounter engine troubles. The SO sent him back to Maddalena, transferring to *636* to continue the journey. Nine hours later, they reached the patrol area. Here they were to enforce the Allied stranglehold on enemy coastal shipping moving north to south. Reynolds says they had barely arrived when Burke announced, "Have a look at Green Three-O, you two. I reckon we've got our first surface target."*

The SO aboard *636* had seen it, too. Instantly a message was passed along, which was relayed on the voice pipe by Burke's telegraphist below. Next to "Sparks" was Reynolds, recently promoted to First Lieutenant of *658*. Reynolds was keeping himself occupied with the logbook:

> *0116 Sighted vessel at Green 30, range approx 4,000 yards, course East. Our course SE. Position 42 ° 56.6' N 10 ° 27.4' E. Speed 12 knots.*
> *0117 "Nuts Starboard" from SO.*

"Nuts" was radio jargon for an enemy vessel. Reynolds says his "heart seemed to be thumping audibly" at the prospect of battle. Minutes later, Burke's voice floated down on the voice pipe, informing him that *636* had fired one of its torpedoes. Reynolds scrambled up to the bridge. He could make out the shape of a large trawler now less than two thousand yards away. It was challenging *658*. Then everything happened at once. The bridge gun buzzer blared. Able Seaman "Happy" Day, aft, reported another ship sighted at Green One-Three-Five. *636* fired her last torpedo—and the trawler's guns began pouring torrents of brilliant tracer in the direction of the MGBs.

"Open fire!" Burke shouted, bringing the wheel hard astarboard. *658*'s guns now blasted away, but only the six-pounder could get a good fix on the target. It was impossible to tell if any

---

* Green refers to starboard, red to port, followed by a bearing in relationship to the boat; in this case, thirty degrees off the starboard bow.

damage was inflicted—none was sustained—before Burke was able to manoeuvre out of the enemy's sights and rendezvous with the SO's boat.

This was followed by a cat-and-mouse game between the MGBs and the trawlers, the latter occasionally illuminating the night sky with cascading starshells. The MGBs were up moon of their quarry and began a slow approach in the midst of the ensuing barrage. Burke relayed an order to his gunners to hold their fire. "I want to wait until we've got 'em right where we want 'em," he drawled. To gain time as they neared the trawlers, Burke asked Reynolds to flash the challenge the enemy had used already. "I seized the lamp and flashed the letter several times and, sure enough, the enemy obediently stopped firing," Reynolds said. He admired his skipper's coolness, knowing the trick might buy them only seconds. But as Reynolds wrote:

> Every second counted now. We had begun our run in at 1,500 yards and were closing the range very rapidly. At 700 yards the enemy opened fire again. Every man on the bridge was half-watching Corny. Why doesn't he order Pick to open fire? I thought. We'll all be killed before we even fire a shot at this rate! No order came, and I gritted my teeth. At last he said: "Stand by, Pick—another 50 yards then we'll let 'em have it!"

With their range now reduced to as little as 250 yards, Burke gave the order, the thunderous din and smoke of *658*'s opening broadside a shock even to her crew. They couldn't miss; every shot left the enemy ship further stricken. Yet Burke kept *658* circling around the trawler, fires now blazing along its length.

In the midst of this bloodbath, one of Burke's gunners reported another ship at Red Two-O.

"Make the challenge, Rover," Burke said to his First Lieutenant. Prior to the war Reynolds had been active with the Boy Scouts, a fact that had only recently come to light with the result that he was permanently nicknamed by his skipper. Reynolds flashed for perhaps a minute. This was answered by a stream of tracer shot across the surface towards *658*.

"Open fire!" Burke snapped. Instantly his gunners pounded the unidentified vessel, which stopped almost as quickly with fire roaring amidships. If there was any jubilation in this success, it was short-lived.

"Cease fire, for God's sake!" Burke ordered painfully. "It's *636!*"

No one could understand why the SO's boat had failed to respond to the challenge, or had opened fire. Seconds later, Burke calmly ordered his grief-stricken crew to "snap out of it" and get busy bringing in the wounded.

But in the midst of this, another vessel was spotted. Now Burke had a terrible decision to make. It *must* be the enemy; he couldn't be caught helping casualties out of the water. *658* sped away from the scene, promising to return.

Again they challenged first, but this time the enemy vessel did not bother to reply before letting go with a hail of gunfire that hit Burke's boat amidships, leaving several men wounded. Burke ordered his guns to reply. "The all-important opening burst was once again devastating," Reynolds said. And as usual, Burke was relentless. "As the enemy turned wildly away, Corny followed every twist until the ship stopped."

Having disposed of this intruder, Burke smartly ordered *658* back to resume picking up survivors from *636*. Again, his work was interrupted. This time a searchlight on the Italian mainland, alerted by the sound of gunfire, caught them in its blinding glare. Shore batteries erupted; even from three miles away, Reynolds said, "shells began to crack and whistle past most uncomfortably."

Burke ordered *658* away at high speed, making smoke as it went. This silenced the artillery. Meanwhile he crept back towards *636*. For an hour or more, Burke's crew picked up the survivors. Then they sped away from the scene for good, leaving behind what remained of the two trawlers and *636* as they returned to Maddalena. One rating died on the way.

He was buried early the next morning. "The silent scene on the gently swaying deck in the pale light was unforgettable," said Reynolds, who had drawn the sombre task of the stitching the body into its canvas shroud. "There was no well-drilled guard, no rifle shots, only a group of bare-headed men in sea kit."

Freddie Warner, the CO of 636, led the service.

> Forasmuch as it hath pleased Almighty God of His great mercy to take unto Himself the soul of our dear brother here departed, we therefore commit his body to the sea....

So had ended the Battle of Piombino Channel—with a simple but moving ceremony of remembrance aboard one of His Majesty's Motor Gun Boats in the Med. Again, it was Rover Reynolds who found the words to describe how they felt as the rating was buried.

"This man's duty was done," he said. "Ours was still before us."

In the autumn of 1943, Tommy Fuller was busy getting into mischief. Shortly after the landings at Salerno he went to Malta, presumably to have his boat repaired, and then Alexandria. The latter appealed to him instantly. Of its many exotic charms, he counted the food at Pastoroudi's restaurant on Rue Solomon Pasha among the most alluring. Evidently he got to Cairo, too, where he luxuriated in the posh atmosphere of Shepheard's Hotel.

Fuller next turned up on the island of Casteloriso—Red Castle—a volcanic speck only a few miles off the Turkish coast south of Rhodes. The island was so badly bombed, he says, he took his boat into the Sporades until he reached Leros, formerly occupied by the Regia Marina and only recently captured by the British, the Italians now supposedly co-belligerents in the war.

The circumstances that led to Fuller's entry to the Aegean and his date of arrival are unknown—although the latter likely occurred in mid-October, when a new 10th MTB Flotilla took up its duties in the Aegean. According to author Bryan Cooper, one of the officers serving with this flotilla was Lt. R. Campbell,

RCNVR, commanding MTB *309*. Little else is known about this individual, perhaps because the early sorties in the Aegean went so badly for the small-boat skippers.

For his part, Fuller alludes only to difficulties with his Italian hosts once he got there. Fuller said they were reluctant to cooperate. He complained of this one day to an Italian admiral at Leros, who replied indifferently, "Well, we've done everything we can. We've made our dockyard available, we moved out of the officers' mess. The officers' brothel has been available to you; nobody's taken advantage of that!"

Fuller was still at Leros in early November. On the twelfth, German forces from the 22nd Infantry Division, under General Müller, invaded the island. The capture of Leros was completed within four days, by which time as many as 3,500 British and 5,350 Italian troops had surrendered. Fuller says he surrendered to Müller in person, who took his pistol—a Colt .45—removed its clip, handed it back and said, curtly, "Your weapon."

Like the reasons that had landed him at Leros in the first place, the details of Fuller's predicament following the island's capture are a mystery. He says he was placed under guard but was allowed plenty of cigarettes and ersatz coffee. Indeed, he gives the impression his guard, whom he called "Fritz," became virtually his batman. Later, Fuller says, he was granted permission to go with Fritz to search for survivors of HMS *Faulkner*, a British ship lost during the attack on Leros. They set out towards Mount Maraviglia. As they wandered along a trail, Fuller came across an abandoned rum bottle. It was just what he might have wanted to slake his thirst after a long hike, but instead he saw in the rum an opportunity to escape.

"I put my tongue in it and went *gurgle-gurgle-gurgle*!" said Fuller. He wasn't drinking it, of course. Then he passed it to Fritz, who took a long tug—for real. In the mid-November heat—he says it was the eighteenth now—Fritz soon decided to stretch out. He was asleep in minutes. Fuller took off on foot in the direction of Porto Largo. He met a British officer en route. Together they crept aboard an admiral's barge commandeered by the Germans, slugged its crew and made their escape towards the Gulf of Mandalaya. Fuller sold the barge in Turkey—at much less than its full value, he adds. He was soon back in Alexandria; shortly thereafter he made several whistle-stops—Haifa and Malta among them—before he was assigned to a new theatre of operations, the Adriatic. He passed through Bari, Italy, on his way—an experience that proved unforgettable. An air raid on the night of December 2–3 had resulted in a catastrophe as hellish as the great Halifax explosion of 1917, if not more so. Four ships were damaged, including one filled with petrol, in the initial bombing run by a few old JU-88s. Then an ammunition supply vessel exploded. Minutes later as many as a thousand men were dead. Sixteen (some reports say eighteen) cargo ships sank, with the loss of thousands of tons of supplies. Among the vessels hit was the *John Harvey*, which in addition to carrying munitions had been loaded with 100 tons of mustard gas. It had been brought to Italy in the event a desperate Nazi Germany resorted to chemical warfare. For months after this disaster, servicemen were inoculated in an attempt to ameliorate the effects of the gas. It was not always successful; Bari continued to suffer in its purgatorial atmosphere. According to Fuller, it was not uncommon to see new arrivals soon tormented by running sores.

And so Fuller departed the Med, on his way to the Adriatic. Alex Joy had left, too, or was leaving shortly. He discovered it was one thing to be granted permission to return to Canada and another to actually get away. For more than a week he languished at Malta with, as he put it, "Priority Z" status while waiting for a flight to England. He finally made it home but not without further difficulties. In Alexandria, he was ordered to report for duty as a naval liaison officer at Samos, one of the small islands in the Aegean. Happily, it proved a brief and uneventful exercise. The urgency in getting back to Canada was that Alex Joy planned to get married— which he finally did, early in 1944.

Thus by the end of 1943 virtually the only Canadians left in the Med were Maitland, Ladner and Burke. Even so, Maitland says he hadn't seen the rest of the 20th MGB Flotilla in several months while operating "pretty well alone" in the Straits of Bonificio between Sardinia and Corsica. Not long after this, however, Maitland was called down to Malta, where he met his friends again. They were there, ostensibly, to repair their boats.

It was during this Christmas hiatus at Malta that Maitland went to see the officer commanding Coastal Forces in the Med, Captain J. F. Stevens—"The Moose," as he was affectionately known, in honour of his large, brooding nose. He seemed in an unusually buoyant mood. Stevens outlined the situation in the Med, adding that as a result of increased attrition among the MTBs and MGBs in recent months it had been decided to consolidate the remaining boats into three new flotillas. He offered Maitland one of the Senior Officer positions.

Word of this quickly made its way to the other boats, although it was not formally communicated until January 4, 1944. Then, a signal was despatched by special messenger to the boats still tied up at Malta but making ready to get underway again:

> *Under a general revision and reconstitution of flotillas, the following boats will form the new 56th MGB/MTB Flotilla, under the command of Lt. Cdr. J. D. Maitland, RCNVR: MGBs 657....*

"Maitland our SO!" Reynolds enthused. "And every one of the boats in the new 56th Flotilla commanded by a Canadian! It looked as though things might hum when we got back to Bastia."

In fact the Canadians had often discussed such a flotilla, even if it seemed a remote possibility. Now, incredibly, Coastal Forces had made it a reality. On paper, it looked especially good:

THE 56TH MGB/MTB FLOTILLA
MGB *657*
Lt. Cdr. J. D. Maitland RCNVR (SO)
MGB *658*
Lt. C. Burke RCNVR

MGB *663*
Lt. T. E. Ladner RCNVR
MTB *633*
Lt. S. Rendell RCNVR
MTB *640*
Lt. C. MacLachlan RCNVR
MTB *655*
Lt. H. M. Pickard RCNVR

Not to be overlooked was Maitland's promotion to Acting Lieutenant Commander. Steve Rendell, formerly Maitland's First Lieutenant, was also promoted and given his own command, as was Herb Pickard. Campbell MacLachlan of Toronto—one of the old "Maple Leaf Mills" family—had come to mind immediately as a suitable candidate for the new flotilla when Stevens had first raised the matter. He was now one of the small-boat raiders assigned to the "all-Canadian" 56th.

Their first operational sortie would be out of Bastia, Corsica, on the night of January 21. The Allied armies were stalled between Naples and Rome, partly as a result of an unexpectedly determined resistance but also due to the appalling conditions that winter. To interrupt the enemy's supply lines as well as leap-frog behind his dug-in positions along the front, a landing was planned for the port at Anzio, some thirty miles south of Rome. Meanwhile the 56th would create a diversion at the port of Civitavecchia, to the north of the Italian capital. This, it was hoped, would forestall the enemy rushing troops to the area of the real invasion. "Our instructions," reported Reynolds, who remained Burke's First Lieutenant with the formation of the 56th Flotilla, "finished with the invitation for us to 'create as much alarm and despondency as possible in the neighbourhood.' "*

---

* Some historians have argued that Civitavecchia should have taken the brunt of the Allied landings, rather than Salerno and the toe of Italy. It is interesting to note that both Field Marshal Kesselring, the German Commander-in-Chief in southern Italy, and his Chief of Staff, General Westphal, afterwards agreed with

Once again the fast-attack craft were being called upon to prove the importance of spectacle—an unlikely discipline perhaps, but one they understood was well-suited to the MGBs and MTBs. Moreover, they were keen to assert their new independence, establish their worth. Here was an opportunity not to be missed.

Their main props in the coming drama consisted of phonograph recordings broadcast over loudspeakers: sounds of anchor cables being played out; instructions shouted to landing craft—in short, all the noise an enemy would expect to hear during an actual invasion. To this would be added certain pyrotechnics intended to convincingly simulate the flashes of big guns. Such means of deception had worked in the past, both at sea and on land; it was hoped they would work again.

There would be another twist to this operation: the MGBs and MTBs would be accompanied by radar-equipped American PT boats. These had arrived at Bône in April 1943 and were led by Lt. Cdr. Stanley M. Barnes, USN, an affable if not overly zealous individual. It was said that shortly after the PTs had arrived Barnes—splendid in his uniform, complete with hip revolver and well-polished boots—went to see Admiral Cunningham to report for duty (the PTs were considered part of the British Coastal Forces). Cunningham's office was by all accounts opulent, befitting the British CiC in the Med. The man, too, was legendary. Perhaps this had an effect on Barnes. In any event, he was told he would find Cunningham at his desk, which was positioned at the end of a grand hall, the full length of which Barnes travelled, his boots echoing sharply on the marble as he approached. Cunningham's head remained fixed on some paperwork while Barnes presented himself and saluted.

"Sir, we are in all respects ready for war!" he added magnificently.

For several minutes, it seemed, Cunningham quietly studied his paperwork. Finally:

---

this assessment, adding that landing at Civitavecchia would have hastened the Allied conquest.

"Thank you, Barnes."

Barnes saluted stiffly and wheeled about. He had marched perhaps halfway down the grand hall when Cunningham spoke again.

"Just a moment." Cunningham removed himself from his desk and crossed to where Barnes was waiting. There, with an impeccable stage delivery, he said, "I say, Barnes, don't kill *too* many Germans."

For more than a year, the Higgins-type boats of PT Squadron 15 under Barnes's leadership were the only US Navy craft operating in the Med. The fact evidently inspired Barnes, who was awarded the Navy Cross for his heroism during actions off Tunisia and Sicily. Later, while operating with the 56th MGB/MTB Flotilla, he acknowledged that he had learned a lot from the British—and Canadians. Such magnanimity was evidently not typical of some other PT skippers. Many were accused of a feckless attitude in pursuit of the enemy. This remains a delicate issue among some of the Canadian commanders particularly, who speak of it off the record only. To this day they cannot understand why in numerous actions the "Yanks" either broke off too soon or fired their torpedoes from impossible distances. Even allowing for the fact that the latter required a greater distance to arm themselves than did the British torpedoes, they seemed at times overly cautious. In view of this, the perceived American propensity to award medals—or "gongs," as they were known—was treated with contempt. Some among the British and Canadians peevishly claimed the U.S. Navy would decorate an officer if he passed wind and survived it.

It was also felt that Americans generally had squandered the excellence of their boats. The PTs were fast and well-armed, except for their torpedoes, which seldom worked. Indeed they were almost laughable. Tommy Fuller paraphrased Mark Twain when he said of the torpedoes: "The guy was firing at the cow, and the cow was perfectly safe until it turned around and walked into one of his bullets."

For all their shortcomings, the Americans did have one huge advantage over the British, which the latter glumly acknowledged:

the radar sets on PTs were vastly better than anything the British and Canadians were issued. British radar was tolerably good for picking up aircraft signals but lamentably weak for detecting surface craft. The sets were also useless near land because of a "back-echo" that obscured the first quarter of any scan. The American sets eliminated many such problems. They also displayed the signal on a small screen that was considered a vast improvement over the British system.

So the Allied skippers worked out an arrangement: PTs would accompany the British and Canadian boats to provide effective "night vision" using their superior radar sets, while the MGBs and MTBs would bring their better torpedoes into action.

The Dogs left Bastia at 1700 on January 21, laying a course directly for Civitavecchia. Maitland in *657* took the lead, followed by Burke in *658*, Ladner in *663*, and Pickard with *655*, the only MTB in the unit that night. Also with them was Peter Barlow in MGB *659* on loan from the new 57th Flotilla. Shortly before midnight, they rendezvoused with Barnes and his four PTs a few miles south of Giglio Island.

They had just started to approach the beach when R/T loudspeakers aboard the boats crackled. This was a surprise: it was understood that radio silence was to be maintained unless something urgent developed.

"Hallo, Wimpy, this is Stan. I have a target at Red 40, range 2,800 yards. Shall I leave it to you and carry on with the main job?"

The other boats listened as Maitland answered Barnes.

"How many are there, Stan? Sure, we'll take them on."

"Looks like one big and two small. They're all yours, Wimpy. Good luck."

The American radar had proven itself again. It was a dark night—according to Reynolds aboard *658*, visibility was less than five hundred yards. The PTs swung to starboard while Maitland flashed to the boats in his flotilla and they followed. They were relying now on their own, inferior radar sets as they closed on the target. Nevertheless, Maitland was able to maintain an accurate heading.

"Dogs from Wimpy. One target right ahead, fifteen hundred yards, and another at Green 20, range seventeen hundred yards, both closing. 18 knots. First attack will be to port."

The new SO was taking charge, leaving little doubt as to his abilities. Maitland said afterwards, "My tactics were to get as close as we could and always to get the following boat fine on my quarter. If the target was to port, the second boat's bow would be slightly to port of my stern, the third boat slightly to port of the second, in what we called 'fine order.' "

By 0207 the enemy vessels were sighted. There, for all to see, was an F-lighter—a cargo vessel with a very shallow draught but also a large number of guns; both convoy and escort in one—and two of the elusive E-boats, one on either beam. Maitland continued to close, an exercise of raw nerve which, if it succeeded, would bring him to within point-blank range of their prey. He was well within a hundred and fifty feet before he signalled the other boats.

"Dogs from Wimpy—open fire!"

Buzzers sounded and immediately the night exploded with the deafening sound of gunfire. Maitland said his boats threw "an awful hail of stuff" at the target. Reynolds, aboard *658*, was almost mesmerized by the attack on the F-lighter. "Five streams of converging, relentless tracer, spread in an arc about him so that he could not possibly reply," he said. "But reply he did, and desperately, too."

Both *657* and *658* were hit repeatedly. They quickly moved away, taking stock of their wounded, and were soon closing again on the target. Now the E-boats were in the thick of the fight; it seemed incredible they had not responded earlier. But evidently they lacked enthusiasm for a prolonged battle. One disappeared into the night after almost ramming Pickard aboard *655*; the other was "very roughly handled" by the MGBs, which left it a flaming wreck bobbing on the sea. The flotilla had begun with a victory—including one E-boat! Later, they counted the cost: most of the MGBs were damaged, although none as badly as Pickard's MTB, which had been badly shaken up by several 20-mm shells. Burke's boat was hit in one of its wing petrol tanks, but luckily it was full or the vapours might have exploded. But this was trifling compared to the toll in human life. Maitland had repeatedly hammered away at the F-lighter, which they subsequently decided had been carrying ammunition. "She just blew up," he said. "God! It was terrible—just terrible." No survivors were found. Of the wounded aboard the MGBs and MTB, all but one was patched up. The exception was Ordinary Seaman Brayshaw, a gunner in Burke's boat who died shortly after he was delivered to the Base Hospital at Bastia. This took most if not all of the pleasure out of their success.*

But they had to go out again to face the enemy. "It was part of our job to accept that the lives of men must occasionally be bartered for enemy ships," observed Reynolds. That night a conference was held, where it was decided to send out only *657*, *663*, and *659*, the others to be available the following night. They left at dusk for a patrol just north of where the previous night's fray

---

* Later Barnes reported that the PT boats had made as much noise as they could during the diversion raid, but that they were unable to surpass that of the real fighting in which the MGBs were involved.

had occurred. For those left behind, it was agonizing not knowing how Maitland, Ladner and Barlow had fared. According to Reynolds, he was asleep down below when at about 0400 he heard the sound of engines revving and felt a boat coming alongside *658*. He scrambled to the upper deck and saw Ladner's First Lieutenant, Derrick Brown, peering at him from the bridge of *663*.

"Any luck?" asked Reynolds.

"Well—it was a bit frustrating," Brown replied. Apparently they had run into a convoy of F-lighters with several big escorts and had had a go at them. But *657* and *659* were damaged, and so they had to withdraw.

"We definitely sank an E-boat and almost certainly got one of the F's," Brown added. In two nights, they had had success. The 56th was off to a good start, yet Brown yawned and stretched nonchalantly.

"Your turn tomorrow, Rover. Hope you make it a hat-trick!"

With this, Brown told Reynolds to "get his head down" as he would need all the sleep he could get. Later Reynolds admitted it was good advice.

The next night was Burke's turn to lead a small unit consisting of *658*, *655* and PT *217* on a patrol south of Capraia Island. They arrived early and settled in to a long search, the PT's radar sweeping the area to alert them of any potential danger. Four hours passed without contact. Then a signal came in from Bastia, alerting the unit to suspected enemy activity in the area of Vada Rocks, and they immediately sped northward on an interception course. Eventually they were rewarded when six F-lighters and a lone E-boat escort hove into view. The PT fired one of its torpedoes. It missed, alerting the E-boat, which began firing wildly at PT *217*. This allowed Burke to approach unnoticed. Thirty seconds was about all it took to destroy the E-boat. The 56th had its hat-trick—and Burke wasn't finished yet! Reynolds explained how his skipper went about increasing the score:

> I swept round with my glasses. The F-lighters were no longer in two lines but had scattered rapidly and were firing bursts of

tracer in every direction. Over the west, smoke which the PT had made in her diversion was spreading towards the convoy and already obscured the first few ships.

The confusion was magnificent. The enemy did not know friend from foe, so we should be able to enjoy ourselves... Corny could move about within the convoy, attack suddenly and then break off and creep to another target, leaving only fear and uncertainty behind.

For half an hour, Burke owned this small patch of the Mediterranean. Like a prize fighter—or, better still, a matador—he was in his element, skilfully, daringly baiting his adversary until ready to land a knock-out blow or the final vanquishing sword thrust, which in Burke's case took the form of deadly accurate gunfire from his arsenal of weapons. His own boat was hit numerous times, yet it survived. Best of all: no casualties were recorded, at least none aboard *658*. The next day various sources confirmed Burke had sunk at least one F-lighter and one E-boat, as well as damaged three other vessels including a 900-ton minelayer, which was aground near Vada Rocks. Later, the Battle Squadron's CO appended a comment to Maitland's action report, observing for the benefit of the navy's brass: "...this was the first time that the newly constituted 56th Flotilla operated as such... It is satisfactory to note that their tails are nearly as high as the explosions they caused."*

Not long after this series of actions, the 56th was dubbed "The Cowboy Flotilla"—a sobriquet that somehow clashed with "The Three Musketeers," identifying Maitland, Ladner and Burke personally, although both were appropriate in their own ways. The flotilla's new nickname was perhaps the result of the Canadians' colourful idiom, which to a British ear might have sounded like that of a cowpoke; Reynolds often recorded Burke and the others

---

*The Battle Squadron was a special unit within Coastal Forces comprising various British small craft—including Maitland's MGBs—and PT boats in the Med. It was led by Cdr. Robert Allan, a veteran of small-boat warfare in both the English Channel and the Med, and at twenty-eight the youngest commander in the RNVR.

uttering such words as "fellers" and "reckon." In any event, the British ratings especially were proud of it. This was demonstrated one day when almost the entire crew showed up wearing spurs. Maitland, who was likely not alone in his bewilderment—like Ladner and Burke he was in fact an extremely cultured individual—called out to his coxswain, Jake, demanding: "What the hell are you up to?"

"Well, sir," Jake drawled, "if they're gonna call us the 'Cowboy Flotilla' we thought we'd better look the part!"

So the all-Canadian 56th had asserted itself early in the game. Maitland and Burke were awarded the Distinguished Service Cross for their actions that won the flotilla its prized hat-trick in January 1944; to everyone's disgust, Ladner received only a Mention-in-Dispatches. For several months after this, the Cowboy Flotilla fought on as a unit attached to Cdr. Allan's Battle Squadron, seeing action mostly in the Tyrrhenian Sea and the Gulf of Genoa, earning more praise and—most important—greater success in their encounters with enemy ships. The press had a field day with their exploits, although few would ever actually penetrate the mystique surrounding the Canadians.

Think of it: Maitland, Ladner and Burke, close friends from well-to-do families in Vancouver, plus Rendell; Pickard of Winnipeg and MacLachlan of Toronto, all "blue bloods," so to speak, each commanding an armed speedboat engaged in a deadly game of hide-and-seek with the enemy's own high-speed craft and coastal convoys conducted far enough away from the restraining hand of authority. Of course it all went to their heads, these brash and pugnacious men who skippered the MGBs of the navy's "other navy," even if at sea they took their work seriously.

They were, simply, the best of the small-boat raiders in the Med. It was likely this, and not their antics, that impressed the navy's brass when thought was given to the promise of all-Canadian units elsewhere—in England, to be precise, where two new flotillas had been formed to continue the Battle of the Narrow Seas.

Rough weather meant tough going for the 29th's "short boats."
NATIONAL ARCHIVES OF CANADA/PA 144590

The 29th ceased to exist following a fire and explosion in Ostend Harbour, February 14, 1945. Five of the flotilla's nine boats were destroyed, 23 of its officers and men were listed killed or missing. NATIONAL ARCHIVES OF CANADA/PA 116484

C. Anthony "Tony" Law, DSC, pre-war artist and yachtsman, was the 29th's popular commanding officer.
NATIONAL ARCHIVES OF CANADA/PA 144588

Oliver Band Mabee, whose sophisticated manners and champagne tastes disguised a courageous spirit. Mabee commanded MTB 745.
NATIONAL ARCHIVES OF CANADA/PA 180068

Charles "Daddy Bones" Burk, DSC, top left, skipper of MTB 461, with his crew. Burk was celebrated as an outstanding tactician in small-boat warfare.
NATIONAL ARCHIVES OF CANADA/PA 176740

Jack "Jake" McClelland, First Officer on MTB 726, "liberated" St. Malo. In post-war Canada, McClelland became a famous publisher. NATIONAL ARCHIVES OF CANADA/PA 180071

Norn "Guns" Garriock earned his nickname after becoming the 65th's gunnery officer. COURTESY A P (BERT) MORROW

Canada's 29th and 65th Flotillas played a vital role in support of the Allied invasion of France during the summer of 1944. NATIONAL ARCHIVES OF CANADA/PA 144576

Albert "The Beard" Morrow, who commanded MTB 726 in the 65th Flotilla, was described as the most photographed officer in the RCN during the Second World War because of his piratical appearance. COURTESY A P (BERT) MORROW

James Kirkpatrick, DSC, commanded the 65th Flotilla. Called "The Brain" for his astuteness on the bridge, Kirkpatrick led what was considered one of the most spectacular and brilliant torpedo attacks against the enemy on the night of July 3/4, 1944, off the approaches to St. Malo.
NATIONAL ARCHIVES OF CANADA/PA 180073

Gunner Tom Jones was the 65th Flotilla's "unofficial" diarist. COURTESY TOM JONES

Motor Mechanic Glen Gander won Mention in Dispatches for his gallant efforts in keeping MTB 745 afloat after she was severely damaged by German fire on the night of September 30, 1944, in the North Sea. COURTESY TOM JONES

A view from the stern of a speeding MTB. Seen is Ross McCallum. COURTESY TOM JONES

The high-speed German Schnellboot, or "E-boat" as it was commonly known, was an able adversary whenever it came into conflict with MTBs and MGBs. COURTESY TOM RITCHIE

Crews of the 65th Flotilla square away their Fairmile "Dog" boats on a "make-and-mend" day in port. Life aboard was crowded and uncomfortable. NATIONAL ARCHIVES OF CANADA/PA 137959

Left to right: Tom Ladner, Douglas Maitland and Cornelius "Corny" Burke, the "Three Musketeers" in London, 1945. NATIONAL ARCHIVES OF CANADA/PA 180065

His Majesty's MTB 640, Campbell MacLachlin's "Dog boat," tied up at Malta in 1943. The photograph, which was taken from an embankment overlooking the harbour, gives an unusual view of a gunboat's upper deck. COURTESY CAMPBELL MACLACHLIN

L to R: Tom Fuller, Tom Ladner, Douglas Maitland and Cornelius "Corny" Burke, together at Buckingham Palace. COURTESY SIMON FULLER

6

All-Canadian Flotillas

A S INDIVIDUALS, CANADIANS WERE familiar figures aboard the Royal Navy's small boats that saw action in the English Channel during the early and desperate days of the war. By the end of 1943, they were fighting as a distinctly Canadian group whose two leaders brought to their commands the same unmistakable flair their countrymen had shown in the Mediterranean.

Yet those same leaders were as different from one another as two men could be.

Tony Law's patrician manners belied the image of a sea-wolf. Aloof and aesthetic, there was an aristocratic air about him. But those who knew him saw a compulsive, driven young man. Even the way he went to war reflected this intense desire to excel. Charles Anthony Law, "Tony" to his family and friends, was on a painting expedition along the Saguenay River aboard his own yacht on the eve of war. Arriving at Tadoussac the last week in August and hearing the latest news of the impending conflict, Law immediately set sail for Quebec City to report for duty in the Royal Canadian Ordnance Corps in which he held a commission as a lieutenant. His family would have been surprised had Law done otherwise.

Law was born in London, England, in 1916, the son of Major and Mrs. A. S. Law, both Canadians. His father, following service in the Canadian Expeditionary Forces during the First World War, settled in Quebec City. The boy's early life was one of comfort and privilege. His maternal grandfather was the Hon. Mr. Justice L. A. Audette, a judge of the Exchequer Court, whose summer home at Rivière du Loup held fond memories for the boy. It was where he had built his first sailboat at age fourteen. Other summers were spent at the Muskoka retreat of his paternal grandfather, Captain F. C. Law, RN, retired, where it was said life on this island hideaway was not unlike the disciplined life aboard a battleship.

But the retired sea captain inspired young Tony in another way. Captain Law was an accomplished painter, and through his association with members of the artistic community the boy's own talent with oils was discovered by no less a figure than Dr. Marius Barbeau, the respected anthropologist. After three years as a student at Upper Canada College, Law enrolled at the University of Ottawa and pursued his art studies under Fred Varley and Franklin Brownell at the Ottawa Art Association. In 1939, Law was awarded the Jessie Dow Prize for landscape with an oil painting called *Cold Winter Day, P.Q.* which the *Gazette* reproduced and on which its critic commented. The canvas was described as having clean, crisp colours. In March 1940, restless to get into action, Law resigned his commission in the army and volunteered for the RCNVR. Within a week he sailed for England to serve in the Royal Navy, getting his first taste of war in small boats. Never in Law's craziest dream would that include taking on the German battle fleet—in broad daylight.

In the summer of 1941, the German battle cruiser *Scharnhörst*, her sister ship *Gneisenau* and the heavy cruiser *Prinz Eugen* had taken refuge in the occupied port of Brest on the English Channel. By the new year, Hitler was convinced that the British were about to attack Norway and ordered the ships north. Leaving Brest under the cover of darkness on February 11, 1942, the ships began a spectacular dash up the Channel, by early afternoon of the following day steaming through the narrows of the Dover Strait. To improve the chances of success of this brilliant gamble, Hitler's three mighty warships were protected by a phalanx of steel in the shapes of six destroyers and a large number of the fast and deadly E-boats. Overhead, a continuous cover of no fewer than fifteen fighters accompanied the fleet throughout the passage.

The British knew it was only a matter of time before the battle fleet would try to break out. On the night of its departure, RAF Coastal Command had three radar-hunting Hudson bombers probing the Channel off Brest, the Brittany coast and between Le Havre and Boulogne. Incredibly, none found the fleet. The radar in two planes packed in, and the third aircraft returned to England before the German ships came into range.

Law remembered the chase as a fiasco. It wasn't until around 11 a.m. on the second day that two cruising Spitfire pilots sighted the enemy and raised the alarm. The first British unit to get away was five motor torpedo boats based at Dover, including MTB *48*, which Law commanded.

Running wide open in a heavy swell and wind, the Senior Officer's boat broke down, leaving Law and the three other boats to press on with the attack. Suddenly, appearing out of a smoke-screen covering the fleet, there appeared twenty E-boats commanded by a famous small-boat fighter, Charles Mueller. The chances of getting through to attack *Scharnhörst* and her sister ships were at best tenuous. Hoping for a lucky shot, the four MTBs fired all their torpedoes but at four thousand yards this was a dreamy long shot. All eight torpedoes missed their targets. Worse, a destroyer turned on Law's boat and bore down on him with guns blazing. Because MTB *48* was so close to the destroyer, it couldn't depress its guns low enough to score a hit. Law decided he would try "grounding" the destroyer and headed for the infamous Goodwin Sands, a treacherous shoal of shifting sands that had previously claimed many an unwary skipper. So alarmed was

Law's navigator, he yelled, "Look, you're going to run aground if you keep on going." Law replied, "He's going to run aground first," meaning the deeper draft of the destroyer would doom it. It didn't. The ship, the *Friedrich Ibn*, peeled off and rejoined the fleeing German fleet.

"It was a real Gilbert and Sullivan affair," Law recollected. There was one brief moment of absurd relief. Law's coxswain, pointing to a group of approaching aircraft, shouted, "Sir— aircraft with two wings—they must be British!" They were. These were the obsolete open-cockpit Swordfish torpedo biplanes derisively known as "stringbags."

Even though the engagement was an utter failure, Law was awarded Mention-in-Dispatches for his tenacity in the brave but futile attack on the enemy battle cruisers. Until then, Law had seen forty-six actions and saw many more over the next year and a half with the Royal Navy in the English Channel. In November 1943, when it had been decided to form two flotillas made up entirely of Canadian sailors, the navy had their man to command one of them, the 29th, in the figure of the aesthete C. Anthony Law. He had earned the reputation of a resolute leader.

The Canadian selected to form and lead the second flotilla, the 65th, was James Ralph Hilborn Kirkpatrick of Kitchener, Ontario, who in appearance and temperament was the opposite of Tony Law. The artist was slight of build and quick of movement, and his hair always appeared slightly longer than the navy allowed, projecting a presence slightly more bohemian than military. Kirkpatrick was tall and muscular; in the memory of Kathleen Barclay, his Wren secretary, he "moved beautifully" like a boxer, which in Kirkpatrick's case was understandable since he had fought as an amateur heavyweight in college.* Kirkpatrick was known as "The Brain" for his clever handling of both the brass and his men. "He had eyes in the back of his head," said Barclay. "You'd be talking

---

* WRNS, affectionately called "Wrens," was the acronym for Women's Royal Naval Service. In the RCN they were known as Women's Royal Canadian Naval Service, WRCNS, but still referred to as Wrens.

with him when suddenly he'd turn and shout out the door at a passing sailor, 'Square off that hat.' " Kirkpatrick never conspired with anyone or played favourites, Barclay recollected. "He would listen and then decide, just like a judge." Not surprisingly, then, it was to the bench that Kirkpatrick went after the war. Behind a desk ashore or on the bridge in battle, Kirkpatrick always held his emotions in check. Cool under fire, he was known to take calculated risks on operations, one risk no more annoying to some of his crew than the way he'd taunt enemy shore batteries by calmly sailing into their range of fire.

A tough sailor and a tough disciplinarian, Kirkpatrick had somewhat of a jump on his fellow volunteer reservists. A graduate of the Royal Military College, Kingston, he was seldom fazed by the order and drill imposed by the traditions of the Royal Navy. At HMS *King Alfred*, the dreaded RN wartime school established to whip civilian-reservists into shape, Kirkpatrick had expected the worst but instead found training there a cakewalk compared to RMC. Following his RMC training, Kirkpatrick had decided to study law and, when war broke out, was enrolled at Toronto's Osgoode Hall. He was overseas by June 1940 and assigned to an armed merchant cruiser that was torpedoed on its second patrol. HMS *Petropolis* was still floating after the first torpedo struck but Kirkpatrick, who had abandoned ship with everyone else, decided to reboard her. Two more torpedoes hit the ship and the Canadian agreed it was time to leave, but not before Kirkpatrick found his way to the wardroom and poured himself a stiff drink. Back again in the water, he clung to a spar for five hours before being picked up by a destroyer. For the next two years, Kirkpatrick served in small boats on various operations from rescuing downed Allied airmen to shooting up mines brought to the surface by minesweepers. But the most exciting assignment on gunboats was boarding schooners in suspicious waters where it was thought they were supplying German subs. The gunboats would roar in at high speed, keeping the suspects covered with their automatic weapons.

"Then we'd slow up and move in, bounce our boats into their rigging and leap aboard—real old pirate stuff," he told an information officer who was doing a story on the small boats. With astonishing modesty, Kirkpatrick told the reporter that "other fellows seem to have a lot more adventure than I do."

This, of course, was debatable but as Law and Kirkpatrick were to discover as senior officers of the 29th and 65th respectively, the worst was yet to come.

In November 1943, the decision was made to form the Canadian flotillas. They would be commissioned as His Majesty's Canadian Motor Torpedo and Motor Gun Boats and manned exclusively by Canadian officers and ratings. The boats were all British built and came under the operational control of the Royal Navy. While the victualling of the boats was the responsibility of the RN, a decision that produced groans among the Canadians who felt British rations inferior to their own, they received Canadian pay and allowances.

Throughout February and March, the crews travelled to backwater boatyards throughout southern England, and in one case Scotland, to commission the boats, eight in each flotilla. The 29th got motor torpedo boats, the seventy-one-and-a-half-footer called "the short boats" or "shorts." The 65th was made up of the latest Fairmile "D" boats known as "Dog boats," longer at 115 feet but more heavily armed and carrying a combination of torpedoes, depth charges and mines; two six-pounder guns, two twin turrets of .5 in. Mk Vs, twin Oerlikons and two twin 303s. The Dog boats were a triple threat and could operate either as a torpedo or gunboat, as well as having the capacity to attack with depth charges. The Ds packed a formidable wallop. Although they were designed for an attack speed of 34.5 knots, 27 knots was closer to reality; boat builders, as aircraft manufacturers often did, exaggerated their crafts' performances, which seldom lived up to the claims. This always was more of a disconcerting experience for pilots rather than small-boat skippers, who occasionally found themselves on take-off on a long runway still on the ground when the manual said they should have been airborne one hundred yards "back there!" The shorts came close to the stated speed of 41 knots, making them the smallest and fastest boats in the Second World War.* The Germans' *Schnellboot*, or E-Boat, boasted a top speed of 44 knots, a fact that Harro Garmsen said was a source of much comfort to the Germans since they "always had a good chance to get away." While the Germans couldn't claim it to be the smallest and fastest small boat, at 115 feet their *Schnellboot* was indeed the speediest. All the boats, Allied or enemy, were equipped too with one vital piece of machinery, the generator that produced smoke or fog allowing a quick get-away in dicey situations, a vital piece of equipment that probably saved more lives than any other gear aboard.

The German boats featured one other comforting advantage. Their engines were diesel, while the Canadian and British boats were powered by highly volatile 100-octane gasoline, a fact that was disastrous for the 29th Flotilla a year after it had become operational.

But by March 1944, no one in either flotilla was looking ahead much more than a week at a time. Boats from both flotillas began arriving at HMS *Bee* at Holyhead, Wales, for what the Royal Navy called "working-up," or what the U.S. Navy referred to as "shake-down" trials.

Holyhead was depressing in appearance, certainly not the inspiration for William Blake's "green and pleasant land." It was perched on a peninsula, the Atlantic winds constantly assaulting the rocky shore flattening the grass like a dull scythe. Today's wandering tourist knows Holyhead as the main ferry port to and from Ireland. It was said that during the war the ferry was used by agents in the pay of the enemy as a convenient platform on which to spy on the Royal Navy. Holyhead was frantic with activity for it was this port that the Royal Navy used for working up newly commissioned MTBs and MGBs, British as well as Norwegian, Canadian and Free French. Despite frequent winter gales that kept

---

*One knot is 1 nautical mile per hour or 1.15 land miles per hour.

the boats in harbour, sometimes for days on end, Holyhead was relatively safe because of its distant location from enemy air attacks.

Kirkpatrick was already on hand when Law arrived and they repaired to *Bee*'s mess where the "rounds of beer came so fast that our back teeth were soon floating," Law remembered. The tempo of training, however, was what most remembered. Mornings were spent in lectures and the afternoons put theory into practice, navigation, aircraft recognition, signals, tactics, gunnery and firing practice torpedoes in day and night exercises. There was little respite from the daily training, although Law found time to do some painting. Stationed at *Bee* was the well-known wildlife painter, Peter Scott, son of Scott of Antarctic fame. One night near the end of the trials, Scott and Law collaborated on a mural for one wall in *Bee*'s wardroom depicting a seascape that featured roaring torpedo boats and soaring birds.

Painting was always a means of escape and a source of relief for Law. Even though he continued to command the 29th, he was also appointed an official war artist, contributing to the impressive collection of Canadian war art. While off-duty painting may have helped alleviate the tension of command, Law found more immediate solace as he ran down the roster of names of the skippers arriving with their newly commissioned shorts that would make up the eight torpedo boats of the 29th Flotilla. All were small-boat veterans with several years' experience in Royal Navy motorboat and gunboat flotillas.

There was Dave Killam of Vancouver, a clever poker player who Law found "quiet and keen." Charles Burk of Toronto, who learned to sail at the RCYC on Toronto Island, was an experienced officer as well whose reputation in action was no less impressive than his celebrated skill at shooting craps, a talent that earned him the nickname "Bones." Later, when he became a father, someone added the prefix "Daddy" and for the remainder of the war Burk was known as "Daddy Bones." Bob Moyse of Winnipeg was a Channel veteran too who joined the RCNVR as an ordinary seaman and officer candidate. From Winnipeg came the soft-spoken Glen Creba, a contrasting personality to Craig Bishop of Sherbrooke, Quebec, dashing in appearance, who set off the already simple but elegant officer's square rig jacket by sporting a white handkerchief in the breast pocket. Another ordinary seaman who rose to command was Charles Chaffey of Vancouver, who had served in the same RN flotillas as the famed Britisher, Peter Dickens. Chaffey was called "Chuff-Chuff," but after all these years no one remembers why. Chaffey had seen action in the disastrous Canadian raid on Dieppe in August 1942. The laconic Barney Marshall of Victoria, British Columbia, completed the skippers' roster for the 29th.

The 65th Flotilla was equally blessed with veteran small-boat skippers. There was the ebullient Bert "The Beard" Morrow. Although he was born in Vancouver, his family were pioneer ship-builders in Newfoundland. He got his first command at age four, a ten-foot sailboat as a birthday present. Malcolm "Mac" Knox of Montreal first saw action in the Channel in the spring of 1943 with a Royal Navy MTB flotilla, a decided contrast to his pre-war sailing aboard handsome Chris Craft cruisers in the St. Lawrence. His brother had been the American boat manufacturer's Quebec representative and there was never a lack of a demonstrator for tooling around on Sunday outings.

Les McLernon was a lanky car salesman from Montreal who brought an exuberance of command more characteristic of the sales lot than the bridge of a fighting ship. He was so tall Katie Barclay remembered McLernon "had to stoop to talk to you." Everyone, too, remembered McLernon's "lopsided smile."

His personality was strikingly different from that of Oliver Band Mabee, a Toronto blueblood of slightly chubby proportions. The Wrens jokingly called him Oliver "Bland" Mabee because of his highly polished sophistication.

Owen Greening came from a prominent Hamilton family who ran a prosperous rope and wire manufacturing company. Older than the others, he was considered "mature." At age thirty-two, Greening was referred to as "the old man." Another businessman-turned-skipper was John Collins of Sundridge, Ontario, where he

operated a propane gas firm. George Moors was from the Lake-
head where he had worked for a grain broker in Fort William (now
Thunder Bay) before joining the navy. Like their commander of
the 65th, all had volunteered for motor torpedo boats.

While all the skippers brought experience in action to the two
newly formed Canadian flotillas, this was not always the case for
the ratings. Some had seen service in corvettes, destroyers and
minesweepers and a few with Royal Navy flotillas, but the remainder of them were arriving freshly trained from Canada. In all cases,
though, the sailors joined their assigned flotillas after passing
through the much-cursed HMCS *Niobe*, the RCN's overseas shore
base that was always cryptically referred to as "somewhere in
Scotland." Actually *Niobe* was located at Greenock, Scotland, an
hour's train trip west of Glasgow on the banks of the Clyde,
appropriately housed, it was felt by its transient inhabitants, on the
grounds of a former mental institution whose main building served
as *Niobe*'s quarterdeck. The place was a madhouse that only
wartime bureaucracy was capable of creating. In the first six
months of 1944, nearly five thousand men underwent advanced
special training at *Niobe*, and more than thirteen thousand ratings
passed through on way to commission fourteen Canadian
ships, two flotillas of landing craft, plus the two Canadian motor
torpedo boat flotillas. When Leading Seaman Dave Wright of
Cloverdale, B.C., arrived at *Niobe* in November 1943, overcrowd-
ing was severe and there was no place to put the arrivals except in
tents soaked by an almost continuous drizzle of rain. "We were
damp, wet, miserable," said Wright. His mates vacated the tents
for refuge on the cement floor of the base's latrines where they
decided to sleep. "It was much drier than it was in the tents,"
Wright laughed. Swedish-born Jack Johnson, who grew up in The
Pas, Manitoba, thought *Niobe* "pretty—pretty grim." RCN flacks
tried disguising life by describing the base as "picturesque," and
its commanding officer, Captain E. A. Brock, attempting to put a
good face on a poor situation, alluded to *Niobe* as a "sort of
'foreign' island in a setting unfamiliar to its Canadian population,
many of whom have travelled little and find it not easy to adjust
themselves happily and quickly to strange customs." Indeed,

concurred Johnson. Halfway between the base and Greenock train station was located a Borstal, a school for juvenile delinquents who Johnson observed were used like horses to pull ploughs through a nearby field. In time, *Niobe* grew to a sprawling camp of a hundred Nissen huts and a weekly complement of two thousand sailors waiting to be sent around the country for asdic training, telegraphy, gunnery, torpedo, fire-fighting, damage control and other specialist courses. Happy were the sailors when they finally departed this huge manning pool to join the two flotillas even if training had not entirely equipped them to perform the duties to which they had been assigned. Johnson, who knew "something about steam and coal" as a stoker, found himself in the engine room of MTB *466* with its three 1,200-horsepower Packard engines. "Christ, I didn't know anything about engines," Johnson said years later. But he soon learned.

By the end of April, most of the short boats of the 29th and the longer Dog boats of the 65th had departed from the working-up trials at Holyhead. The 65th headed to HMS *Cicala*, Dartmouth, while the 29th found itself scattered in different ports along England's south coast undergoing refits or repairs, in one embarrassing instance as a result of damage caused to both the flotillas' senior officers' boats. Law's and Kirkpatrick's boats had been in a minor collision on March 31 at Holyhead and in backing off, Kirkpatrick's boat was in collision with a third vessel, putting his boat out of operations for several weeks. Another of the 65th's boats suffered even more extensive damage when she went into dry dock at Holyhead for normal maintenance. The gate gave way on high tide and she was so extensively damaged by the flood of water that the boat was decommissioned in the 65th since it was thought her repairs would take too long to be of any immediate value to the flotilla.*

After moving from Holyhead to Dartmouth, the 65th suffered another kind of casualty. Able Seaman Alexander Duncan

* This was MTB *744*, which never did see action with the 65th. Eventually, she was repaired and turned over to the RAF as a long-range rescue craft.

apparently got into some bad liquor and "suddenly went blind in the night." He died the next day in the Royal Naval Auxiliary Hospital at Newton Abbot.

The 29th completed its working-up period with fewer mishaps but not without moments of comic relief. One entire crew, except one sailor, arrived from *Niobe* less their lifebelts, causing Law to write a sarcastic note to the Senior Canadian Naval Officer at King's House in London "that life-jackets are of more value to a seagoing sailor than to HMCS *Niobe*." He would appreciate sailors getting their life-jackets back before joining a seagoing ship, Law informed the brass.

Kirkpatrick and Law nonetheless reported they were pleased with the results of the arduous working-up period, commenting on the dedication of both officers and men. Other than the sudden demise of Able Seaman Duncan, Kirkpatrick reported to his superiors that in the 65th "the general state of health amongst the crews is excellent and the morale good." Law was equally enthusiastic. "The crew are keen to learn and seem to be of a high calibre in the 29th Canadian Flotilla," he said. His words, however, disguised a note of bitter disappointment. During the working-up period, the 29th received a signal from the British Admiralty that the Canadians interpreted as completely asinine. The flotilla of short boats was ordered to strip its torpedo tubes and to replace them with racks to carry depth charges. "Mere words cannot express the effect on the flotilla's morale," Law later wrote. "Our faces were long and sad as we watched our main armament and striking power being taken away." The Admiralty said the changes were required to counter the presence in the channel of the German W-boat, a strange submarine whose turbine engine was said to be powered by hydrogen peroxide that gave it speeds of 40 knots on the surface and 30 knots submerged!*

---

* There were in fact eight of these unique submarines called type XVII using "ingolin" fuel (hydrogen peroxide), which when mixed with diesel and steam, powered the Walter turbine. Like so many of Hitler's so-called secret weapons

Law immediately appealed the order to Vice-Admiral Percy Nelles, Senior Canadian Flag Officer, Overseas [SCFO(o)] in London, but without success. Torpedo tubes were in such demand that as soon as they were removed from the Canadian boats they were quickly snapped up elsewhere in the fleet. Law was told in a letter from a desk-bound naval assistant in London that "you and your chaps will do your utmost to do a good job with the tools you have."

The job that was to be done was an urgent one. Throughout England, but especially along the southern coast, the atmosphere was tense and vibrant as preparations quickened for the invasion of France. No one exactly knew when this was going to be launched, but as the small, grey fighting boats slipped their mooring lines from various ports along the Channel there was a pervasive air of impending battle. By early May, the 29th was tied up in the quaint little harbour of Ramsgate in Kent, and by mid-May the 65th reached Brixham in Devon, a fishing port that it would call home. It is important to pause to record the roster of boats and the identities of the young Canadians who commanded them, if for no other reason than continuity, but more important to document their names from an already fading record.

29th Flotilla

MTB	Skipper	Rank	Hometown
459	C. A. "Tony" Law, DSC (SO)	Lt. Cdr.	Quebec City, Que.
460	Dave Killam, DSC	Lt.	Vancouver, B.C.
461	C. A. "Daddy Bones" Burk, DSC	Lt.	Toronto, Ont.
462	Robert J. Moyse	Lt.	Winnipeg, Man.
463	D. Glen Creba	Lt.	Winnipeg, Man.
464	L. Craig Bishop, DSC	Lt.	Sherbrooke, Que.
465	Charles "Chuff-Chuff" Chaffey	Lt.	Vancouver, B.C.
466	Sherwood "Barney" Marshall	Lt.	Victoria, B.C.

---

that emerged in the last year of the war, only two of these subs were operational, and only then in experimental trials.

65th Flotilla

MTB	Skipper	Rank	Hometown
726	Albert "The Beard" Morrow	Lt.	Vancouver, B.C.
727	L. R. "Les" McLernon, DSC	Lt.	Montreal, Que.
735	John Collins	Lt.	Sundridge, Ont.
743	Malcolm "Mac" Knox, DSC	Lt.	Montreal, Que.
744	George Moors	Lt.	Fort William, Ont.
745	O. B. "Ollie" Mabee	Lt.	Toronto, Ont.
746	S. Owen Greening	Lt.	Hamilton, Ont.
748	J. R. H. "Kirk" Kirkpatrick, DSC (SO)	Lt. Cdr.	Kitchener, Ont.

Seen as part of the broad canvas being composed on the eve of the invasion, the two Canadian flotillas were minuscule both in their numbers and size when compared with the battle cruisers, destroyers and corvettes standing ready and poised to strike the enemy. The officers and men aboard each one of these tiny flotillas who went to sea in battle scarcely ever exceeded 328 souls, yet the legacy of their deeds was disproportionate to their numbers. Anyone on the jetty who saw them return from their nightly forays into the Channel over the next year, with decks awash with blood and their hulls battered and holed, may well have wondered if indeed they led charmed lives.

"Oh golly," recollected Katie Barclay, "oh boy, they were the best. The *very* best." And their presence is as vivid in Barclay's mind's eye now as it was then; McLernon with his Jean Chrétien mug; Kirkpatrick with the sometimes deprecatory smile; and Ollie Mabee's Rosedale manners. And the letters that Mac Knox asked her to post home to his wife—every day.

7

The Battleground

EW OCEANS OR SEAS anywhere in the world come as close to matching the history of intrigue and conflict as the English Channel. Its shores and waters have been the home and the workplace for a parade of pirates, spies, smugglers and invading armies and navies for countless centuries. Caesar, the crazy Caligula and Claudius all launched troublesome enterprises there. So did the Danes, the Dutch and the Normans. Spain sent its fated armada into these waters but the treacherous winds and Sir Francis Drake scattered the ships like a bathtub fleet, a costly lesson that did not, however, deter a succession of invaders bent on holy war or other nefarious undertakings.

Compared to the vast expanses of the Mediterranean Sea, the Atlantic or the Pacific, the Channel always seemed the merest of puddles. Yet this watery obstacle was to perplex the most rapacious military machine ever assembled in this century, the grey, marching legions of Adolf Hitler. While the Germans never actually attempted an invasion of England, their threat of waterborne attack pervaded from the fall of Dunkirk in the spring of 1940 and throughout the following summer that year. Hitler's grandiose invasion plan called "Sea Lion" was never to be realized. To

131

succeed, Hitler knew he needed to command the skies above the Channel and to do that the RAF had to be wiped out. The Luftwaffe began its attacks in July and reached a crescendo by August 13 when the Luftwaffe mounted 1,485 sorties. When this effort failed to clear the skies of British fighters, the Germans concentrated on destroying its air enemy on the ground, attacking airfields and vital control centres. Still, the RAF resisted even though it was perilously close to defeat. Instead of hammering home a final blow on the RAF bases, Hitler changed his strategy and began pummelling London in a terrifying series of raids that became known as the Blitz.

The merciless bombings only served to stiffen British resolve, but more important gave the RAF the time needed to organize its defence and patch up its shattered bases. By mid-September, faced with disastrous losses, the Luftwaffe suspended daylight raids and Hitler called off Operation Sea Lion. The invasion of England across the Channel was scuttled in the skies in what became known as the Battle of Britain. Instead of Sea Lion, which would have seen thirteen divisions hurled across the Channel from bases in Belgium and France, it was the Royal Navy that continued to command and rule these disputed waters, often precariously, until the Allies themselves launched their own invasion four years later.

It was in these contested waters that the two Canadian small-boat flotillas found themselves in the spring of 1944. As a battle-scape, the English Channel was a small one. Nigel Calder likened it to the shape of a megaphone, the corners of the narrow mouth-piece representing Dover on the English shore and Calais on the French side, the corner ends of the wider opening rest on the Isles of Scilly at the top, and the Island of Ushant of the western approaches at the bottom. From the narrow opening at Dover Strait to the broader end facing the Atlantic is a distance of only 350 miles. The width varies from a mere twenty miles in Dover Strait to just over one hundred miles between Scilly and Ushant.

In the post-war peace, thousands cross the Channel daily in comfort and with ease by ferry and hovercraft, a journey that the present generation of Europeans will soon make by the "Chunnel," an underwater tunnel of Olympian proportions now being blasted out under the Channel seabed, while above, pleasure yachtsmen from England, France, Belgium and Holland routinely flit back and forth under sail.

But when the Canadian flotillas stalked and sailed these waters forty-five-odd years ago, it was anything but fair-weather cruising. Then, the Canadians operated in the worst kind of weather and invariably at night. In summer, they knew there was fog one day in five. In winter, they faced bone-chilling winds and temperatures that turned the bow spray from their boats into tiny pellets of ice that stung their eyes and faces like frozen bullets. There were no wet suits then and no Gore-Tex either. They bundled themselves up like mummies. Over their working rig, they put on a first layer called a "goon suit," which in appearance was similar to the snowmobiler's coveralls. On top of that they wore oilskins and since there was no Velcro either, they stuffed towels around their necks like scarves to try to seal out the waters cascading over the bow and drenching the open bridge. On their feet, they pulled felt-lined sea-boots and on their heads woollen toques. Gunners on the open deck topped it all off with chamber-pot-like helmets. Then came the bulky life-jacket and on top of everything a primitive flak jacket that looked for all the world like a baseball catcher's chest protector.

Despite all the layers of clothing, "you were constantly wet," said Mac Knox laconically. "It was a fact of life." Tony Law remembered that no matter how much clothing he put on to combat winter winds he was always "frozen before the night was out." Law invested in an RAF flying suit that worked like an electric blanket when plugged in. The first time he tried using it, the suit nearly electrocuted him when a gigantic wave hit the bridge, shorting out the suit's circuitry in an alarming blue flash of light. He never wore the "ridiculous garb" again.

In anything other than a dead calm, both the short boats and the D-boats were always wet and noisy. The level of discomfort increased as sea and wind conditions worsened, particularly on the shorts because of their planing hulls; when running at top speed, they took on a pounding motion as they leapt through the water bucking and slamming the surface with a cadence that went whump, whump, whump. This repetitive and bone-jarring motion was worse driving into a head sea. When it became debilitating, the skippers altered course so the waves would come on the quarter, which then added another sensation of rolling and por-poising. Running before a heavy following sea created a roller-coaster motion as if aboard a combination of escalator going up and elevator going down. The rolling crest of the wave slowly lifted the stern out of the water and in a micro-second sent the boat plunging down the face of the breaking wave. Steering in these conditions required a skilful touch by the coxswain for too much wheel to either port or starboard to counter the thrust of the cresting wave meant a danger of broaching.

The Dog boats, longer than the shorts by forty-four-and-a-half feet, were slightly better sea boats but not significantly. They were "hard chine" hulls, that is, from the waterline to the keel they were flat rather than round. However, the chine line swept dramatically up from just forward of the bridge to the bow, giving the bow the appearance of being V-shaped. In theory, when driven at high speed, this V-shaped bow was supposed to produce a drier boat by creating a bow wave that was supposed to lift the hull out of the water and reduce the pounding so characteristic of the shorter boats. In moderate seas this was so, but in heavy weather they thudded through the water the same as the shorts, and the sea swept the forward deck, crashing against the chart house and bridge with the same ferocity as felt by the seventy-one-and-a-half-foot shorts. Knox, in a statement of considerable generosity, said sea conditions aboard the motor torpedo boats were probably no worse than a corvette, which it was said "would roll in a mild dew." In both the shorts and Dog boats, no matter how diligent the crews were in buttoning up the ship, it was always wet in anything but the calmest seas. It was a toss-up whether daily life was worse on deck or on the bridge than down below, especially in the engine room. The noise from the three engines in the shorts and the four Packards in the Ds was completely deafening, making it impossible to speak and to be understood. Jack Johnson remembered the stokers crouching beside the roaring engines, communicating by hand signals with each other like mutes, and with cotton batting stuffed in their ears.

And the boats smelled. The 100-octane fuel permeated the decks below in both the Dog boats and the shorts, unsettling the strongest of stomachs. Mixed with the cooking odours from the galley and the perspiration of the crew, it was a combination that was often overpowering. The smell of the fumes too was a constant reminder of just how vulnerable, how potentially deadly their existence actually was. Even though the tanks contained a self-sealing substance in the event they were hit, the thought of a tracer igniting the fuel tanks in battle was seldom out of mind. The inside tanks were always used up first because if a bullet hit the half-empty outer tanks first, the theory was the tracer could ignite the fuel more easily because of the fumes.

Motor Mechanic Leslie Bowerman, who was born on Pender Island in the Gulf Islands, drew on his pre-war boating experience in checking out the gas tanks on Kirkpatrick's boat after one shoot-out. He insisted that a line be rigged around his waist when he crawled over the tanks, fearing he would pass out because of the strength of the fumes. "I could feel myself numbed," he recalled.

The Channel was rarely calm and for good reason. The huge Atlantic swells rolled into the wide western end of this watery "megaphone," producing the infamous Channel chop because the sea floor was much shallower than the ocean that sent its rollers boiling eastward towards the narrow neck of the Dover Strait. Because the French coast was more irregular than the English shore, this tumble and swirl of incoming water also created vicious tides and currents, particularly around Ushant where it was said a sailor "who sees Ushant sees his blood." Further east in the Gulf of St. Malo there was, too, an alarming tide that when the sun, moon and pull of the earth combined their mysterious forces produced what is known as the Alderney Race between the Channel Islands' most northern rock of Alderney and the tip of the Cherbourg Peninsula. Despite the thousands of horsepower the torpedo boat engines generated that could power them out of a tight spot, the presence of these watery black holes of nature demanded constant vigilance on the part of the prowling Canadians.

Bert Morrow said while the sound of the engines moaning below decks was reassuring, it was the skill of his cox, Les Hubbert of Weston, Ontario, "a guy with fingers like two bunches of bananas" wrestling the wheel on the bridge, who gave him an extra measure of confidence.

A skilled cox was as vital as a boat's navigator in these treacherous waters, but it was the confusion of battle that made the job nightmarish. Norm Garriock, Morrow's navigator, recalled that it took constant vigilance. The only possible way to know where they were in these shoot-ups was to keep a continuous plot on the chart. With stopwatch in hand, Garriock recorded the exact time of each heading the boat took, painstakingly marking the information down. It was the only way he'd know after all the twisting and turning of battle what the position was when they broke off the engagement. Since the boats were travelling 20 knots or more and covering a lot of water, this was not easily accomplished. Adding to this onerous job was the fact it was carried out amid the roar of guns and shouts of commands from the bridge just a foot away. "I was never more than five miles out," laughed Garriock years later.

In May 1944, the 29th and 65th Flotillas were finally ready to begin operating in this inhospitable battleground.

The choice of location for the 65th's operational base was a fortunate one. The small Devon port of Brixham lay sheltered behind a headland known as Berry Head, a picture-postcard town whose houses clustered around the port and on the surrounding hills above. The jetty where the 65th tied up on May 14 had wisely been located around the hook of land, protected from the Atlantic. It faced Tor Bay, and beyond, the charming town of Torquay whose palm trees enchanted the northern sailors. But it was Brixham where the welcome was immediate and warm. The town was a historic fishing port and the Brixham fishermen and their boats were renowned. Perhaps it was the townsfolk's empathy with the sea that drew together the town and the newly arrived Canadians, that special bond that exists between all those who go to sea. No one knew better the perils of the English Channel than the fishermen of Brixham. They were resourceful and innovative in their calling, having developed over the centuries new kinds of nets and lines but their most brilliant achievement was the way they developed and built their famous sea boat, the Brixham trawler, a boat so perfectly presented with its gaff-rigged sails that the mere sight of it can still agitate deep emotion in the breast of today's amateur yachtsmen. The 65th quickly settled in and Kirk-patrick informed his superiors the flotilla was to be found on "New Pier, Brixham, telephone numbers Brixham 2328 or 2329."

Tony Law's 29th Flotilla meanwhile had already assembled at Ramsgate, farther east up the Channel and twenty miles beyond Dover, at the very lip of the Channel where Dover Strait ends and the North Sea begins. Ramsgate was a picturesque yachting centre where, curiously enough, those same Devonian fishermen had established a colony in pursuit of the unpredictable herring two centuries earlier. Now, however, except for the presence of the Royal Ramsgate Yacht Club, there were few signs left of the sporting life. The Royal Navy had taken over the town and harbour and the artifacts of war gave the place a besieged look. Barrage balloons lazed in the sky at the end of their tethers, the barrels of anti-aircraft guns poked skyward from behind sandbag pits and coils of barbed wire lay tangled along the shore. After all, the enemy was only twenty miles away, across the Channel.

Unlike the crews of the 65th who lived aboard their boats, the 29th was always in search of shore billets wherever it was based. Their seventy-one-and-a-half-footers were simply too small and cramped to live aboard. The ratings moved into a hotel that had been expropriated by the navy where they slept dormitory-style in the dining room. Although the hotel was new, it bore a faded and dingy appearance. Law ordered the hotel swabbed out and a fresh coat of paint for the walls and ceilings to brighten up the place. The officers took over quainter quarters in the yacht club that evoked an air of gentler days with its faded yachting photographs and yellowing silver trophies spotted throughout the building.

The 29th's settling-in period was brief. Shortly after it arrived at Ramsgate, Law, Moyse, Killam, Bishop, Marshall, Chaffey and Creba were ordered to report to Dover with their boats to escort another group of Royal Navy torpedo boats to land a small force of army engineers on the coast of France. The Dover briefing at dusk had all the trappings of a B-grade movie. The army infiltrators arrived with faces blackened in grease paint, watches were "syn-chronized" and the boats departed in the falling light, the crews silhouetted against the horizon. The engineers were to be taken as close to shore as possible where they were to be transferred to small rubber dinghies to search for, and steal, enemy land mines planted on the beaches and bring them back to Dover for examination. The Army wanted to study the mines to learn how to neutralize them. All this effort was in preparation for the invasion that everyone knew was imminent. But as the Canadians crashed through heavy seas of the wind-lashed Channel, it was apparent that conditions were too risky for recovering the mines, and all the boats were ordered back to Dover. This was the first operation the 29th performed as a unit and there was a feeling of disappointment when it was called off. The following night the wind abated, the sea settled down and the mine-stealing caper was remounted. The operation succeeded without incident; the mines were brought back to Dover, loaded aboard army lorries and speeded off to London to be taken apart and examined.

Still, the 29th hadn't fired a shot in anger. The new flotilla wanted a greater test, an opportunity that came on the night of May 22. Rarely did the flotilla ever sail without an objective in mind. All offensive patrols were the result of a very effective intelligence network, a combined effort of radar aerial reconnaissance and first-hand observation by agents located throughout the French ports. As Allied air superiority grew in 1944, the movement of food, guns, ammunition and men by the Germans using the French rail system during daylight hours had become for them a risky undertaking. More and more they were forced to mount sea convoys at night, even if it meant venturing into the Channel where it was almost certain they would meet the prowling motor torpedo boats. The decision whether to try to intercept these convoys was based on a number of factors. Aerial photos taken over a number of days would be studied and when high-riding hulls of the merchantmen were seen getting lower in the water, the departure of the convoy was likely imminent. Resistance operators lurking around the French ports and talking to dock workers helped to know sometimes when the ships were thought ready to leave, and perhaps even their destinations. Knowing the convoys would not depart until dark and by plotting their projected course, the navy usually arrived at a respectable guesstimate where the MTBs were likely to make an interception for attack.

Law, Bishop, Chaffey and Marshall joined up with four British MTBs for this night's operation. Intelligence reports also said the convoy was being escorted by at least four enemy flak trawlers. These heavily armed boats had a formidable reputation because of the immense firepower they possessed. As the Canadian boats swept out of Dover harbour, Law "felt in my bones that tonight we should meet the enemy."

At 0224 on the morning of May 23, the 29th Flotilla found what it was looking for. The action that followed was so typical of an offensive patrol that it might have been taken from a textbook of tactics. The attack began in total darkness. Then, abruptly, a symphony of noise: a deafening sound-and-light show conducted in a frenzy of confusion. As the group approached the convoy, there was the predictable overture to battle. Starshells suddenly screamed skyward, turning night into day. Starshells were powerful projectiles used by both sides. Exploding overhead in a burst of brilliant light, the shells illuminated the sea below. Red in colour for the Canadians, green for the Germans; vivid, gigantic canopies of falling colour, like huge exploding inverted tulip petals that blossomed and fell seaward, psychedelic really, long before and not entirely unlike the pulsating effect of a ballroom discothèque.

The first burst of starshells caught Law's boat illuminated between the enemy and the group of British MTBs peeling away to find safety in the darkness. Over the Canadian boats came a vicious barrage of heavy-calibre shells aimed at the fleeing British torpedo boats. Law and Chaffey countered with ten of their own starshells under whose cascading light the Canadians spotted the enemy convoy, some E-boats, and beyond the convoy one or two of the fearful flak trawlers.

The Canadians attacked, guns blazing. All around them the sky was criss-crossed by red and yellow tracer fire as Law, Chaffey, Bishop and Marshall pressed towards the enemy—flat out, at full bore.

In the turmoil of the attack, Bishop was separated. Besides finding himself alone, he suddenly found himself in a one-on-one duel with a much faster E-boat. They had closed within a couple of hundred yards, sweeping past one another at a combined speed of sixty miles an hour, pounding each other with everything they had.

Uncertain of Bishop's whereabouts in the mêlée, Law ordered "smoke," a blast of manufactured smoke to cover their getaway in the hope of reassembling his group. For the next hour and fifteen minutes, Law, Chaffey and Marshall probed the area trying to make contact with the German convoy and the chance for another attack. Nothing. The convoy and her escorts melted away in the darkness.

At 0415 the three boats turned back towards Ramsgate, all the skippers nagged by the thought of what might have happened to Craig Bishop and his balls-out run at the enemy. They needn't. Bishop joined up with four British MTBs, reaching Ramsgate before Law and the others.

On that night Law, forever the perceptive painter, remembered: "The sun rose in the east, tinting the sky and water and distant land a warm pink, and with it the morale of the flotilla rose."

With their pennants flying, Law, Chaffey and Marshall leap-frogged towards the white cliffs of Dover, arriving at Ramsgate at 0710 where, to their relief, they found "the bad boy [Bishop] of the flotilla" waiting to greet them with a grin.

In the morning sun they took stock. Law's boat was slightly damaged by gunfire on her port bow. Bishop's had been struck by a shell on the afterpart of her bridge, a shot that had been deflected because of the bridge's armour plating, and which probably saved the lives of all on the bridge. The rigging of Bishop's boat had been shot away as well, along with the little torpedo boat's white battle ensign.

In his formal action report, Law wrote, "This small action was a great uplift to the morale of the 29th Canadian MTB Flotilla, as well as learning a great deal from it, and from what we have learned we hope that the next time we will be more successful."

Unlike the celebration that followed the "commando caper" a

few weeks previously when Law and the skippers went on a piss-up, this night they all bent to the dreary task of filing reports and lengthy descriptions of their first action as a flotilla. The shoot-out raised one important question, a troubling question that could not easily be dismissed. The four British boats had become separated from the Canadian boats early in the action, as well as Bishop from his own unit at the height of battle. The perplexing question posed was: Who was the enemy and who was friendly when a unit got separated? "It was a rather difficult action," Law wrote to his superiors. Once they were separated, "all boats had to be assumed friendly until they proved themselves hostile." It was a question that would confound the small-boat warriors, the most unanswerable worry perhaps throughout the entire Channel campaign. It was a question that went on to ask: Who was steely-nerved enough to hold fire when an unidentified boat came roaring at them? For to hesitate, even for a split second, might invite disaster.

And that is what happened the night of May 22–23, when the 65th Flotilla went into action for the first time. At sundown that evening, four of the 65th's boats slipped their moorings in Brixham harbour and, running at 22 knots, headed directly south across the Channel to the northernmost tip of Brittany, off Les Heux and Les Sept Iles. Conditions were near perfect. There was barely a wind, the sea was calm, there was no moon but the sky was cloudless. The group consisted of Bert Morrow, Les McLernon, John Collins on whose boat Kirkpatrick had embarked as Senior Officer, and Ollie Mabee on the bridge of the fourth MTB. At 0327 radar contact was made. Ahead, but out of sight, was a convoy of ships, and around it a phalanx of small blips that most certainly were E-boats or flak trawlers. Fourteen minutes later the enemy was sighted, the convoy at a range of thirty-five hundred yards, and the escorts at two thousand yards. A minute later, the German escorts spotted the approaching Canadians and turned to intercept them, dashing all hope that they might launch a massed torpedo attack unobserved.

Instead, Kirkpatrick decided to split his formation, ordering Mabee and McLernon to take on the main convoy while he and

Morrow attacked the escorting E-boats, drawing them away from Mabee and McLernon.

Kirkpatrick and Morrow closed to within one hundred yards of the fast-approaching German gunboats, all guns firing—extremely accurately as it turned out, for the two E-boats were blasted into silence, stopped dead in the water. Still the Germans managed to strike Morrow's boat with withering fire before they themselves were knocked out.

Two of Morrow's gunners were immediately hit. Donald Evans, of Saint John, New Brunswick, was instantly killed as he blasted away with his .303 twin-mounted Vickers on the starboard side of the chart house. The portside gunner, Roy "Shorty" Mason, of Cloverdale, B.C., was grievously wounded. The German gunfire severed his left arm. Two other ratings were wounded, but not seriously.

Meanwhile, as this action unfolded—it wasn't more than a minute—Mabee and McLernon were pressing on with their torpedo attack on the three merchant ships in the heart of the German formation. Dave Wright, Mabee's radarman, hunched in his tiny radar shack beside the chart house, called out the distance as they closed the convoy. It was not clear in the subsequent action report at what distance Mabee fired all his four torpedoes, but whatever the distance no torpedoes found a target. All of this action had been observed by Kirkpatrick and Morrow, since the Germans had illuminated the sky above the two attacking Canadian MTBs with their eerie green starshells. In making their getaway from the convoy, McLernon dropped a smoke float to cover their retreat but when he and Mabee tried rejoining Kirkpatrick and Morrow, disaster struck involving Bert Morrow's MTB and Ollie Mabee's boat.

Exactly what happened that night remains contentious. Off the starboard bow of Morrow's boat there suddenly loomed out of the smoky blackness the barest hint of a boat's hull coming at full bore. Was it an E-boat? Brian Jones, a forward torpedoman on Morrow's boat, may well have seen it first.

"Look out! Starboard bow!" he yelled to no one in particular.

Barely had he sounded the alarm when all remaining guns opened fire at the mystery vessel. Jack McClelland, who was on the bridge as Morrow's first officer, was convinced the approaching boat was firing at them. They later concluded the tracers were coming from behind the mystery boat, being fired by the enemy. Morrow in MTB *726* had poured everything he had at Mabee's MTB *745* at nearly point-blank range. The result was devastating.

Charlie "Moe" Allison of Trenton, Ontario, the third man in the crew of Mabee's forward six-pounder gun, was horribly mutilated by the rain of bullets. Tom Jones, the gunner, took one look at Allison and knew "he was dead as soon as he hit the deck." Even so, Jones grabbed the first aid kit from the gun turret, took out a syringe of morphine and gave his mate an injection. "He had a huge hole in his chest," Jones remembered.

Someone later counted ninety or more hits on MTB *745*. Besides two gaping shell holes in the hull, the boat was splintered from bow to stern by light automatic gunfire, the engine room had been hit and the fuel tanks pierced. It was a miracle no one else was killed, although four ratings suffered superficial wounds.

What did happen? McClelland remembered many years later, "She [Mabee's MTB *745*] emerged out of the smoke, just the bow, and it looked as though it was firing on us; it wasn't, but it was the fire from the [German] flak ship beyond it. We unfortunately opened fire on our own boat because we didn't identify her quickly enough."

It seemed incredible but the entire action had lasted a bare seven minutes. At 0335 the battered boats and shaken crews formed up and steered north across the Channel. When Mabee's boat, because of the hits to the engines, couldn't keep up, her casualties were transferred to Morrow's boat, ironically so since this was the MTB that had inflicted their wounds. On the return journey, McLernon's boat broke down because of contaminated fuel and was taken in tow by Kirkpatrick.

Morrow's boat carrying the wounded was the first to reach Brixham, but in doing so the crew later learned that they had completely burned out all four engines, recalled Norn Garriock,

Morrow's navigator. The scene, by chance, was vividly recorded on film. That very week a film crew from the National Film Board had arrived in Brixham to make a movie about the 65th Flotilla. On the morning of May 23, it was on the jetty to record the terrible results of the 65th's first action, including a brief shot of a grim-faced and disconsolate Jack McClelland watching the dead sailors being brought ashore by stretcher, a sequence so powerful that in a few seconds it captured the enormous loss felt by the entire flotilla. Forty-five years later when the footage was shown at the Canadian Coastal Forces Association's 1989 Toronto reunion, there was utter silence.

The following day the 65th buried its dead—Evans, Allison and Shorty Mason, who had succumbed to his wounds shortly after being brought ashore in Brixham. For radarman Dave Wright, their deaths were especially poignant. Allison had been his best mate on Mabee's boat, and it was Mason's father who had driven his son and Wright from Cloverdale to Vancouver when they took their medical exams to join the navy in 1941.

On May 24, 1944, the flag-covered caskets of Evans, Allison and Mason were carried through the winding streets of Brixham on the flatbed of a truck, up the steep hilly lanes to the old cemetery of St. Mary's. Behind, the flotilla crews marched in silence. All along the route, small groups of Brixham townspeople bowed their heads as the procession passed. Brian Jones remembered he had to drop out of the march. One of his shoelaces had come undone. To keep up with the marchers, he was forced to slide the loose shoe along the ground as he walked. "I thought this was ridiculous," Jones recollected. He stopped, tied up his shoe and then ran after the procession until he caught up with his mates.

At the graveside there were a final rifle volley of farewell and the sounding of "The Last Post," their echoes drifting over the town and out to sea, the Channel battleground that had claimed the 65th's first victims. They were the first but not the last for both the 65th and the 29th. The biggest battle of all was soon to be contested. The invasion of France was mere days away. D-Day.

8

The Endless Summer

O N THE MORNING OF June 6, 1944, Lt. John Ritchie Cunningham, RCNVR, of Vancouver, stepped on to the deck of HMS *Ambassador* moored in Torquay harbour across the bay from Brixham and was greeted by a scene that astounded him.

There were virtually no ships left in port!

Only the day before, the harbour had been packed with scores of fighting ships. Cunningham had missed being part of the greatest naval attack force ever assembled in the history of the world.

Cunningham missed, too, much to his chagrin, the invasion of France.

There was little comfort in the fact that the Royal Navy had decided, probably wisely, that *Ambassador* wasn't quite up to the fighting standards required that historic morning. The ship was an old wooden paddle-steamer that had lain idle since the evacuation of Dunkirk four years earlier. Still, Cunningham felt that he had earned the privilege to be part of the "big show" off the coast of Normandy. He had served in corvettes during the really tough days of 1942 and '43 on convoy duty in the North Atlantic. But when Cunningham arrived in Londonderry, Ulster, in January 1944, to deliver a newly built U.S. frigate to the Royal Navy, he was assigned to *Ambassador* as First Lieutenant with an all-RN crew, bringing the ancient steamboat from South Shields, near Tynemouth on the North Sea, through the Channel, and into Torquay. The brass took one look at the old ship and decided that she was too decrepit even for the minor role *Ambassador* was intended to play as a search-and-rescue ship to pick up downed Allied airmen in the Channel. Her only armament was twin .303s mounted on each wing of the bridge.

Cunningham remembered that the days leading up to the invasion were like a holiday at a seaside resort, occasionally interrupted by a few air raids. One day he rented a bike and scooted around Tor Bay for Brixham and a visit with the 65th Flotilla. "It was then I decided that after my stint with the Royal Navy was over I would try to get into MTBs instead of going back to the North Atlantic." Although he had no way of knowing, before the month of June was out, Cunningham would join, not the 65th but the 29th Flotilla, a replacement officer for the mounting casualties the 29th began to suffer in the wake of the invasion.

Tony Law moved his flotilla from Ramsgate to Portsmouth on May 28 to begin preparations for the great attack, the first of many moves over the next year that gave the 29th the air of a gypsy unit—and all the attendant headaches the frequent moves involved. As the flotilla roared down the Channel that still and muggy day, evidence of the impending sea invasion was everywhere. At Portsmouth the 29th slipped in among hundreds of other MTBs, rafted together like so many yachts on a weekend outing in the overcrowded sailing grounds of post-war Canada. There was no accommodation ashore for the crews and they immediately began makeshift arrangements to live aboard the tiny, cramped shorts. Double-deck bunks were squeezed in and since the seventy-one-and-a-half-footers carried only a single hot plate for cooking, extra stoves were also installed. It was crowded and uncomfortable. Fuelled by constant rumour that D-Day was imminent, tension mounted.

That night, some of the 29th's officers went ashore to a Royal

Navy mess for some serious poker; at the same time, just a few miles away, the Supreme Allied Commander in Europe, Dwight Eisenhower, on whose shoulders rested the terrible responsibility of launching the invasion, left his Advanced Command Post at Southwick, seven miles north of Portsmouth, for perhaps the most important meeting of his life. The date was June 4. At nearby Southwick House, Ike met with his commanders-in-chief, but more important with Group Captain James Stagg, RAF, the chief meteorological adviser to the Supreme Allied Commander. About the time the 29th's poker game was breaking up, Stagg met Eisenhower in a tense, dramatic conference. Outside, a wet wind lashed the window-panes of Southwick House and down below in Portsmouth harbour, rain drummed on the decks of the waiting invasion fleet. On Stagg's advice, Ike had on June 3 already delayed the decision one day from the designated date of June 5. Now Stagg informed him that conditions would improve for June 6 but they would still be rough, far from ideal. Ike's dilemma was a terrible one. If June 6 was out, troop convoys that already had embarked would have to be recalled and tidal conditions on the French coast would not be favourable until June 19. It is not known what Eisenhower's exact words were, but the import was something like, "Gentlemen, I can't see us not proceeding."

It seemed ironic that the man who was to bear this tremendous responsibility of launching the largest naval operation in history was never a sailor but a mere infantry battalion commander on the eve of war in 1939, a farm boy who was born in Texas and grew up in the waterless wastes of Kansas, a balding soldier with an engaging smile and an extraordinary gift for command.

Even now, two generations later, the colossal size of the invasion fleet and the land forces unleashed against German-occupied France that Tuesday morning in June tests the limits of comprehension. Those who witnessed Operation Overload and the naval side of the assault, Operation Neptune, struggle to this day to find words to describe the momentous event. C. P. Stacey, Canada's professor emeritus of Canadian military history, called it a triumph, "a triumph so complete that many observers, laymen and soldiers alike, found it for a moment scarcely believable," an undertaking of such scale that it still "staggers the imagination."

There were so many ships, the invasion fleet stretched beyond the horizon. So many aircraft, their formations blackened the sky. Five thousand ships, landing craft and boats; 20,000 aircraft, 154,000 soldiers, sailors and airmen. So much equipment, guns, tanks, trucks, field hospitals and kitchens, ammunition and rations, tents; tons of beer and toilet paper; a mountain of supplies and materiel of such weight that some wag said if it hadn't been for the barrage balloons tethered over England's south coast, it would have sunk.

Canada's contribution to this immense effort was considerable, if not remarkable. For a country on the eve of war whose navy's fleet consisted of two coal-burning minesweepers, six destroyers and a handful of harbour and patrol craft, she was now able to contribute 115 ships of the five thousand that made up the invasion fleet; as well, more than nine thousand Canadian sailors took part in Operation Neptune. Part of the invasion contribution included the sixteen boats that made up Canada's two motor torpedo-boat flotillas, whose exploits were soon to make blazing headlines across the front pages of the nation's newspapers.

Shortly after Eisenhower made his decision in the early morning of June 4 in that stately manor house, the commanders of the 65th and 29th Flotillas received their orders. Kirkpatrick's 65th was assigned to defensive patrols on the western flank of the fifty-mile Normandy bridgehead. Law's 29th was given an offensive role to protect the eastern flank of the invasion front, an assignment that, as the seemingly endless summer dragged on, was a most enervating experience, a campaign that in barely six weeks would leave the 29th exhausted, battered and bloodied.

On D-Day, Bones Burk took the first flotilla boats into action.

Lt. C. A. "Daddy Bones" Burk by all accounts was an exceptional skipper, a natural leader, and a brilliantly instinctive tactician who won the respect of both his officers and crew for a host of reasons, but mostly perhaps because of their admiration of Burk's consummate skill as a small-boat captain.

Burk grew up in Toronto and because he had learned about boats and sailing as a member of the Royal Canadian Yacht Club, he figured he'd "be valuable to the navy." After graduating from University of Toronto Schools, Burk joined the company of Moore Business Forms as an office boy while he took night courses at the University of Toronto. By the time war was declared, Burk had become a salesman with the firm, hardly the kind of training that prepared him for command of an MTB. Years later, Ian Robertson, Burk's "pilot" or navigator, fondly remembered his old skipper.

"First, he was a natural leader of men, in the best sense of the word, and of a kind I've met very few in my life," said Robertson. "He was extremely natural. There was no bluster about him. He had infinite patience, and on top of that he was (certainly in the MTB business) an ace in the full sense of the word and he proved that in engagement after engagement."

Burk had made a name for himself back in the early days of the Royal Navy's light coastal forces where he once got down on his knees on the side of a speeding power boat and pushed a depth charge over the side under the bow of a German merchantman. When that failed to stop the enemy ship, they circled back and he pushed another depth charge by hand over the side, all the while under fire from German gunners. The merchantman was sunk.

When Robertson joined Burk's boat, he was equally impressed with MTB *461*'s dark, stocky first officer, Keith Scobie, Burk's Number One. Where Burk excelled with the "ivories" in craps, Scobie was skillful with the deck whose "cards never seemed to fail him." On the eve of D-Day, they'd wanted all the luck they could get.

The 29th's assignment for the invasion was an extremely arduous one, to protect the eastern side of the British and Canadian assault lanes stretching to the beach, and to attack the German E-boats that were sure to emerge from their base at Le Havre to the east and to their left.

"This was one of the toughest assignments received by any of the flotillas," Law concluded years later. "I felt it was a privilege to be given the responsibility." It was an onerous one, an assignment that meant patrolling from dusk to dawn. To achieve its objectives, Law split the flotilla into two divisions. Burk, with Bobbie Moyse, Glen Creba and Craig Bishop would form one division, while Law, Dave Killam, Chuff-Chuff Chaffey and Barney Marshall, the other.

On the night of June 5, Burk's division left Portsmouth for the Canadians' patrol area. True to forecasts, the weather was abominable, high rolling seas and a raging wind, dreadful conditions for small-boat operations. Instead of heading to the eastern flank, Burk's boats were directed to the western side, north of the Cherbourg Peninsula. While the 29th's first invasion patrol was an exception to the general plan, all subsequent operations took place on the eastern flank. But that first night of the invasion they were to watch and intercept anything leaving Cherbourg, where navy intelligence had warned a large proportion of the enemy's fifty or sixty available E-boats were thought to be based. No enemy craft in fact were detected and Burk, Moyse, Creba and Bishop spent a miserable night trying to maintain formation in a sea later described as "almost too much for our MTBs." At first light at 0500, the tiny shorts turned and headed for the four-hour return trip to Portsmouth, pounding and crashing into a head sea. They reached England at 0900, the crews "sodden and weary," Law remembered. "Their eyes were red-rimmed and their faces caked with salt."

Although the first night lacked action for the 29th, this was seldom the case from then until the first week in August. As Burk's division returned, Law's division of boats was ready to depart for its first taste of action. This pattern of operations was to be consistent. As one division returned, the other departed. So seldom did they see one another that Burk and Law were left to scribble notes to each other, leaving them pinned on a clipboard in a shack on the docks at Portsmouth.

In the early afternoon of June 6, Law, Killam, Chaffey and

Marshall gunned out of the harbour, observing the time-honoured tradition of "dressing ship" to pipe the Admiral's flag, a "ceremony," Law recorded, "which under no circumstances [could] be omitted." While the first officers and crews lined the foredecks on their tiny boats, it must have been with some apprehension. The 29th Flotilla was going into battle without its torpedoes. The tubes still had not been replaced. They were to fight as gunboats and they knew that almost any enemy ship they encountered would heavily out-gun them.

The battle that followed introduced a new tactic. The MTBs would work with a mothership acting in a similar way that RAF fighter control did with its aircraft. Now destroyers, frigates and MTBs would be directed to targets from a central command. In this case, the controller was HMS *Scylla*, flagship of Rear-Admiral Sir Philip Vian who commanded the British landings in the invasion. Sir Philip had earned his knighthood for blasting his way from Alexandria across the Mediterranean with a cruiser squadron that protected the convoy that eventually reached and relieved a besieged Malta in 1942—a tough bird.

At a few minutes past 4 a.m., following a storm-tossed night in their small boats, and with visibility down to four miles, Law, Killam, Chaffey and Marshall found themselves alone on station in the waters off Le Havre.

Drifting with engines idling and constantly adjusting their position, they waited. Suddenly, to their south the proverbial hell broke loose when a British unit of MTBs came upon six R-boats, not as fast as E-boats but viciously armed. The Canadians went to full power and headed for the action. As they closed the enemy, the British MTBs were seen withdrawing. Running parallel to the Germans, the Canadians inched closer. At 0430, and at a distance of only 150 yards, the Canadians opened fire with two-pounders, Oerlikon and Vickers, sweeping the fleeing R-boats at nearly point-blank range; the German boats responded with everything they had as well. Burning tracers slammed into the chart house of Law's boat raking the pom-pom gun crew. Able Seaman William Bushfield was hit twice in the back, his left arm ripped open. On

Barney Marshall's boat, Able Seaman J. A. Wright and T. Howarth were also wounded. On Killam's boat, Phillip Durnfield—also an able seaman—was hit by the German fire.

The exchange lasted barely three minutes but it was so intense that the Canadian boats had blasted the Germans with 2,920 rounds. More alarming, the Germans, in trying to evade the attacking Canadian boats, led them and themselves into a German minefield. Law's boats peeled off at full throttle, amidst exploding mines, starshell bursts and a wall of tracer fire. The flotilla claimed one R-boat sunk. Throughout the shoot-out Bushfield, although seriously wounded, stayed at his post as loader for the pom-pom gun in Law's boat.

So did Wright in Barney Marshall's boat. Even though wounded in the back, the gunner kept up rapid fire until the action was broken off. Later when fire broke out in the demolition jelly, Wright risked his life to neutralize the charge by cutting the detonator fuse leading to it, all of this happening as the Canadians roared off in the smokescreen they had laid over the battlescape to cover their escape.

Then began a frustrating several hours as the Canadians tried to find a hospital ship willing to take aboard their wounded crew members. *Scylla*'s sick bay was already overflowing with wounded sailors, as was a nearby hospital ship. Finally, a landing craft that had been converted into a hospital ship was located and the wounded Canadians, especially the indomitable Bushfield who by now was in severe pain, were taken aboard, all of this unfolding in a high wind and rising sea. With the wounded gone came some respite. The boats were stood down for the rest of the daylight hours, tying up behind a battleship for a fitful few hours of sleep that were constantly interrupted by the booming guns from Allied battleships and cruisers.

That night, June 7, Law, Killam, Chaffey and Marshall were again back in action under a sky blossoming with hundreds of starshells. At one point, the 29th's four boats were bombed by enemy planes dropping mines. Later, investigating a radar contact, the tiny boats mixed it up with two German destroyers, gunning within five hundred yards, firing as they closed the enemy. But the German barrage was so fearsome that the boats made smoke and sought safety. As they withdrew, geysers of shells dropped around them like raindrops, one so close it drenched Chaffey's speeding boat; so close, thought Barney Marshall, that he swung out of the line-astern formation, fearing if he continued on course he would run over Chaffey's wreckage. Although the barrage was perilously close, no damage was done.

On June 8, weary and exhausted, Killam, Chaffey and Marshall headed back to Portsmouth. Law, who was detained to meet Admiral Percy Nelles, returned alone, all of them arriving back at Portsmouth running on empty. Each boat had used up nearly all of its twenty-five hundred gallons of the high-octane fuel. Despite fatigue, they celebrated their first operations of the invasion with appropriate drink, Amontillado sherry.

On the way into Portsmouth, Law's boat had passed Burk's division heading over to the assault area for its second round of operations. As Bones Burk swept past, Law flashed the action-bound MTBs the following message: "Good luck. You'll need it."

Burk, Moyse, Creba and Bishop began their patrol with a spirited chase of E-boats who suddenly appeared but just as quickly vanished at high speed. The E-boats invariably outran the MTBs whenever they chose to open throttles. The Canadians returned to their patrol area and waited, listening in the dark. A half hour later two enemy destroyers loomed up in front of Burk's division of boats, probably the same two destroyers that Law's division had taken on the night before. At first, Burk's team went unobserved but the destroyers quickly broke off their shelling of the assault area, turning their guns on the four Canadian boats. Still without their torpedoes and obviously outgunned, they made smoke for their getaway in a shower of salvoes from the enemy. Bishop's boat, which was last in line and making smoke for the others, took a direct hit, instantly killing Able Seaman Fred Armstrong. Four days later Burk survived a near miss when dive-bombed by an enemy plane that had spotted the phosphorescent wake below in the night. The bomb was so close that its blast blew all the gas out of the engines' carburetors, causing the boat to stall.

In the third week of June, there was a brief lull in the action. Law, whose turn it was to be in the patrol area, along with Chaffey and Marshall, got caught in an incredible storm that at its peak reached the fury of a hurricane, finally forcing them into the tiny, protected harbour of Courseulles-sur-Mer, which had been captured by troops of the 3rd Canadian Division on D-Day. Before running to Courseulles, they struggled offshore, fending off the mounting waves, a force of nature so powerful they wondered if in fact they could survive its fury, its mountainous seas. Lines parted, a pounding sea tore off rubbing strakes and battered the chart house and bridge. Wet, bounced around like India rubber balls dropped down a stairwell, the crews struggled to prevent the boats from broaching in the crashing sea. For four days they were cold, nearly always wet and hungry. It was impossible to cook and they had to make do with hastily slapped-together meals of cold bully beef. On June 22 the storm eased, allowing Law, Chaffey and Marshall to make the bruising run in high seas back to Portsmouth and much-needed food and sleep. No sooner had Law's division returned than Burk's took off to patrol four miles west of Le Havre where he, Moyse and Bishop ran smack into three E-boats. In the old trick of the American Indian wars, all three boats concentrated on the last German in line, peppering the straggler with all their guns. Because of the combined speed of the Canadian and German boats, they closed rapidly, passing so close Burk feared he'd collide with the E-boat, so close the heat of careening bullets could be felt on their faces.

On and on the action went. It was now July and with the month barely two days old, tragedy struck Law's division. On July 1, Law, Killam and Chaffey left Portsmouth for yet another patrol. Pounding along at 20 knots in a heavy rolling sea, whump!... whump...whump! they sped towards Normandy. Suddenly Law felt a tremendous shudder, the boat shaking and violently vibrating. He had hit some kind of half-submerged debris. It was useless

to go on. Killam took over as acting Senior Officer and, along with
Chaffey, continued to France. Law reluctantly turned towards
Portsmouth, barely limping over the undulating swells, the return
journey taking until late the next afternoon; on Law's arrival, the
news of Killam's patrol left him devastated.

That very morning, after having patrolled the western flank off
Le Havre, Killam and Chaffey themselves turned for Portsmouth
and home. It was early morning and a low mist hung over the
water. Killam was leading, Chaffey following, when there was a
horrendous explosion on Killam's boat, which literally disintegrated. The blast was so powerful that a column of water, lifting
bits of debris, shot over two hundred feet into the air and rained
down on Chaffey's boat bringing up the rear. Everyone in MTB
460 was blasted overboard and those who weren't were blown out
in a second explosion that followed the first. In poor visibility
caused by heavy mist, recovery of the victims was difficult. Killam
apparently survived the first explosion, and throughout the rescue
attempts he was seen swimming among the survivors offering
encouragement to dazed crew members struggling in the oily
water. Chaffey moved in as close as possible, rigged scrambling
nets over the side and launched Carley floats in an attempt to
snatch to safety as many as possible. The search went on for an
hour and a half before Chaffey decided to get the six wounded
survivors to the nearest hospital ship. As Chaffey pulled away, a
British MTB arrived to continue the search. Somewhere in the
mist, the rescuers heard the voice of Dave Killam. "Carry on!"
Killam called out. "Don't worry about us!"

Although no one ever said it, they all thought that Killam was
living on borrowed time, that he was into extra innings. Ever since
he joined the navy in 1940, Killam had been serving in small boats,
having commanded various landing craft, motor launches and
torpedo boats, winning the Distinguished Service Cross for his
role in demolishing certain German installations on the French
coast just prior to Dunkirk.

There was no sign either of Killam's first officer, the likeable
Howie Hunt of Toronto, who everyone had often teased that the

Churchill-size cigars he smoked were bigger than he was. Perhaps the luckiest aboard was Able Seaman André Rousseau of Montreal. Below, Rousseau was knocked semi-conscious by the first explosion, but miraculously the second blast blew him from the sinking MTB, flinging him into the sea.

On board Chaffey's boat as he departed with the survivors were two dead sailors whose bodies had been recovered, Able Seaman George Grant, of Prince George, B.C., and George Ashmore of Lachine, Quebec. Besides Rousseau there were six survivors: Phillip Durnford of Orillia, Ontario, who had been wounded just weeks previously; J. Letters of Toronto; J. Allingham, of McAdam, N.B.; Maurice Lay of Cedarvale, B.C.; and M. Costello of Charlottetown, P.E.I., all able seamen.

Missing along with Killam and Hunt were men whose names and hometowns vividly reflected the small-town nature of those who had volunteered for wartime duty with the RCN: Petty Officer D. George, of Wolfville, Nova Scotia; Telegraphist P. Thompson, of Kindersley, Saskatchewan; Leading Seaman J. Lee, of Kingston, Ontario; Stoker Mechanics L. Lawson, Port Dalhousie, Ontario; E. A. Button of Winnipeg, Manitoba; and J. Hartley of Ashmount, Alberta. A Royal Navy rating, Telegraphist A. W. Rowe, of Colchester, Essex, England, who was aboard on temporary duty, was never found.

Of the crew of seventeen, only six survived the explosion and rescue.

Back at Portsmouth, where Chaffey arrived the following day with the bodies of the dead sailors, the atmosphere was palpable with gloom. Sitting alone with Law in the flotilla's office on the jetty, Chaffey recounted the tragic story, still in shock from seeing his friend blown up in front of him. No one was more shocked or surprised than Chief Motor Mechanic Fred Walden. Only four days earlier he had been transferred off the doomed boat.

There was little time to mourn. That afternoon Law, Moyse and Bishop, steering their little fighting ships towards the coast of France, growled across the Channel with a vengeance.

For five days, from July 4 to July 9, the 29th Flotilla struck back at the enemy in a series of attacks, attacks that were to be called the longest continuous action in the history of the Allied Coastal Forces.

In those five days, Law, Moyse and Bishop, later joined by Burk, Creba and Marshall, lashed out at the Germans, inflicting terrible retribution, almost it seemed as a cauterization of their own feelings. One strike followed another where the Canadians did not count odds. In those five days, they took on 30 E-boats and 10 R-boats in a series of vicious encounters. When it ended, the Canadians chalked up one E-boat and two R-boats destroyed, sent to the bottom. Three more E-boats were severely damaged, and a German *Heinkel* who dive-bombed Law's boat was blown from the sky.

Not surprisingly, the Canadian losses mounted. These fierce, running gun battles took their toll, as did enemy mines the Germans had seeded over the battlescape. On July 8, Creba's boat hit a mine and sank. Only the day before, Creba and Marshall had survived the blasts of twenty-five mines that they had detonated as they ran the patrol area at high speeds. Amazingly, there were no casualties, but Creba's boat, MTB *463*, went to the bottom of the Channel.

The next night, Burk's boat was shot up as was Bishop's who, even though he suffered painful wounds, was able to bring a smile to the lips of all who heard him reporting his wounds over the radio. "Tony, Tony," Bishop called. "I've been shot in the ass."

A week later, Law's boat was hit by shore batteries and had to be abandoned. With the loss of MTB *459*, the flotilla's Senior Officer was without a boat. Law scrambled back across the Channel for a replacement as Burk took over as acting Senior Officer. About the same time, nearly all the flotilla's remaining boats had been refitted with their torpedoes and tubes, which gave the 29th a wider tactical role and provided Burk with the opportunity to pursue his forte as the consummate tactician, a talent that was most admired by Burk's crew.

"He, of course, was older than I and he had a feeling for the broad picture of the battle in the Channel, and what it meant," Ian

Robertson recollected. "In addition, in close-in fighting he had a sense of what was needed to be done quickly, and an almost instinctive ability to set about it in the most economical and most effective way. It's hard to describe it more than that. But to watch that man in the middle of an action was really an education.... You'd have a few seconds of blinding light and deafening noise as ships would pass each other going at enormous speeds in the middle of an action. Then we'd come out of that and within a second he'd have given the coxswain immediate instructions as to where to go to find the enemy. I never saw anyone else like that."

On the night of July 25–26, this extraordinary skill was put to the test once more. Burk led the flotilla in its first massed torpedo attack against the enemy.

Burk, Moyse, Chaffey, Marshall and Joe Adam, who had taken command of Bishop's boat (Bishop was still recuperating from his painful buttock wound), found themselves in coastal waters between Cap d'Antifer and Cap de la Heve. Alerted that an enemy formation was moving into their patrol area, Burk led his boats inshore where they lay virtually undetected, placing the German convoy in silhouette against the horizon. Moving stealthily towards the Germans in line-abreast formation, the Canadian boats had crept to within nine hundred yards before being detected and before the Germans opened fire. Under heavy enemy fire, the Canadians pressed the attack. Within fifteen seconds, six torpedoes were speeding towards the enemy ships. There would have been two more torpedoes launched but Barney Marshall was wounded in the shoulder by German gunfire and crumpled to the deck of the bridge. Moyse's boat, which had not yet been re-rigged for torpedoes, acted as a gunboat. As if the fire of the enemy convoy escorts was not enough, German shore batteries also suddenly began hammering the Canadians as they turned to escape; their retreat was covered by Moyse's boat. The getaway was as dramatic as any the flotilla had ever experienced. Slowing down, speeding up and changing course every minute to escape the pounding shore batteries, the flotilla ran full-out for eleven miles, being straddled all the way by shells constantly exploding all around them and sending huge geysers of water into the air. It was as hair-raising as any shoot-out the 29th was ever in. In the mêlée of the attack, the Canadians observed one large blip disappear on their radar. They were credited with possibly sinking an enemy minesweeper. The high quality of leadership displayed by all the skippers was equally exemplified by their first officers. When Marshall was hit, Joe Brampton immediately stepped in to take command.

These frantic and spectacular actions finally began to take their toll on the crews and their boats. Anyone who watched them return each morning, the crews haggard and drawn and their boats splintered, riddled and patched up, began to wonder how much more punishment they could take.

The brave 29th Flotilla, as courageous as any unit in the naval history of Canada, was a shambles. It had lost three of its eight boats since the beginning of the invasion, and had suffered 37 per cent casualties, an alarming and disproportionate number of dead and wounded for any outfit in combat whether in ground fighting or at sea.

Moreover, the remaining boats were in desperate need of repair and refit. Of those nerve-racking days, Law was to write: "The stress and irregular meals were responsible for many of us losing weight. The 29th was battle weary, and we were beginning to feel that we could not last much longer under the severe conditions— mine threats, pounding shore batteries, and vicious dive bombers roaring out of the night."

Even worse, Law remembered, was the emotional stress being felt by all, both officers and men who "were falling victims to horrible, haunting fears."

Yet the flotilla licked its wounds and struggled on. But as the Allied campaign ashore finally began moving further inland and eastward to liberate the so-called Channel ports, the 29th was pulled back to England for the rest and refit that it so desperately needed. But before the summer was out, the fighting 29th Flotilla was back in action. Although it did not seem possible after what the flotilla had been through, the cruel if not perverse hand of fate touched the fighting 29th Flotilla in the struggle ahead as it followed the action up the Channel, delivering a devastating blow, an assault yet to come but one so catastrophic that even the indomitable 29th would never recover.

More boats would be destroyed; more flag-draped coffins and processions; more sounds of bugles in the morning.

At the western flank of the invasion bridgehead, the 65th Flotilla was making history, too, that summer of 1944, a summer for those who lived through it and survived that seemed eternal.

The personalities of the senior officers of the two Canadian flotillas differed as much as the images of the boats under their commands.

From the day of its formations, the 29th exuded an air of élan, impetuous in many ways, as it dashed and darted back and forth across the Channel, from the high rooster tail of water the boats made going flat out to their dishevelled appearance after battle, their decks littered with ammo casings and jury-rigged accoutrements. Even in port, the tiny boats presented a tumble of extra mooring and spring lines, spare fenders, shell boxes and general clutter, a presentation that would certainly boil the blood of any weekend admiral in post-war yachting circles. Part of that image was the simple reason that the short boats were so small. There just wasn't enough space to properly stow all the gear the crews required to go to sea and fight. As the Channel campaign dragged on and moved eastward, the 29th was either continuously pulling up stakes or settling in. Worse, the boats had never been designed to live aboard, but all through the invasion action this was what the officers and men were forced to do, a situation that promoted a certain camaraderie, an informality.

Jack Johnson, the stoker on Barney Marshall's boat, remembered after returning to Portsmouth from the invasion beaches that he and his mates were so tired and exhausted that "we just slept on the decks," but only after the boat had been re-ammunitioned, refuelled and generally squared away. "You live together with twelve guys or more day in and day out, you become pretty close to each other," Johnson said. "There was never any of the bullshit of the big-ship navy." In the shorts, many of the young officers looked the other way even though they knew the ratings were storing away their daily tots of rum issue.

The Dog boats of the 65th Flotilla, on the other hand, reflected the look of the big-ship navy, despite the fact at only 115 feet—just a little over one-third the size of a corvette—their appearance in profile resembled a larger fighting ship. In enemy action reports, the Ds were sometimes mistaken for destroyers in certain light conditions.

Besides, they carried double the crew, up to twenty-seven officers and ratings, though these numbers varied depending on kinds of equipment and armament added or taken off. Because the crew lived aboard, the routine was more like a larger ship with its wardroom for officers, however small, and a galley properly laid out to feed everyone.

Underway, the Dog boats' motion and entry through the water was less jaunty than the shorts'. The fact was, with their sombre grey hulls and darker grey, almost blue, decks, they presented a menacing look that was supported by the armament they carried. They were the most heavily armed of any boat in the Allied Coastal Forces of the war.

Kirkpatrick had earned a reputation as an extremely skilled commander and a tough leader. Years later he said, "I was extremely proud of my flotilla. I thought they were really well trained and well disciplined; and a good bunch too, a *very* good bunch."

There was another aspect of Kirkpatrick's personality that belied his age, a maturity that one would not expect in a young commander. When he found or believed someone wasn't pulling his weight, the man was shifted out; not merely transferred or sent packing, a move that might affect morale, but the shirker or incompetent was promoted out of the flotilla.

And like nearly every one of the small-boat skippers who

possessed some panache in this tense enterprise of war, Kirkpatrick was certainly no different.

After all, it was Kirkpatrick and Tommy Fuller, one of the most colourful Canadians to serve in small boats, who arrived in England from Canada wearing monocles and carrying cricket bats, asking people ashore after landing "where the nearest cricket pitch was."

For the first week in June, the 65th Flotilla found itself playing a defensive role on the western flank of the bridgehead, patrolling with various other Allied warships in the protection of their own convoys supplying the invasion forces. There was little enemy contact. Like the 29th, the 65th also had to contend with heavy weather and they themselves were knocked about by rolling seas and lashing winds. But after June 11, it went on the attack. On June 17, Kirkpatrick, Mabee, Morrow and McLernon were able to hit one German convoy a double blow. Prowling off the shore of the Cherbourg peninsula, the Canadians sighted two German merchantmen, E-boats and several trawlers. Spotted by the enemy, they were challenged by a signal that they ignored, silently boring in on the convoy. At fifteen hundred yards, McLernon fired two torpedoes, followed at twelve hundred yards by Kirkpatrick, who fired two more. All the boats continued the attack, closing within four hundred yards, all the while blasting the Germans with shell and gunfire before breaking off. Speeding ahead, the boats lay in the darkness offshore for another go around and another attack. When they broke off the second engagement, they found comfort in the sight of the German boats firing on each other in the confusion, not an uncommon development in the heat of small-boat warfare.

On June 22, Kirkpatrick, Mabee and McLernon were out again, joined in this patrol by Knox. The encounter was yet another typical battle whose chief elements were equal parts of sheer terror, noise, streaks of tracers lacing the night sky, smoke and fire. In attacking this convoy that night, Mabee's boat was badly shelled, shuddering to a limp. Dangerously exposed, Kirkpatrick rushed to the stricken Mabee, covering the area with a smokescreen. Meanwhile, McLernon and Knox carried on the attack, Knox pounding into point-blank range riddling a minesweeper and knocking out a defending E-boat. After covering Mabee's boat with smoke, Kirkpatrick now turned to attack the convoy, laying a wall of fire into the path of a tanker and setting it ablaze. He had gone in so close that Kirkpatrick nearly struck the sinking minesweeper that had been Knox's target. Kirkpatrick and Knox then joined together to take on two small coastal craft that had been converted to gunboats, knocking both of them out of action.

These sustained actions, one would have thought, might possibly dilute the depth of emotions experienced by the crews and their officers. The contrary was true. All were constantly having to balance fear and apprehension. No one, or very few, ever became inured to being shot at, even though some were laconic in retelling these actions, such as Tom Jones, the gunner of the forward six-pounder in Mabee's boat, who was shot up the night of June 22. Jones, who kept a diary, strictly against regulations, was downright terse in recording the June 22 action. "Four large holes in our ship and several in our other ships," he wrote after the battle, "but nothing serious." The fact was that the engines were so badly damaged, all had to be replaced.

The Canadians discovered very early on in their nightly sorties that there were no lone wolves in battle, that all the boats and their skippers were interdependent in battle, that teamwork was vital. No better an example was the battle of June 22–23.

This teamwork was brilliantly displayed a few weeks later in a spectacular torpedo attack by the 65th on the nights of July 3–4 on a German convoy off the approaches to St. Malo.

The night was as brilliant as the conduct of the action that followed. There was a bright luminescent moon, far from ideal for attacking the enemy, and the sea was quiet. Because it was so bright, the German convoy of three merchantmen and their escort of gunboats could clearly be seen with binoculars several thousand yards away. That night Kirkpatrick was leading Knox, John Collins and George Moors. They had been running at 10 knots but after sighting the convoy they all throttled back. A post-war generation of movie-goers who watched the likes of John Wayne leading torpedo boats into action, going full blast and firing his "fish" as the boats porpoised over the waves, would be disappointed with the realities of this particular engagement. The Canadians came to learn that a slow steady approach increased their chances of success.

"The problem with motor torpedo boats is getting steady enough so that you can get your sight on the enemy as they came along," Kirkpatrick recollected. "Of course, you have to have a very steady coxswain too. But, for instance, if you were in a following sea, you would be wallowing all over. And you see, speed had nothing to do whatsoever with a torpedo attack. We found out very early on that you could get a great deal more accuracy if you could go in very slowly and discharge your torpedoes."

Running line-abreast (side by side) and down to 7 knots, the Canadians crept to within eight hundred yards of the convoy before being detected, pre-selecting their targets. Kirkpatrick and Knox would attack the first merchantman; Collins and Moors, the second one.

Kirkpatrick fired first and almost immediately observed two strikes. Swinging away with guns blazing, Kirkpatrick's boat was severely hit by German fire, seriously wounding Lt. Bob Campbell-Smith, of Vancouver, his first officer, and wounding four ratings. Hit in the mess decks, the bilges began filling with water.

Knox continued his run-in and thirty seconds later fired his salvo of torpedoes, hitting both the first merchantman and the second, as well as a third ship following. Knox finished off the attack with withering gunfire on the crippled boats before swinging away himself.

Collins now fired all his four torpedoes, hitting the second merchant ship and two other ships, one ahead and one astern. As he bore away, his gunners raked an approaching German gunboat, but in the exchange of fire took a pounding himself. His boat was holed at the waterline and began to sink. The hole was plugged and emergency pumps put into action.

Now Moors fired at the second merchant ship as well, scoring a strike. Another of his torpedoes struck a ship astern, which exploded and sank in a column of fire and smoke.

The spectacular attack, which sent three ships to the bottom, lasted exactly one minute. Ironically, one torpedo, fired by Moors, missed its main target but was responsible for sinking the third vessel.

Of the four attacking motor torpedo boats, three were badly damaged, Kirkpatrick's, Knox's and Collins's. Only Moors's boat escaped hits. The 65th's Senior Officer was so impressed by Knox's remarkable performance that he recommended him for a Distinguished Service Cross, but the application got lost in navy bureaucracy! Later Knox was awarded a DSC for another action which, if the navy hadn't fouled up, would have been his second.

In any case, the 65th Flotilla was on the front pages of newspapers back home. Kirkpatrick was quoted as simply saying, "It was the perfect setting for a torpedo attack and we took full advantage of it."

Collins was quoted too. He had been holed at the waterline not once, but twice. "The crew worked feverishly," he said, "some up to their shoulders in water, plugged up the holes and bailed like hell. We couldn't make much speed, so when we arrived home the crew were exhausted from bailing and pumping water."

The brilliant attack would have done justice to Hollywood.

It was characteristic of Kirkpatrick, the complete professional, that the publicity that followed the action "was out of all proportion" to the flotilla's status in Coastal Forces. In fact, he said, it was embarrassing.

"If it is desired to publicize Canadian MTBs," he wrote to his superiors, "there is enough human interest in the individual ratings without resorting to such bland phrases as 'dare devils,' 'bone crushing,' 'back breaking,' 'finest ever,' 'knocking the stuffing out of,' 'knock 'em down, drag 'em out battle,' and many other phrases which only a newspaper reporter suffering from severe nightmares could construct."

If such phrases, some of which appeared as well in navy press releases, were designed to sell war bonds, then fine. But limit the hoopla to Canadian distribution. To hog the limelight in face of the terrible beating that the 29th Flotilla was taking and the courageous effort it was making was in Kirkpatrick's mind totally unfair.

The remainder of July was less hectic than the beginning for the 65th. Thirteen patrols had been mounted but no contact was made with the enemy. Besides, more often than not, sea conditions were too bad for the small boats.

August began literally with a bang, an incident that unnerved the Canadians, leaving the Senior Officer of the 65th in a cold rage. Operating with the Allied fleet was a Polish destroyer *Blyskawica*, whose name the Canadians couldn't pronounce, calling her "Bottle of Whisky." By any name, the ship was to be feared. The story making the rounds through the Allied fleet was that the Poles, whose country was first to be invaded by Hitler, had built up such a fury to strike back that they had gained a reputation for being trigger-happy. On the night of August 4–5, the flotilla was returning from a patrol off St. Malo, taking up station offshore hoping to intercept possible enemy shipping.

Jack McClelland recalled what happened. "We had been lying there just waiting until the end of our watch and we were to leave the station at four o'clock in the morning. We were just drifting, and we had drifted a little bit out of station."

Suddenly the night exploded with a rain of shells around Kirkpatrick, Morrow and McLernon.

Blyskawica and her sister ship *Piorun* had opened fire on the Canadian MTBs.

"They [the Polish destroyers] opened fire on us with all their goddamn guns and I will tell you that was an experience," said McClelland, who was first officer on Bert Morrow's boat. "I have never before experienced a 4.7-inch shell going over my head. It was like a bloody railroad train going by."

The Poles later claimed that the Canadians had not properly identified themselves, so they opened fire as they were entitled to do.

Even when the Canadians signalled, *"Blyskawica, Piorun*, for Christ's sake, we are Canadian MTBs," the Poles continued firing. Years later McClelland said he always felt the Poles knew who they were firing at, but because the Canadians hadn't properly identified themselves, the Poles were going to teach them a lesson. If true, the lesson was costly. Two sailors on Kirkpatrick's boat were slightly wounded and a third, Able Seaman William Calverley of Nanaimo, British Columbia, the third man on the forward gun, was instantly killed. The next day the captain of the *Blyskawica* received from the 65th a neatly wrapped package. Inside was a piece of shrapnel the Canadians had dug out of the deck of the Senior Officer's boat. The Poles took this as an insult and so told some crew members of the 65th a few days later. "This resulted in an incredible dust-up between our fellows and the Poles," recalled Norn Garriock. "Unfortunately, it happened in a pub which left the place practically demolished."

For the rest of August, the flotilla carried out a total of ten offensive patrols, frequently being shelled by enemy batteries, none more terrifyingly so than the night McClelland later joked that the 65th Flotilla "liberated" St. Malo.

Morrow, Collins and Greening, encouraged by news reports that the historic French port had been captured, tooled into the harbour in the early hours of August 10. As they approached, the Canadians saw a radar scope training on them as well as an enemy range finder. All this activity was most suspicious, so the Canadians turned about and began heading to sea when the German batteries opened up.

"We zigzagged and made smoke and the other boats were calling up to us on the radio cheering us on," McClelland remembered years later. "Shots dropping everywhere. We were bloody lucky we got out without even being touched. We were soaked from shells landing."

Ten days later Kirkpatrick was not as lucky. Patrolling off St. Mathieu just after dawn, a salvo of shells from a shore battery hit his boat, spraying the chart room and ripping into a torpedo tube, one gas tank and the radio aerials. Because of the time that MTB

748 had been in port for repairs following the Polish destroyer attack, and the subsequent shelling of St. Mathieu, she had seen little sea time, earning a derisive nickname from the crews, the "one-punch kid."

The first real break in the constant patrolling and shelling didn't come for the 65th until the end of August. The only boats operating now were under command of Collins, Mabee, McLernon, and a new MTB to join the 65th under command of G. D. Pattison. Dangerous weather conditions forced them into the port of L'Aber-Wrac'h on the north shore of the Brittany coast almost directly above Brest. It was here on August 20 that Mabee's boat became the first Allied ship to sail past the harbour gates and into the port since the war begun. The relative prosperity of the town surprised Tom Jones. "The fields are full of cattle and plenty of vegetables," Jones wrote in his diary. "We get a few souvenirs from the inhabitants for cigs and chocolate bars. We also get plenty of fresh eggs, milk and pork. The only thing they seem to be short of is sugar."

From August 28 to September 3 the flotilla, to its relief, was weatherbound in the tiny port. The Canadians were only twelve miles from German-occupied Brest, which was now feeling the brunt of massive Allied bombings from the air and shelling from the sea, close enough that the men heard the rumble of battle and saw the constant gun flashes like so much summer lightning.

The break from the routine was sorely welcomed for the weary crews. They borrowed two whalers from a Royal Navy sloop riding out the storm in harbour with them, staging a series of races. Mabee's crew took all challengers and the prize, ten shillings each per man and an extra large tot of rum.

The sailors also got a chance to go ashore, getting a look at the abandoned equipment the Germans left behind before fleeing L'Aber-Wrac'h and an opportunity to pick up a little booty.

Tom Jones's diary:

> Most of the boys go ashore to collect German souvenirs and they sure bring plenty aboard. We also do a lot of trading with

the French who flock out in their boats with eggs, chickens, etc. We go through all the German underground fortifications and a big U-boat quarters equipped with a periscope overlooking all the entrances to the harbour. There is a fortune in ammunition and equipment on the Island. We bring several things back including a complete telephone system in good working order. We have all kinds of fun firing a signal pistol.

On September 3, the flotilla slipped L'Aber-Wrac'h and steered north across the Channel for Brixham. Above, a formation of five hundred Flying Fortresses headed for the battlefront. That same day the British army had reached Brussels. Two days before, a unit of Canadians swept into Dieppe, only to find the town had been evacuated by the enemy. Le Havre was about to fall to the British and the first Canadian units had already crossed the Somme.

Normandy was now safely secured behind the advancing Allied armies, safe enough that entertainers were beginning to arrive to put on shows for the troops. Two performers were the then relatively unknown comedians, Wayne and Shuster. Years later when someone asked Johnny Wayne to suggest suitable punishment for Hitler, the irrepressible Wayne thought that if Adolf were captured, tied up and forced to sit in the front row to watch Wayne's rendition of "Blah, in der Fuehrer's Face," this would be supreme justice.

Had the dictator appeared before either the 29th or 65th Flotillas, in the wake of the costly Normandy campaign at sea, any one of its members would have surely shot the son-of-a-bitch right between the eyes.

As the ground war moved eastward, so did Canada's small-boat raiders. The gruelling summer was over. Ahead lay the battle of winter and, even though he was now on the run, the enemy, as implacable on defence as he was on attack, continued to challenge Canada's fighting sailors—not only in the English Channel, but in the sunny Adriatic, too, where the Canadian-led Cowboy Flotilla was conducting its own unique brand of small-boat fighting.

9

Pirates of the Adriatic

B Y THE MIDDLE OF 1944, the men of "Wimpy" Maitland's
56th MGB/MTB Flotilla were tired—dead tired. Several
times Burke had returned to Malta, leaving *658* in the care
of his First Lieutenant, Rover Reynolds, while he lay in a bed at
Bighi Hospital recuperating from a variety of ailments. He missed
several noteworthy actions as a result, including Operation Bras-
sard, the invasion of Elba on June 17. For this, the 56th was
assigned to the island's east coast, where it was thought an
evacuation might be attempted. Meanwhile the Cowboy Flotilla
itself had begun to encounter a few setbacks, not the least of which
was the loss of several ratings killed in action. Then, at the end of
June, Cam MacLachlan's boat struck a mine while returning to
Bastia and was destroyed. Five more ratings were lost in this
tragedy. Nevertheless, with the crude calculus they used to deter-
mine whether they were winning or losing in their private war with
the E-boats and flak trawlers, they had to admit they were ahead,
even if the mounting casualties suggested otherwise. And so it
came as a surprise when they discovered their time in the Med had
all but run out. According to Reynolds, Maitland flashed word of
this to *658* as though the idea had suddenly occurred to him.

171

"Say, Corny, how would you like to trot down to little old Malta again and then move round to the ro-mantic islands of Yugoslavia?"

Within days, they were back at their familiar berth at Hay's Wharf, opposite HMS *Gregale* at Malta, to undergo extensive refits prior to sailing for the Adriatic. There they caught up with developments in the Balkans that had resulted in their new assignment.

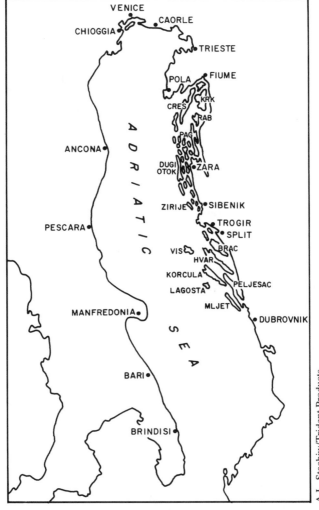

A.L. Stachiw/Trident Products

Shortly after the fall of France in June 1940, Britain established a secret organization called the Special Operations Executive (SOE). Its mandate was to support resistance movements in occupied Europe, but Winston Churchill saw it in more colourful terms. He reportedly told the organization's first director, Hugh Dalton, also the Minister of Economic Warfare in Britain's coalition government, "Now, set Europe ablaze!"

With this, the first SOE agents were committed to fomenting revolutions abroad, supplying insurgents with arms and ammunition, lending technical and logistical expertise to resistance movements and generally interfering as much as possible with the enemy's economic interests in Europe. From the outset, SOE seemed preoccupied with supporting the resistance movement in France, a policy that attracted a large number of Canadians to join the clandestine organization.* Yet the theatre in which SOE had perhaps its greatest impact was in the Balkans—and, in particular, Yugoslavia, where the communist Partisans led by Josip Broz Tito were fighting a bloody civil war against the royalist Chetniks of General Drazha Mihailovich as well as various occupying armies.

For a while, Britain supported the Chetniks, much to the pleasure of King Peter II and members of his exiled cabinet in London. But soon intelligence reports from various SOE missions sent to Yugoslavia suggested the Partisans were more aggressively fighting the enemy. The downfall of the Chetniks—and, it should be added, the royal household in Yugoslavia—had begun. The arrival in September 1943 of a military mission led by Brigadier General Fitzroy Maclean—dubbed "The Kilted Pimpernel" by the British press, he had served as a diplomat and was at the time a Member of Parliament—marked Britain's *de facto* recogni-

---

* The best source of information regarding Canada's role in providing agents to SOE is Roy MacLaren's *Canadians Behind Enemy Lines: 1939–1945*, published in 1981 by the University of British Columbia Press.

tion of Tito's Partisans as the leading resistance movement in Yugoslavia.*

Elsewhere in the region—in Albania, for example, which was mired in its own tortured complexities—SOE achieved somewhat less than its expectations, yet still had a bearing on the war's conduct. The Albanian communist leader, Enver Hoxha (pronounced *Hoe*-jah), whose avowed aims included the end of monarchial rule under the much-despised, self-appointed King Zog I—who was also a refugee in London—received substantial aid from SOE agents, despite his lethargic approach to defeating the Nazis. Still, as much as Britain's policy throughout the Balkans seemed based on the rule of political and military expediency—as Winston Churchill put it once, inquiring of the Partisans and their rival Chetniks: "Who is killing the most Germans?"—it was not an unprofitable exercise backing Hoxha's communists as long as they, like the Soviets, were allies and in this case could provide a few safe harbours.

For this was another pressing reason to support resistance movements that, at first glance, appeared contrary to Britain's best interests: they, in turn, could help the Allied cause. This was almost certainly a factor when an invasion across the Adriatic was contemplated. The plan was discussed at the Teheran Conference in November 1943; indeed it dominated the talks. Churchill favoured such landings for purely political reasons: already he was fearful of the Soviet Red Army moving in to the Balkans, which would have a profound impact on the post-war balance of power in the region. Surprisingly, the Americans were less inclined to take a similar view, evidently preferring a strictly military strategy. The English Channel, they argued, led to the largest concentration of enemy troops. Churchill reluctantly dropped the matter, although

---

* Shortly after this, the British began sending desperately needed medical supplies to the Partisans. Later, a few surgeons were dispatched. Of these, Major Colin Scott Dafoe of Madoc, Ontario, was the most admired for his tireless efforts on behalf of the wounded. His story is told in *The Parachute Ward: A Canadian Surgeon's Wartime Adventures in Yugoslavia.*

it was revived occasionally for propaganda purposes to divert the enemy's attention from plans to invade elsewhere—namely, along the coast of Normandy in June 1944.*

Meanwhile the Allies continued to harass the enemy's coastal convoys along the east coast of Italy, just as they had in the Tyrrhenian Sea. Operating out of Taranto (captured in September 1943 by British and Canadian troops), Coastal Forces had enjoyed some success against enemy installations on the Albanian coast as well. Eventually a Coastal Forces base was established at Brindisi, followed shortly thereafter by Bari. But few targets were found along the east coast within patrolling range of the small boats, so in conjunction with the Allied decision to support the Partisans a Special Service MLs, under the direction of Lt. Cdr. Morgan Giles, was established only a few miles off the Yugoslav mainland, on the island of Hvar. In no time it was realized the indented Yugoslav coast and numerous islands offered a perfect setting for the hide-and-seek type of warfare practised by MTBs and MGBs. By October, operations were moved to Komiza Harbour, at Vis, which was captured by the Partisans with British help.

For months, small-boat raiders operating along the coast of Yugoslavia enjoyed a clear-cut advantage, but by the middle of 1944 "the juicy plums of the early days had withered to tough bitter prunes in the shape of heavily armed escorts, F-lighters,

----

* It was at the Teheran Conference as well that the Allies formally decided to abandon Mihailovich. This was, arguably, a terrible mistake. For an in-depth analysis of the subject, see David Martin's *Ally Betrayed*, published in 1946, and *The Web of Disinformation*, 1990. Mr. Martin, a Canadian journalist who flew with the RCAF in Burma and later settled in the United States, has devoted almost his entire post-war life to the study of Mihailovich's puzzling treatment by the Allies. He has recently shown that field reports of Partisan activities were often grossly exaggerated, while accounts of successful Chetnik activities were routinely suppressed or, in BBC broadcasts, falsely attributed to their rivals. The outcome of this was tragic, to say the least, as millions of Yugoslavs were virtually delivered by the British into the hands of Tito, whose post-war regime was brutal. The chilling consequences of the decision at Teheran are further explored by Nora Beloff, in *Tito's Flawed Legacy* (1985), and Nikolai Tolstoy, in his book *The Minister and the Massacres* (1986), *et al.*

E-boat flotillas, and schooners mounting 40-mm and 20-mm guns," said Reynolds, "so that in many cases they were now at least as powerful as our boats."

This ominous fact emerged when the 56th Flotilla arrived at Brindisi in late July. It had left Malta on the twenty-first, made a brief refuelling stop at Augusta, Sicily, and then sailed to the Italian mainland. From Brindisi (or Bari; according to Maitland it was the latter, as they were able to confirm the lingering effects of the air raid that had resulted in an explosion aboard a ship carrying mustard gas), they moved north to Manfredonia, the stepping-off port to the Dalmatian Islands. Reynolds added that everyone in the flotilla felt ill at ease and "uncomfortably green" as they prepared to join this new theatre.

"We were unquestionably regarded as 'those chaps from the other side' and, with the disadvantage of having to learn a new set of conditions, we were obviously going to have to prove our worth. The reputation which had preceded us cut little ice, so we kept quiet and prepared ourselves for the new job."

They might have drawn at least some comfort from the rumour mill, when it emerged that one of their ilk was already legendary in the Islands. Of course this was Tommy Fuller, who was known, simply, as the "black-bearded Pirate of the Adriatic." Looking at his record, it is not hard to understand why.

Take, for example, Fuller's action on the night of April 2, 1944. Just after 1800 on this warm, still evening, Fuller, now a Lieutenant Commander and Senior Officer of the 61st MGB Flotilla, left Komiza Harbour on the island of Vis and made his way south along the coast. He went ashore at one point in his journey to speak with a local Partisan leader. There, Fuller also picked up several OSS agents who had an Italian prisoner with them.*

"It was our intention to proceed inside Zulana Harbour and strafe the local German garrison," Fuller later wrote of his mission

---

*OSS—Office of Strategic Services—was the U.S. equivalent of the British Special Operations Executive. Later it became the Central Intelligence Agency.

that night. "However, on the information of our American friends that the Germans had 155-mm and anti-tank batteries there, we decided otherwise and proceeded along the coast east of Zulana."

It's almost laughable, reading Fuller's succinct and polite action report prose, knowing that if he were narrating this in person the air would be full of the purplest language. He *is* a natural story-teller.

Within an hour of arriving, Fuller's prudence was rewarded when a small thirty-ton schooner hove into sight.

"All guns on target," Fuller ordered.

Normally, he would have closed on the vessel and sunk it with gunfire. But not tonight. Fuller knew the base at Vis was experiencing a supply shortage. It seemed a waste to destroy all the materiel the schooner, low in the water, was obviously carrying.

"Don't fire," Fuller countermanded, leaving his crew perplexed. He called down the voice-pipe to several British commandos on board and their Partisan cohorts.

"We've got some fun coming up. There's a boat for you to capture!"

With this, Fuller brought his gunboat alongside the schooner, crashing into its side. To the accompaniment of the Partisans' blood-curdling yells, the boarding party vaulted over the rails. There was hardly any resistance. Once captured, the schooner was towed back to Vis, where it was handed over to the Partisans who added it to their "Tiger" fleet of commandeered vessels. Fuller's booty that first night included explosives, a jack-hammer drill and compressor, land mines, mail for the garrison at Korcula, and, perhaps best of all, cigarettes and a cargo of good Bavarian ale!

He did it again the following night. In fact, Fuller made a bet with Morgan Giles he could do better next time. Off the tiny Prznjak islands southwest of Korcula, Fuller sighted a one thousand-ton merchant ship that had run aground. Standing off were two schooners. Fuller took both of them back to Vis, his haul that night including firewood, wheat and ammunition. By now the pattern was set. Two nights later, Fuller captured a four hundred-ton schooner carrying food; three nights after that he captured two more as well as a motorboat, while sinking two ships that resisted. On the night of April 14, Fuller, accompanied by another MGB, destroyed a tug and a four hundred-ton tanker it was towing, but captured a two hundred and fifty-ton lighter. In the month of April his tally came to eight captured schooners, a lighter and a motorboat; he had sunk four vessels.

Fuller's success did not go unnoticed by the navy's brass. In fact he earned rare praise from the Admiralty, which had seen reports of his boarding operations. Noted one desk-bound admiral, evidently caught between a need to exercise restraint and his obvious envy, "The tactics evolved date from the 18th century and earlier and are evidently as effective now as then.... These forces have brought their boarding and cutting-out tactics to an exceptionally high standard. Some people have all the fun—and deserve it."

According to Maitland, who along with the others waiting in Italy heard a number of tales regarding their fellow Canadian, Fuller was busy capturing everything from canned sauerkraut to goulash, ten tons of Danish butter and countless drums of petrol. And invariably, as he returned to Vis, the Partisans would meet him with a brass band. There was even a song about his exploits. But "Old Tom Fuller With His Eight-Five Sledge" alluded to those few occasions when he couldn't tow one of the captured schooners. Fuller used a large eight-and-a-half-pound sledgehammer obtained from the base supply depot to knock the schooner's bilge valves off and scuttle it (he had also put in a request for a long ladder, which he used to make his boarding raids less hazardous). Fuller made sure he shared his booty, too. In fact, he says he sent three kegs "with the compliments of Tom Fuller" to every Mediterranean flag officer: "Insurance," he explained afterwards, "in case anyone tried to court-martial me for looting!"

As a result of his raids, Fuller dined magnificently in the town hall at Komiza with his Partisan hosts and, when he arrived at Vis in June 1944, Marshall Tito himself. The meals were lavish: pork and beans and lobster, octopus garnished with nuts and olives, and a red-fleshed fish baked whole in its skin. Fuller, as guest of honour, got the head. Festivities accompanying such banquets were as spirited as the menu. Notwithstanding Tito's edict against the consumption of alcohol, there was always plenty of it to be had, and not just the Bavarian ale Fuller had seized. The local plum brandy, known as *rakija*, and a deliciously sweet wine called *prosek* enlivened every meal. Toasts were ongoing. With each, the diner yelled *"Ziveli!"*—"to life!"—before tossing back the potent drink. It has been said that whenever a diner collapsed at one of these boisterous meals, a sentry unsheathed his bayonet and prised the bolts from the room's only door. Then, stretched out on the door, the latest casualty was paraded outside accompanied by a string quartet's version of "The Dead March." The story is likely exaggerated if not apocryphal, but no less amusing.

Life at Vis could be entertaining for more than just the meals. Fuller said that nobody had bothered to cut the submarine telephone cables connecting the island to Hvar, which was now occupied by German troops, so whenever the mood struck him he would ring at night and tell the other side what he thought of it. "It was all very friendly," he said. This easygoing arrangement suited Fuller. It was also appropriate in the "really screwy" atmosphere of Vis. The scenery was hardscrabble, but strangely idyllic: gnarled olive trees set against ochre earth and rolling hills. But there was barbed wire, too, and ammunition dumps, brightly painted signposts, and an airfield nestled in the middle of a nearby valley. The island's narrow roads were crammed with trucks and jeeps. Living with the Partisans, who were about as colourful a lot as you could find—they were ill-equipped, wore ragtag uniforms and wedge caps adorned with the red star, saluted impressively and were ardent guerrillas—was equally unforgettable for its multitude of surprises, not all of which were pleasant. Fuller recalled one such incident. It occurred during the Partisans' May Day celebrations at Vis, not long after Fuller had brought back a number of prisoners who the Partisans had decided should be hanged in the market square. Fuller objected. Indeed, he says he sent a message that was relayed to Fitzroy Maclean, who informed Winston Churchill. The prime minister appealed directly to Tito, demanding that under no circumstances were the PoWs to be subjected to such inhumane treatment. Tito, now currying Allied favour with as much zeal as he could muster, acquiesced. Word was passed along to the Partisans not to publicly execute their prisoners. So the Partisans, according to Fuller, quietly hanged them from the apple trees of an orchard that was *behind* the square.

The Partisans were as brutal sometimes with their own. Fuller said that among the Allied personnel at Vis were a number of U.S. Rangers, including a fellow named Rogers with whom he had become friendly. Rogers had lately had a dalliance with one of the female Partisans; in fact he was madly in love with her. Fuller and Rogers were talking one day when they saw the woman being marched outside under guard.

"What's up?" Fuller asked. Rogers wondered if she was about to be given a medal. Following a brief speech, a firing squad formed up hastily, and—BANG!—the woman was summarily executed. Rogers was beside himself with grief and rage. Fuller sent his young interpreter to investigate.

"She had a self-inflicted wound and couldn't fight any more," the fellow reported.

"What did she do?" Fuller asked. "Shoot her fingers off—or what?"

"No, she was pregnant," was the reply. Tito, in addition to prohibiting the consumption of alcohol, had forbidden sexual relations amongst his Partisans. Fuller said that Rogers, who no doubt had fathered the child, went "nuts" upon hearing of this.

But as Fuller remembered also, the Partisans could be equally self-sacrificing and heroic. Those who worked with the Partisan Medical Service particularly stood out. They were mostly young and inexperienced. Fuller said that wounded Partisans brought back to the makeshift hospital at Vis were put in the care of young female nurses, most of whom laboured without the benefit of formal training. There was, however, one young woman who prior to the war had been a fourth-year medical student in Zagreb. But even this training did not prepare her for the variety of injuries she had to treat, or their severity. According to Fuller, in one day she performed fourteen amputations in facilities that were deplorable—usually a wooden door put down as an operating table in a crowded, filthy room, while rusting instruments were "sterilized" outside using water boiled in a forty-five-gallon drum with a bonfire under it.

Of course the purpose of Fuller's being at Vis was to engage the enemy, which as the record shows he did with extraordinary success. Perhaps as a result, he lamented loudly the rare occasions when little or nothing happened. These he called Stink Patrols, the equivalent of Zizz Patrols as they were known in the Med (and Z Patrols in the English Channel). Still, they could be amusing. Fuller said he often came upon small craft hiding close to shore and upon investigating found they were full of people. Fuller challenged each with the few words of Serbo-Croat in his vocabulary. Invariably, he said, some old geezer would call out from the dark, "Speak English, bub!"

"For sure he'd run a fish shop in Los Angeles, come home and retired," Fuller explained.

The shore was Fuller's best friend, too. "We used to put an iron bar in the heaving line and throw it up in the rocks and pull ourselves in to the shore, because the shorelines were, you know, forty feet deep. It's mountains right down to the sea. And not even on a great moonlit night, if you look into the shore, can you ever see anything except black. So I always figured that was the best camouflage."

It worked best when Fuller planned to board and capture an enemy vessel. That way he could lunge unseen at the last moment, maintaining the element of surprise. "They'd think that they were in close, but you would be in closer still." It helped that the enemy boats almost always had their guns trained to sea, the direction from which trouble was expected. If he intended to destroy a boat, he manoeuvered as quickly as possible to the ocean side, placing the enemy between him and the shore. "The reason for this," he explained, "was that when…you fire back at them, all your 'overs' would set fire to the bush ashore. In no time there'd be a conflagration of the dried brush which put them in silhouette."

Fuller used a variation of this tactic during his last action in the Adriatic, which he fought in July 1944. Hiding with three other boats in a cove, he waited until a schooner hove into sight. Emerging from the darkness, he realized that as many as five E-boats were fanned out around the schooner. Fuller closed anyway.

"Fire starshell!" he ordered. By then the schooner had opened fire. According to one source, Fuller's starshell landed on the schooner's foredeck, igniting fuel that lay exposed in buckets. The schooner exploded, taking with it one of the E-boats. The others quickly vanished. Fuller sped after them, pressing the attack even as he was hit. Then, for reasons that remain unclear, the E-boats got caught up in a duel with each other. "The crew cheered as we watched the bits and pieces fly," Fuller said afterwards. Coastal Forces called this "one of the most successful actions fought in the Adriatic," and gave Fuller a second Bar to his DSC for his role in leading it. Not long after this action, it was decided Fuller had seen enough action. He was relieved and sent back to England.

But Vis had not seen the end of Canada's contribution to the small-boat war in the Adriatic. Not long after Fuller left, the skippers and boats of the 56th MGB Flotilla arrived. They tied up at Komiza Harbour at noon on July 30, met Lt. Cdr. Morgan Giles and were given their first assignment: a "false-nose job" that would take them out three days in a row escorting various other craft landing men on the island of Korcula to the south and on the Yugoslav coast itself. There was a considerable element of risk involved inasmuch as they would be vulnerable to attacking aircraft. Happily, the operations proceeded without incident. The only worrisome note to the exercise was Burke's absence from it. He had remained in Italy while the other boats sailed to Vis and was in a hospital again. His presence was felt nonetheless when Rover Reynolds, temporarily in command of *658*, encountered a suspicious vessel off Korcula and chased after it. "Tony [the boat's acting First Officer] shouted through his megaphone: 'Let go everything!' and we were off—as Corny would put it—'in a cloud of heifer dung!' "

But within days, Burke joined the Cowboy Flotilla at Vis. He was heartily welcomed, too, in the otherwise glum spirit that had come with several uneventful post-Korcula patrols. Reynolds reported overhearing one of 658's ratings remark as they came alongside the jetty at Komiza: "The bloody skipper's back: I bet we find some bloody Jerries now!"

He was right, of course. On the night of August 17, the boats of the 56th MGB Flotilla left Vis to patrol the narrow channel between the island of Mljet and the Yugoslav mainland. There, hunting together for the first time in months, the "Three Musketeers" would find more trouble than they could possibly imagine.

They had one small job to do before they could move into the patrol area. Maitland landed two Royal Marine Commandos at the northwest end of Mljet, where they were to act as spotters, reporting on enemy shipping passing through the channel. This done, they moved off to start their patrol. They had barely arrived when Maitland hailed the other boats.

"Hallo, Dogs, this is Wimpy. I have a possible target. Four small ships moving fast up Mljet Channel. Am steering to intercept."

Maitland, as Senior Officer, now had the luxury of a U.S.-built radar set on his boat. This vastly improved the flotilla's operational abilities, allowing it to detect and track enemy ships well before the Dog boats were in a position to intercept.

Burke, on 658, was soon hunched over a chart on the bridge.

"Looks like E-boats," he said to Reynolds. "I don't think we can catch them."

They gave up the chase, taking this near miss with "bad grace and ill humour," as Reynolds reported. But as it was a dull, moonless night they could safely assume they had not been spotted, either.

They resumed their patrol.

Within an hour Maitland, using a megaphone, hailed the other boats.

"Say, fellas—I think we're in luck! There are three targets at range three miles just entering the channel and running down towards us. Come to action stations and get into cruising line to port. I shall wait as long as I can before attacking."

They were in a perfect position to meet the enemy: close inshore, in a shallow bay. Maitland kept everyone informed as the convoy approached. The plan was to wait until the ships were almost on top of them before breaking out and attacking at close range on a course running opposite to the enemy's.

Twenty minutes passed. R/Ts crackled periodically with curt signals from Maitland's boat. Then: "Target now clearly eight or nine ships."

Minutes later the first of the enemy ships was visible through binoculars.

"Here they are," said Burke, standing next to Reynolds on the bridge. "Three in sight, right ahead."

Then the hardest part—the heart-in-the-mouth, head-pounding, palms-sweating part everyone but the skippers hated—waiting for Maitland to give the order to attack. God, how he waited. Waited until the enemy ships were virtually on top of them.

Then: "Here we go, Dogs! Speed eight knots, fine Seven Order. Attacking on port bow. Tommy—light please! Range is five hundred yards!"

Engines crash-started. The noise was incredible. Starshell went up. This was what truly terrified the enemy ships, realizing in that instant they were caught. Five seconds later Ladner's boat fired its pom-poms, and so did the others. It was madness.

Incredibly, the enemy ships recovered from the opening barrage and were soon pounding the Dog boats with their own tracer.

"All guns shift right," ordered Burke. "Group of small craft. Open fire!"

In the exchange that ensued, *658* took several nasty hits. Burke asked Reynolds to have a look at whatever damage they might have suffered. Below, Reynolds found the chief motor mechanic stripped to his waist and clambering over the engines. There was a large jagged hole on the port side of the boat's hull where a 40-mm shell had entered, knocking out all but one of *658*'s engines. Fortunately they were clear of the convoy now and could take a moment to effect repairs. But even this would give Burke only his starboard engines.

Ten minutes passed. Reynolds issued a few reassuring words to the gunners as they moved back towards the enemy convoy nicely silhouetted by a brush fire on the shore (evidently Fuller was not the only one to make use of this tactic). Reynolds says they went even slower during the second run—less than 8 knots. How they did it and remained calm while facing the enemy's own torrent of gunfire is beyond an outsider's imagination. Years of Hollywood gangster movies with cars racing past at breakneck speed, a phalanx of thugs pouring hot lead from their Tommy guns at some helpless victim on the sidewalk, have left the impression this is the best way to go about such business. Evidently not so. Reynolds said they approached from astern of the convoy and found an E-boat and two landing craft. These began to fire at the MGBs, but again Maitland waited until the last moment.

According to Reynolds:

> At two hundred yards we sailed relentlessly and slowly past, pouring out a deadly hail of fire which silenced all reply in a few seconds. When I sounded the "cease fire" signal, all three were left as burning, lifeless hulks.

Immediately the MGBs moved on to catch up with three other boats at the head of the convoy. From six hundred yards, the enemy ships opened fire. The MGBs continued to close, now selecting their targets: Maitland would take the leading schooner, Burke would have the one in the middle, and Ladner's job would be to finish off an F-lighter closest to them. Again, Reynolds provides the best account of the action:

> I looked aft. The six-pounder crew were steadily passing ammunition from hand to hand and I could feel the jerk as every round was fired. Good lads! They were the men who could win this fight, not Doug, or Corny, or me. By putting 658 in a good firing position, we could give them the opportunity to win it—but they had to do the shooting. If they couldn't shoot low and hit, then we had wasted our time and we should all pay the price. I thought of my gunnery instructor. "The quick—and the dead." He had known.

The gunners on all three boats were in top form. From 658 they hit an ammunition locker on their target. The schooner exploded, "like a set-piece of fireworks at the Crystal Palace," said Reynolds. Meanwhile Burke's coxswain continued to fill the air with invective regarding the poor quality of the enemy's shooting.

"I reckon they don't do any drill, sir. Perhaps they 'aven't got bastards for gunnery officers like we 'ave!"

In fact the enemy ships had counterattacked with all they had. "That wasn't too pleasant, was it?" Burke said to Reynolds during a brief lull in the fighting.

"Well done so far," came Maitland's reassuring voice on the R/T. "Let me know when you're all set."

There was more work to do. Two more boats were detected on Maitland's radar, now approaching. The guns were soon reloaded. Reynolds watched his skipper.

> We moved in at 8 knots, and were astonished to see the leading schooner challenge us with the letter "H". Corny's brow knitted. "I wonder if she's expecting more escorts to join?" he muttered.

The MGBs weren't interested in waiting to find out. Twenty

guns opened fire at Maitland's command, and in an instant the schooner swung away, silenced.

"Hallo, Dogs. Two of these jokers are still holding course," Maitland signalled.

It was decided to lie in wait. Fifteen minutes later another schooner loomed ahead with a smaller vessel alongside. From three hundred yards the MGBs opened fire. Reynolds was amazed the enemy ships could take such punishment. "But they had by no means our accuracy or fire-power... and in a very short time were both silenced."

Maitland's radar screen no longer showed any moving vessels. He decided to search the channel to "mop up" what remained of those they had attacked already. One of the wounded schooners proved elusive, but was eventually tracked down with the help of more brush fires set along the shore. With this, Maitland ordered the boats back to Komiza Harbour. Five hours after their work had begun, nothing seemed to be left afloat along the entire length of the Mljet Channel.

Maitland's report of the battle received the highest praise from Coastal Forces.

> *This action may well be regarded as a 'peak' performance of the 56th MGB/MTB Flotilla, with all its RCNVR commanding officers under the magnificent leadership of Lt. Cdr. J. D. Maitland, DSC.... In the light of the reports from Intelligence, it is thought that this action may be described as the shrewdest blow that the enemy has suffered on the Dalmatian coast, and well may have speeded his evacuation of the Islands.*

It was true the Dog boats of the Cowboy Flotilla had dealt a serious blow to the enemy's shipping along the coast. Whether this in the context of other successful operations in the Adriatic or a need to reinforce troops elsewhere prompted the decision to begin evacuating the major islands, the Battle of the Mljet Channel remained an overwhelming victory.

Now that the enemy was pulling out, the pace of activity altered dramatically. Following a brief period at Manfredonia again to repair the damage to their boats, the 56th—along with virtually every other flotilla in the theatre—was hastily summoned to Brindisi. There the boats were assigned to patrol off Corfu, an area one hundred and fifty miles away, to prevent the enemy's withdrawal of men and materiel from the islands to the mainland. It turned out to be another Zizz.

Next they went to Ancona, which had only recently fallen into Allied hands. Here the action was centred at Rimini, some fifty miles farther up the coast, where the Canadians and British were hammering at the enemy. For the 56th it was the closest they had come to a main front since Sicily. Their job was to deter E-boats from laying mines in the path of Allied warships operating along the coast. But several nights out proved as monotonous as their earlier exercise off Corfu.

It was not surprising. Even if they had found action it would be hard to imagine anything with the intensity of the Battle of the Mljet Channel. The fact was that only a few months after their arrival in the Adriatic, the men of the 56th discovered there was hardly anything left for them to do. Moreover, the Midas touch they had enjoyed until now was about to show signs of diminishing.

First, *657* boat hit a mine off Rimini that blew its stern away, killing five ratings who were aft. Maitland was not aboard when the incident occurred; in fact, it was the only time he had not gone out in command of his boat. His First Officer, Freddie Mills, had taken it out while Maitland was in Corsica getting spare parts for *657*'s radar set. Reynolds, temporarily in command of *658* while Burke was visiting his brother-in-law on the mainland, towed Maitland's boat back to Ancona where it was berthed in the "graveyard" alongside an ML crippled the previous week. And that was where Maitland found his boat the next morning. "It was a pretty sad day," was all he said.

There were more such days to come. Within a month, Ladner

announced unexpectedly he had had enough and was taking a posting as Senior Operations Officer at Malta.

"I was sick and I weighed one hundred and thirty-odd pounds," he said. "I didn't realize how sick I was, actually."

He spent a month at Bighi Hospital recovering from pneumonia. The setting, a large Palladian building dating from Nelson's days, was restful, even in the midst of so much rubble from years of bombing of this island fortress. But Ladner's convalescence was troubled by the loss, only days after he departed Ancona, of *663*. It, too, had struck a mine on its first patrol with a new British skipper.

The flotilla was now down to three boats from the original six.

Then Maitland left. Like Ladner, he had been actively engaged with Coastal Forces for four years and needed a break. He ended up as the Senior Operations Officer at Ancona, residing comfortably in a sumptuous flat overlooking the Adriatic. Meanwhile Burke was appointed Senior Officer of what remained of the 56th MGB/MTB Flotilla. His first night out, operating again from Vis, he destroyed an I-lighter (similar in design to an F-lighter but smaller) in a spirited action. By all accounts he led the flotilla throughout the following weeks with the same daring and zeal that were his custom when the Three Musketeers were together, but it was clear to all that a lot else had changed. It was only a matter of time now before Burke's two years of active duty expired and he, along with Maitland and Ladner, would be entitled leave to Canada again.

They were reunited at Malta for Christmas 1944. There, *658* began a long period in which it was virtually rebuilt. Sadly, Burke's days as its skipper ended long before it put to sea again. The Cowboy Flotilla was no more.

Its legacy, however, remained. The tactics it had practised in both the Mediterranean and the Adriatic, first learned from "the immortal Hichens" in the English Channel and improved upon since to reflect the maverick style of the Canadians, were duly handed down. Fittingly, it was Maitland who best described this hard-won appreciation of the ethos of small-boat warfare.

"You've got to get in close," he said, "as close as possible—a hundred yards, fifty, less. And slow speed. You must go slowly, preferably on the same course as the target, so you can stay alongside her. If you're close enough, she can't depress her guns sufficiently to hit you. *That's* when you get them. Fire tracer. Set them on fire. Rake them fore and aft, fore and aft. Again and again. *That's* the way you get them."

The small-boat skippers who accepted this chillingly stern principle usually succeeded. Those who did not were either ineffective, or soon dead—leaving aside the question as to which was worse in the minds of the Canadian skippers.

It emerged elsewhere, too, as the foremost rule of action aboard small boats. In the English Channel, where fighting continued to rage, the Canadians with the 29th and 65th flotillas had embraced the same creed of close combat, regardless of its toll.

10

Back into the Fray

A T NOON ON SEPTEMBER 7, 1944, the 65th Flotilla slipped
Brixham harbour for the last time, bound for new hunting
grounds and a new operational base at Great Yarmouth on
Britain's east coast. In the memory of some of the flotilla's
members, it was a departure accompanied by dreadful hangovers.
The crews had come back from a three-day leave in Brixham,
Paignton and nearby Torquay with its waving palms. In Kirkpatrick's monthly report on the flotilla's operations, the 65th's
commander noted officers and men were "extremely sorry to
leave Brixham where we had been so well looked after." The day
before the boats shipped their mooring lines at New Pier, the crews
had entertained the townspeople aboard the Dog boats. Torpedoman Brian Jones remembered "we were pouring a lot of drinks for
the folks and everyone was feeling no pain." Tom Jones noted in
his diary that the flotilla was given "a rousing farewell and crowds
of people come to see us off." Commander R. Pierson, who headed
the Royal Navy's HMS *Cicala*, under whose command the flotilla
operated, "gives a speech and wished us the best of luck and hoped
we did as good at our new base."

Kirkpatrick was anxious to move on. "The past month of

offensive patrols had proved to us that there was little opportunity left encountering the enemy except perhaps further south in the Bay of Biscay," he said. Many operations had been planned for that area, but only a few had been carried out. It was simply too long a haul for the boats to make it there and back the same day, forcing the flotilla to operate in daylight hours, opening itself to possible air attack.

The 29th Flotilla, meanwhile, had also departed its operational base at Portsmouth, returning to Ramsgate where the flotilla had formed up prior to the invasion. There was a brief break from routine when the 65th pulled into Dover on September 8. Law and his skippers journeyed there to join Kirkpatrick and the 65th's officers in a party in Kirkpatrick's tiny wardroom aboard MTB *748* where Law remembered receiving "a royal welcome" followed by a night of imbibing.

Despite both commanders' favourable reports to their superiors on the health and morale of their crews, living conditions aboard the cramped boats had been difficult throughout the summer, especially for the 29th.

Lieutenant-Commander P. W. Franck, an accountant officer from *Niobe*, who travelled from Glasgow to the south coast in June to settle numerous pay queries, reported to the Canadian Naval Mission Overseas (in London) that not all was well.

"It is depressing to find that the morale of both officers and men of this flotilla is at a very low ebb," Franck wrote. "The chief reason for this is the accommodation and messing arrangements which appear most inadequate."

While at Portsmouth, the 29th was supposed to be accommodated ashore at HMS *Vernon*. Franck said that the harbour transportation was poor, occasionally non-existent. It meant that the crews returning from their exhausting nightly sorties would have to wait hours for a vehicle or a duty boat to take them to the other side of the harbour. Instead, after re-ammunitioning, refuelling and cleaning weapons, the weary sailors began sleeping aboard the boats. If they wanted to eat at *Hornet*, it meant waiting for a vehicle or a boat to take them there and back. In any case, the meals were poor.

"The evening meals served in HMS *Hornet* are of extremely poor quality and the quantity is quite insufficient," Franck had reported. "An example of one evening meal was a small meat pie, one piece of bread and very poor cocoa. This was a night when the boats proceeded to sea on a ten-hour operational patrol."

It was understood that the crews were to be given a soup ration to take to sea for the night, but no soup was ever issued.

"The ratings would not go to the trouble of waiting around for duty boats to cross the harbour for meals. As a result [they] are obtaining their own food and cooking it on board on one small hot plate. It is felt that they are not being properly nourished and that this has seriously affected both morale and fighting efficiency."

Eating arrangements were only marginally better aboard the 65th Flotilla's boats. Torpedoman Jones remembered a monotonous concoction of baked corned beef and mashed potatoes as "just terrible" although the cook "thought this was just the greatest thing in the world." Franck had also inspected the 65th in June where he found "the messing is reasonably satisfactory despite some difficulty in obtaining a variety of diet." He was more concerned that "living conditions are extremely crowded."

Fifteen to nineteen men in the seamen's mess were living in a space where they could not stand or sit at one time. "When they are all sleeping," Franck noted, "one cannot move in or through the mess. As the boats are on patrol duty at night only, sleeping must be done during the day and the quarters are none too well ventilated. Sleep is frequently disturbed by maintenance work being carried out on board."

But what really caused "great discontent," Franck said, was the navy's bureaucratic interpretation of the regulation for paying what was called "hard-lying" money at full rates for seagoing days and half rates for days in harbour. Some other ships' crews with more spacious living quarters were getting the full rates while the MTB crews were only on half pay while in port, an anomaly

Franck pointed out because MTB crews in Canada received full rates of hard-lying money continuously even though they were operating "in smooth waters and certainly much more safe waters than do the MTBs" engaged in the Channel war. But all this was in the past. By September, they were rested and their boats in good fighting shape.

Back at Ramsgate, the 29th Flotilla soon discovered, however, that the hotel, which they called HMCS *Canada*, and which they had put considerable effort into cleaning up in May, was now occupied by Polish sailors. Again the 29th took on its orphan image. The crews rejected the accommodations the Royal Navy had assigned them, "very unsatisfactory," in Law's memory, and went back to sleeping aboard the shorts. The food situation however, improved. The Canadians were now receiving Canadian rations, which were issued in larger amounts and were better quality food than the Royal Navy rations they had been on all summer.

Kirkpatrick's 65th fared much better. Great Yarmouth was a seaside town with many of the trappings of a resort city with its wide esplanade, flower beds and small hotels. The flotilla berthed up the Yar River, taking over a shack on the jetty as the flotilla office beside a "depressing coal dump," said Katie Barclay, who had now joined the flotilla as Kirkpatrick's secretary. Oddly enough, even though Great Yarmouth was favoured by Londoners for their holidays, she didn't particularly find the place appealing. The beaches were mined and covered with barbed wire. Barclay, who was billeted in one of the hotels the navy had taken over, walked to the 65th's "office," arriving each morning as the boats came back from patrol, taking a line and helping the crews to tie up.

Beginning September 10, the 65th patrolled the North Sea for eleven consecutive days before a week of storms kept the boats in port. With autumn at hand and winter approaching, both flotillas would be dogged by gale-force wind and seas. But on September 30, Kirkpatrick led six of his boats into the North Sea to patrol off Holland's West Friesian Islands from Texel to Ameland. Shortly after one boat turned back because of engine problems, the five remaining MTBs sighted an enemy convoy in the distance and began to close the range, jockeying for a favourable position to attack. Unfortunately, the Germans spotted the approaching Canadians, blasting them with very accurate fire at a range of eight thousand yards. Later air reconnaissance confirmed that the "convoy" Kirkpatrick was trying to attack was in fact a group of heavily armed escort M-class minesweepers and that there were no merchant ships among them. Ollie Mabee's boat took a direct hit in the engine room, the shell knocking out two of the four engines. Shrapnel also cut the fuel lines to these two remaining undamaged engines. Moreover, fragments smashed two small four-cylinder engines that pumped fresh water from special tanks that cooled all of the engines. With the engines out, the gun turrets lost power. MTB *745* was a sitting duck until Chief Petty Officer and Motor Mechanic Bill Goodhew and Motor Mechanic Glen Gander set to work. First, they plugged the four-inch hole with wiping rags, alerted the bridge to start the deck pumps to take out the water, which had now reached the engine mountings. Besides the damage to the engines, the blast also knocked out the main steering works, forcing the boat's coxswain, James Gregory, to rush aft from the bridge to man the small wheel of the emergency steering. All the while, shells continued to rain down from the German guns. Below, Goodhew and Gander feverishly worked to get the two undamaged engines started. They jury-rigged a new fuel line and got one engine going. At the same time they had to re-route another line from the fresh-water cooling tanks to keep this one engine from overheating. Kirkpatrick meanwhile moved in and laid smokescreen to protect the stricken motor torpedo boat. Shortly, the makeshift repairs made by Goodhew and Gander enabled MTB *745* to limp back to Great Yarmouth on its own, with one engine ticking over despite a very high sea building up as they journeyed homeward. For the quick-thinking motor mechanics whose efforts most certainly saved the boat and the lives of her crew, Goodhew was awarded a Distinguished Service Medal, and Gander was mentioned in dispatches. Forty-five years later, the events of that dramatic night were hazy in Goodhew's memory because, as he said, "there had been so many actions that they kind of get mixed up in your memory." Gander was still able to vividly recall in detail those horrifying hours.

October passed uneventfully for the 65th. Raging storms kept the small boats harbour-bound for most of the month, a situation the Germans took advantage of. On October 15 and October 22, the small boats carried out an offensive sweep off the Dutch coast from Tershelling to Ijmuiden. Despite the fact these sweeps carried them directly down the enemy convoy route, including a close-in investigation of Texel harbour, they did not encounter a single enemy merchant ship or escort. The MTBs had their limits in the gales that left the North Sea in a fury for most of October. Kirkpatrick later reported "that the Hun was moving his merchantmen in weather which he would know kept our boats in port." Nevertheless, the 65th Flotilla managed twenty-five patrols in October and a record-breaking seventy-two patrols in November, an excessive amount of sea time even for the hard-driving Kirkpatrick.

The gloom of October was replaced by a hectic pace in November. This was an assignment that the flotilla felt was the most important since its formation, to protect the channels that had been swept of mines leading from the sea into Antwerp, Belgium. While Antwerp was now in Allied hands, it was useless as a port until the banks of the Scheldt Estuary could be cleared of enemy guns. While the land to the south of the Scheldt Estuary was virtually all in Allied hands by the end of October, the Germans still held a key piece of geography, Walcheren Island, which guarded the sea approaches to the estuary. When the island was assaulted in early November, the 65th Flotilla's boats were used to protect the flanks of the landing craft and were at sea for sixty hours, a long time for small boats. Ollie Mabee's and John Collins's MTBs were given the not-too-healthy assignment, as Kirkpatrick described it, of laying smoke between minesweepers and enemy shore batteries, coming under constant fire.

In the middle of the month, Kirkpatrick's *748* raised the spirits of the entire flotilla with an attack on six E-boats in the Scheldt Estuary, a brilliant hit-and-run assault that combined all the essential elements of small-boat fighting: stealth, surprise and heavy fire at close quarters. It was just after midnight of November 15. There was no moon, the sky was overcast and the sea was fairly calm. Suddenly, ahead off his starboard bow, six E-boats loomed out of the darkness moving at slow speed, perhaps ready to begin seeding mines, Kirkpatrick later concluded. Going to full boost of the throttles, MTB 748 roared down the line of German boats, hammering each boat as they swept past, and cutting through the wake of the last E-boat in the formation. Caught napping, the E-boats did not return the fire until 748 had passed the last boat in line, and then their fire was short, wide and high. The Germans made smoke and in sweeping back for a second crack at the E-boats, Kirkpatrick had to suddenly swerve to avoid colliding with one.

That's how close MTB 748 had pressed the attack. Her crew counted numerous hits on the German vessels, even though in the opening seconds of the run-in, 748's six-pounder had jammed after only six rounds. Had it not jammed, 748 would have surely added an E-boat to their list of victims. Still, in these brief seconds, the Canadians had blasted the enemy with nearly two thousand rounds of shell and shot.

There was little relief from the constant patrolling and the stresses that the patrols imposed on both men and ships. In late October, there had been a brief interlude in the fighting. The Canadian flotillas had become part of an umbrella group consisting of RCN and RN flotillas known as Coastal Forces Mobile Unit No. 1, which operated out of the recently liberated port of Ostend, Belgium. All sailors delight in the surroundings of a new port and they were no exception at Ostend. Despite having been heavily bombed, the city's grim appearance did not deter the Canadians from spending a few hours ashore. Tom Jones, faithful to his daily diary, recorded his impressions.

We all go ashore and visit the German fortifications and

E-boat pens. We spend all afternoon looking the place over. The Germans certainly made a good job of demolishing the docks but we soon get things well under way again and the supplies are coming in steady. We see German prisoners plenty. We see hundreds of prisoners from the front, most of them Russians, Poles, Siberians, Chinese and Mongols. We also see our own casualties coming back from the front which is only 18 miles. The boys think the town of Ostend is really OK. There are lots of brothels here and are operating wide open as they are licensed and examined by [the] Army Medical Officer. They line up about 50 or more to wait their turn to see the girls. There are 12 girls.

While the Canadians continued to use Great Yarmouth as their main port, Ostend came into frequent use, requiring Katie Barclay to travel from the flotilla's base in England to Ostend. The paperwork generated by the 65th's activities was burdensome, copies of the nightly action reports, Kirkpatrick's monthly summary of activities and the ubiquitous requisition forms all had to be typed out—in triplicate. She worked out of an office in a building only recently vacated by the retreating Germans, ironically the same building that had been occupied by the E-boat crews they were hunting down and whose presence was still felt. All the signs in the building were still in German. Barclay discovered on her first tour of the place that there were no separate toilet facilities for women either, so the perky Canadian Wren used the same toilet stalls when need arose alongside the men.

A different kind of surprise awaited Tom Jones. The Canadians were able to buy many food items that had not been seen in England for years; ice cream, a large variety of fresh fruit and vegetables and plenty of good wine were readily available. To Barclay this was an anomaly. She was struck by the presence of a large number of undernourished children playing in the rubble, two of whom did not endear themselves in her memory. Barclay, who spoke French, was taken aback one day when she heard one little ruffian telling another that Barclay's Wren uniform designated her as a prostitute for the Canadian officers.

Ostend lives in her memory for another reason. It was from this port that she departed for an operational trip on one of the flotilla's fighting ships. Any time she made the journey from Great Yarmouth to Ostend to tend to the books, it meant a long roundabout trip involving trains and eventually a ferry from Dover to Ostend. Once while preparing to make the return trip to England, she mentioned this to Bert Morrow, skipper of MTB *726*. Morrow, who himself was just leaving to take his gun-laden boat back across the Channel, invited her aboard. When the senior Wren officer in Great Yarmouth discovered this, Barclay was severely reprimanded, a tongue-lashing she ignored. The pesky westerner had become perhaps the only Wren to have made an operational voyage in a Canadian warship in enemy waters in World War II.

Souvenir hunting was a favourite pastime too for the sailors, and German weapons were much sought after.

"I managed to get a German rifle from one of the Belgian patriots for a few packets of fags and a couple of cigars," the entry in Jones's diary for November 8 tells us. A month later back in Ostend for a brief shore leave, Jones was off to nearby Brugge "to see if we can pick up some automatics. We visit the Canadian hospital there and manage to get a *P38* and a Browning automatic. We then get in touch with a Belgian underground family and get another Browning."

The trip nearly ended tragically. A shipmate accidentally fired one of the weapons while waiting on the platform at the Brugge train station, which was crowded with people, the spent bullet missing his foot by an inch, sending a few Belgians diving for cover.

Kirkpatrick wrote in his monthly report that "the officers and men found Ostend and Belgium extremely interesting and amusing. The amusement side quickly palled as the novelty of it faded, and time would have been very heavy in the boats had they not been worked as hard as they were."

The boats in truth were in a deteriorating condition, the result of battle action and frequent heavy weather. Engines were being removed after five hundred hours and replaced with rebuilt ones.

Underwater obstacles constantly damaged propellers. But more frustrating perhaps to the skippers and crews, already stretched to their physical and emotional limits by the constant threat of death or injury, was an attitude that combined petulance and disinterest displayed by many of the workers and their foremen who were doing refits and repairs in some of the British boatyards. In postwar Britain it was an attitude that became known as the "I'm all right, Jack" syndrome. Just as maddening was the condescending personality of some of the so-called experts who obviously disliked dealing with these civilians-turned-sailors, and colonials at that.

Kirkpatrick's own boat, MTB *748*, and Ollie Mabee's *745*, both of which had seen punishing service since the flotilla was commissioned, were out of action for nearly two months. The boats had been badly hauled out of the water and improperly shored. So obvious was the shoddy work "that one could see with the naked eye the hog [the bulge] in the hull," reported the 65th's commander to his superiors. "The energy shown by most of the dockyard workmen has certainly not raised an ounce of praise from the commanding officers of the boats who have stood by their boats during this refit." Mabee's boat was taking so long in the refit yard that her crew eventually ended up with nearly forty-five days of leave, so long that the sailors ran out of money and began moonlighting for fifteen shillings a day in a London brewery, a job which of course had its advantages. The owner allowed them to take home every night as many bottles of beer as they could get into the pockets of their mackintoshes. When Mabee's boat was finally refloated with her full war load, it was discovered the dockyard experts had not taken this fact into account. The shafts of the propellers were so much out of alignment that the boat shook excessively, bucking and shuddering so much that it felt she would fall apart.

Poor workmanship also dogged refitting of the 29th Flotilla's boats when they were hauled. In Tony Law's monthly report for September, his anger was barely concealed. The dockyard at "Ramsgate have an extremely bad habit of accepting a refit knowing perfectly well they have not got the base staff to undertake this work. The result is that the operational boats suffer and the boat being refitted suffers," he complained.

The 29th was now back at full strength following the battering it took off the assault beaches. Law got a new MTB *486*, as did Bones Burk, MTB *491*. Law's original boat, MTB *459*, which he had abandoned in July when it was holed by a mine, had been transported back to England where it was miraculously rebuilt. It was recommissioned by Law's former first lieutenant, John Shand. Keith Scobie, who had served as Burk's No. 1, took command of their old boat MTB *461*.

For Law, September began with both good and bad news. One day there were two letters awaiting him, the first a reprimand from the Admiralty for the collision he suffered with Kirkpatrick's boat during the working-up trials at Holyhead the previous spring. It seemed petty to Law after surviving the mad summer of combat that had seen three of the flotilla's boats shot out from under it. The second letter brought better news. "In flowery English," Law learned he had been awarded the Distinguished Service Cross for his daring leadership during the invasion fighting.

The 29th Flotilla was very active in September with numerous sorties to the French coast. But it was obvious the action had moved eastward towards Belgium and Holland in face of the Allied advances. At the end of the month Law requested the Canadian Naval Mission in London that the 29th "be placed in a more strategic position" where he pointed out Coastal Forces were "meeting with great success in action against the enemy off the Dutch coast." On October 21, the 29th departed Ramsgate to crowds of waving townsfolk who had come to the jetty to wave goodbye, heading to yet another new operational base, this one at Felixstowe on the coast of Suffolk where the crews found themselves living ashore in newly built homes, one boat crew to each house. The officers moved into separate quarters in two hotels, one close to the docks, the other five miles outside town. Yet the new quarters got little use. For the rest of October there were constant patrols, nearly all the boats having spent half the month at sea, an impressive record in face of the time that was lost leaving Ramsgate and settling into the new base.

The weather was slightly better closer to the Channel where they patrolled than it was farther north, where it kept the 65th in port. Still, October was wet and cold.

November was equally active and the month began with a fierce engagement. On November 1, Law, Creba, Scobie, Burk and Bishop were off the Hook of Holland in search of a German convoy reported in the area. Shortly after the patrol began, one of Scobie's engines packed in and he was forced to return to Felixstowe. The others continued the search and soon the Canadians' radar picked up the convoy, estimated to be seven miles distant. As Law, Creba, Burk and Bishop moved slowly towards the enemy, they saw that the convoy consisted of several flak trawlers, a gunboat, a tug towing a barge, and, most promising of all, a three-thousand-ton merchant ship. As the Canadians approached still undetected, there appeared on the scene yet more enemy vessels. There were seven E-boats approaching from the opposite direction. Breaking up the formation, Law and Creba turned to attack the E-boats while Burk and Bishop sped towards the convoy. Law's diversion attack allowed Burk and Bishop to move into position for a torpedo run. Selecting the merchant ship as the target, Burk and Bishop throttled back to 10 knots to give them a steadier platform from which to launch their torpedoes. Under heavy fire, they pressed on to within eight hundred yards before Burk emptied his two tubes. Two enemy hits on Bishop's boat prevented him from launching torpedoes, but he joined in with Burk in sweeping the convoy with rapid fire. The gun attack was so fierce and rapid that Burk's six-pounder ran out of ammunition and Bishop's main gun was knocked out by enemy shrapnel. But as they ran down the line of escorts guarding the convoy, they saw a huge blinding white flash amidships of the merchant vessel followed by a cloud of black smoke that they felt certain was the result of a torpedo hit. As was almost always the case, the Canadians suffered casualties. Two sailors were hit on Bishop's boat; Harry Broadly was killed instantly, and Allan Bevan was wounded. The waterline hits on Bishop's boat sent the sea pouring in through the holes, flooding the forward part of the MTB where, below, Petty Officer Motor Mechanic Fred Walden was faced with trying to keep his boat afloat as had Bill Goodhew and Glen Gander a month earlier.

Walden was the boat's damage-control petty officer. When he got to the ratings' mess deck where the shell came through, "the boat was shipping a hell of a lot of water." Walden got a bucket brigade going while he tried to block the hole. Taking a fire axe, he smashed the table in the mess deck for use as planking. Plugging the hole with clothing and covering it with the smashed-up table, Walden made a wedge from the axe handle to hold everything in place. By now the boat was heavy in the bows from all the water it had taken in. A suction pump in that compartment was useless until the boat could pick up speed, creating enough suction to make it work. When the boats regrouped it was obvious Bishop's boat was severely damaged and ordered to make for Felixstowe offering Bishop an escort. This offer was refused by Bishop, who didn't want to weaken the remaining group of MTBs who were setting off to try to make contact again with the enemy. Of his Commanding Officer Craig Bishop, Walden said, "He was a great guy. Nothing would stop him. Nothing. He put his duty ahead of everything." After back-breaking bailing, the water level in the boat was lowered enough to increase the speed to activate the suction pump. They reached home port safely, the final voyage for Harry Broadly.*

The remaining boats continued their patrol with Law, Creba and Burk playing a tense cat-and-mouse game with four German flak trawlers known as The Four Horsemen of the Apocalypse. These ships heavily outgunned the small torpedo boats and were viciously armed with the devastating 88-mm gun—lots of them.

By the end of November, the boats of Law's flotilla were in as

---

*Except for Dave Killam, all of the 29th Flotilla's skippers survived the war, including Craig Bishop. He was to die in a peacetime yachting accident off the coast of Nova Scotia.

poor condition as Kirkpatrick's 65th, if not worse. The recurring patrols in the cold pounding sea, and the damage as a result of enemy gunfire, meant the boats were constantly being repaired and out of action. Everyone had a cold or the flu. Adding to the misery, the crews got moved out of their comfortable little houses to make room for another flotilla, taking over a large nursing home as a barracks. Located beyond the port, the building required extra staffing but because of a shortage of replacements, these duties fell to the exhausted crews after returning from their sea duty at night, robbing them of sleep they so desperately needed.

The plight of the 29th Flotilla couldn't have been worse, until two incidents occurred that plunged the men into deeper gloom. A riot broke out between the Canadians and the men of a Polish flotilla whose presence had resulted in the Canadians being moved from their quiet house quarters into the nursing home. Not only did their pride suffer, three Canadian sailors ended up in hospital from the donnybrook.

On top of that, seventy men became violently ill through food poisoning on November 30. Suddenly the men began vomiting with severe stomach cramps and dozens of them fainted. Contaminated meat at the noon meal that day was believed responsible.

Sullen and sick, the men petitioned their officers for redress. They had had it. Although it was later referred to as "the mutiny," the situation was serious. This was the last straw for Tony Law, whose own reserve of energy was tapped. Law blasted the brass with the proverbial rocket.

In a tersely worded report, the 29th's commanding officer told his superiors that because of the sickness, and the quality of the sailors being drafted as replacements for this arduous and highly dangerous hit-and-run warfare, he could not maintain the boats at their peak fighting efficiency.

"At the present time there are no ratings in reserve, and personnel from boats undergoing slipping, repairs and short refits are being used to complete the complements of operational boats. It is predicted," he said, "that unless sufficient personnel can be supplied from HMCS *Niobe* ... boats will have to be withdrawn to keep other boats at sea."

The report went off like a bomb at *Niobe*. The manning pool's commanding officer was livid at the suggestion his command had let down the 29th Flotilla by failing to provide suitable replacements. He was further incensed when the Canadian Naval Mission in London instructed him if the flotilla was not up to authorized strength, "early arrangements should be made to rectify the condition."

A few replacements arrived shortly after the Naval Mission's order, but the challenge of getting the right people was a continuing problem. Of course, all officers and men in the wartime RCN, the RCAF and the Canadian Army Overseas were volunteers. When the small boats were commissioned, most of the officers and many of the sailors had asked to be on the small boats. But the fact was that serving in the MTBs was a high-risk occupation. As the Channel war progressed, the news of the flotilla's mounting casualties followed in its battle wake. Only the very bravest were willing to accept the risks that went with service on small boats.

By the end of December, living conditions for members of the 29th Flotilla had improved slightly and in his monthly report of proceedings Law wrote that "everything was running satisfactorily." This was not the opinion of an investigating team from *Niobe* that arrived to inspect the 29th a few weeks later.

"The dormitories were in a state of confusion with kit bags and personal gear scattered all over the place," the investigators reported to *Niobe*'s commander. The officer in charge "assured that measures would be taken immediately to clear up this disgraceful condition, and that ratings would be out of bed and have their bunks made each day before 'Hands Fall In' unless they had obtained prior approval. While making rounds it was obvious that quite a number of ratings found sleeping all day a pleasant way of passing time and avoiding work."

It did not occur to the desk-bound *Niobe* team that these men were at the end of their limits of endurance.

The investigators observed that sailors reporting back to their quarters in the nursing home from shore leave simply went out again by the back door. Despite the numerous discomforts being endured by the MTB crews, the investigating team recommended a barbed wire enclosure be erected around the building.

The *Niobe* investigators then journeyed to Great Yarmouth to inspect the 65th Flotilla, reporting it was impressed with the efficiency of the base organization. Of course any comparison is odious and should not be made. The 65th always lived aboard their ships and made less frequent changes in its base operations. The 29th invariably was left to shift for itself both in billets and messing arrangements, all of which made daily routine more difficult.

One recommendation the investigators made was to strengthen the number of Canadian sailors on shore patrol with Royal Navy personnel. When the 65th arrived back at Great Yarmouth just before Christmas, there had been a "dust-up" between the Canadian sailors and Royal Navy ratings. Kirkpatrick immediately discontinued a Canadian shore patrol and instead agreed to a joint shore patrol of British and Canadians, but this wasn't satisfactory either because, as the investigators discovered, "a rating on patrol duty was reluctant to take appropriate action against another rating whom he serves with or knows very well."

Kirkpatrick's flotilla spent the Christmas of 1944 quietly. The 65th's flotilla lorry drove to London to pick up mail, turkeys and plum pudding, which had been supplied by HMCS *Niobe*. The crews of the three boats of the 65th stuck at Ostend got the same comforts sent to them by a dispatch boat. They were supposed to be relieved by crews from Great Yarmouth, but too many of the flotilla's nine boats were up on blocks for repairs.

The 29th Flotilla sent boats out for patrol on Christmas Day and Boxing Day, but most of its nine boats were under repair; too, Scobie's boat was leaking so badly it was declared unseaworthy. Others were out with shaft and propeller damage suffered when they hit submerged debris, or were being patched up from hits made by German fire.

So it was that 1944 ended wearily for the Canadian motor torpedo flotillas at war in the North Sea. The new year promised the hint of victory if the sailors were able to continue to conquer fear, fatigue and the grey rolling seas. "By this time some guys were starting to go hairy on us," said Garriock. "After all, how much stress can somebody take?"

It was all relative, of course. Had they known, the Allied crews might have felt some relief in their circumstances compared to the truly desperate situation their adversaries faced. Instead, they studiously followed the land battles trying to interpret the meaning of the victories or set-backs. Even though December's Battle of the Bulge in the Ardennes was fatefully costly for Hitler, the sea battle continued in January with renewed intensity. The odds of surviving were still perilous, so great in the mind of one sailor of the 65th that he decided they couldn't be beaten.

One day he took a hand grenade, pulled the pin and jumped overboard.

11

White Ensign, Black Swastika

I F NOT FOR A chance encounter in, of all places, the Annapolis Valley of Nova Scotia in 1957, Harro Garmsen might have easily kept a significant part of his life to himself—not to hide anything, but rather to avoid offending certain lingering sensibilities and to preserve his own sense of dignity. He was, you see, born in Germany. In 1924. And during the Second World War young Harro Garmsen did what many of his friends were obliged to do: he served in the navy—the Führer's Navy. Losing the war was a good thing, he insists genuinely. But losing, in itself, is *never* a good feeling. The subtlety is difficult enough to express let alone find understanding.

It was certainly not an easy task in 1957, four years after Garmsen settled in Canada. Then he was working as a film cameraman for the CBC when a director from Toronto turned up in Halifax to shoot a documentary. To save costs, it was decided to hire the crew locally, and so Garmsen got the assignment. By an ironic twist of fate, the director was Norn Garriock, who only a few years before was known as "Guns Garriock" when he served aboard MTBs in the English Channel with the 65th Flotilla, mainly in Bert "The Beard" Morrow's *726*.

They met again in October 1989, at the Canadian Coastal Forces Veterans Association reunion in Toronto. There was Norn Garriock, a garrulous "old sport" now past seventy, murderously handsome in a navy blazer that offset perfectly his shock of white hair and magnificent moustache. He bears an uncanny resemblance to the veteran character actor, Keenan Wynne. And there was Harro Garmsen, a slim, well-groomed man with few pretensions (only his white shoes seemed quaintly out of place during an interview earlier in the year). It was Garriock who introduced his former enemy to the membership by recalling their first fateful meeting on Canadian soil.

From Halifax they left for Annapolis Valley, Garmsen behind the wheel. For reasons now forgotten, they had with them in the back seat a Member of Parliament, whom they all but ignored. Garriock and Garmsen started talking. They had barely met, after all, but would be working together shortly. According to Garriock, the conversation went roughly as follows.

"So, Harro, how old are you?"

Thirty-three, or thereabouts. And Garriock?

"Oh, we're about the same age."

"No, you're a little younger," said Garriock.

"Not much, though."

"When did you come over—from Germany?" Garmsen told him. "Well, then, you were there during the war."

"Oh yeah, I was there during the war."

"Were you in the services?"

"Oh yeah," said Garmsen. "I was in the navy."

"In the navy? I was in the navy!"

"Oh."

"What service were you in, Harro?"

Garmsen said, "I was in E-boats."

"Well, gee, I was in MTBs!"

The animosity resulting from this extraordinary coincidence was instant. They continued to probe—until:

"You weren't by any chance on that caper going in to Dunkirk, were you?"

Evidently a shocked look of realization crossed Garmsen's face as he drove, his attention barely on the road. He understood immediately which "caper" Garriock meant.

"Well, as a matter of fact...yeah, there were four of us trying to go into Dunkirk!"

It had happened on the night of February 22–23, 1945. Norn Garriock was aboard Bert Morrow's *726* when it and a British MTB intercepted a unit of four E-boats, one of which was *S 221* of *2. Schnellbootflottille*. *S 221* was Harro Garmsen's boat.

"Well, I was on one of the two boats that engaged the four of you!" said Garriock.

The more they talked, the angrier they became. The battle that night had been particularly vicious—and bloody. Obviously both men had survived it, but it had been so violent it stood out in their memories of the war.

Forgotten in the back seat, of course, was the Member of Parliament, who was listening "flabbergasted," as Garriock says. The odds against such an encounter as he was witnessing seemed astronomical. Worse, Garriock and Garmsen seemed ready to slug it out again right there, in the car, barrelling along a highway to Annapolis Valley!

Perhaps one of them glimpsed the anxious look on the member's face—and laughed. That did it.

"Wait a cotton-pickin' minute!" said Garriock. "The war's over!"

There was a palpable break in the tension while Garmsen agreed. Then they both looked at the road.

"And where the hell are we?" asked Garriock.

In the argument, they had missed a turn-off and were some fifty miles beyond where they were supposed to go!

Of his initial encounter with Garriock in 1945 and their shoot-out, Garmsen told the audience in Toronto, "Mercifully, we both missed, leaving him free to organize this reunion and me to be your guest." If this seemed at all chivalrous it should not have surprised anyone, for even during the war a curious code existed between the small-boat raiders that flew the White Ensign and Black Swastika.

Like many of the British and Canadians who volunteered, Harro Garmsen had experience with the sea from an early age. He was born in Leck, Germany, but raised in Flensburg, which is close enough to the Danish border to be within sight of the Baltic. "Father had a sailboat—a good-sized one," he says in his cultured accent. "I always wanted to be on small boats because that was what I knew." Finishing his high school in 1942, Garmsen became an officer cadet at the Naval College at Flensburg. He was later sent to Gdansk, Poland, in the Gulf of Danzig, where he spent seven months aboard a pre-First World War battleship. Then it was back to Flensburg to finish his training in seamanship, navigation and gunnery. He finished as a midshipman, a rank two notches below officer status, and went to sea still longing for his chance to join the Kriegsmarine's fleet of fast-attack craft. Like midshipmen elsewhere, he realized his fate was in the hands of others. "You just went where they sent you and that was that," said Garmsen. But by 1944 he got his wish. Ironically, by then "the good times were over."

In fact they had begun to subside as early as 1942, when the British began outfitting their escort destroyers with radar. This made it increasingly difficult for E-boats to exploit poor visibility in the English Channel as successfully as they had in the past. By the autumn of 1942 both east and south Allied convoy routes were also fully covered by shore radar, adding to the E-boats' woe. An undetected approach and lying in wait for passing ships were no longer possible.

To reassert at least a minimal element of surprise in their tactics, the *Fuhrer der Schnellboote* (Commander, E-Boats, henceforth referred to as FdS), a position created in April 1942, devised the concept of *Stichansatz*, a term without suitable English equivalent but which amounted, roughly speaking, to a hit-and-run style of warfare. Said Hans Frank, a naval historian in Germany's post-war Bundesmarine, it "involved an approach made in closed formation, dispersal at the limits of the enemy's detection capability, high-speed advance against the convoy route, firing, reassembly, and retirement in company." Such tactics further relied on absolute radio silence. This was crucially important in view of the Allies' effective use of radio intelligence and code-breaking capabilities.

For a brief period, *Stichansatz* worked. It was helped by the capture of a British MGB in September 1942, which provided charts marking the exact points along the convoy routes where MGBs were to intercept attacking E-boats, a fact that was unknown to the British until the war's end.

But even with this vital intelligence in enemy hands, the British were able to mount sufficient countermeasures against the E-boats. Sending MGBs to wait off the coast of France until the enemy boats returned from their sorties, then blasting them out of the water also had a demoralizing effect on the E-boat crews.

The loss of North Africa and Allied landings in Sicily in 1943 also affected policy regarding the E-boats. Naval strategists admitted that in grand terms the Third Reich had gone from being "the hammer to being the anvil." The principal solution to this dilemma was to defend occupied Europe as long as possible. The only other option, as Grossadmiral Karl Dönitz saw it, was to step up the tonnage war against the Allies. This was the assignment given to the E-boats in the winter of 1943–44. They were the only ones who could do it, really. For the Luftwaffe, overextended on all fronts, it would have been impossible.

So a new round began. For the E-boats, there was certainly no lack of targets. Every week as many as four hundred ships entered or left the Thames Estuary, two-thirds of which moved along the north and south routes. The remaining third followed the south coast of England, sailing east and west. To engage the Allied convoys, FdS had in the English Channel area five E-boat flotillas, each with an average of eight boats.

But again the E-boats were limited by a number of factors. "Lack of support by powerful surface warships or the Luftwaffe meant that FdS ran his show pretty much on his own," said Hans Frank. This was both good and bad. Independence and freedom from the meddling of higher command echelons was cherished by the small-boat raiders on either side of the English Channel, but only to a point. British air superiority meant the E-boats still had to operate at night and were restricted in their radius of action to roughly 300 to 350 nautical miles.

In other words, they had to be home before dawn or the RAF's Beaufighters would blast them out of the English Channel.

Navigational conditions off the English coast at least partly compensated the E-boats in their new role. These imposed certain predictable routes on the convoys, allowing improved opportunities to attack. For the British the critical area to defend became the stretch between Great Yarmouth and Cromer, where the convoys moving north and south passed each other and the offshore sands left little room for evasive actions during an E-boat attack.

But the E-boats did not always rely on *Stichansatz* or any other form of direct confrontation. Laying mines in the path of approaching convoys worked equally well and did not risk losing boats in duels with MGBs. Sometimes the E-boats merely exploited their better sea-keeping qualities to go out on nights when weather conditions prevented Allied craft from venturing forth to meet them. That is what happened on the night of November 5, 1943. Radio intelligence persuaded the skippers of several E-boat flotillas based at Rotterdam and Ijmuiden that they could operate unmolested, their adversaries having been forbidden to sail in a severe storm. From their perspective, they were right to go. In a sea that would have likely smashed most MGBs and MTBs, the E-boats sank at least two ships by laying a mine barrier and torpedoed several others from a large northbound convoy.

But, as Harro Garmsen discovered, such moments became increasingly rare in the small-boat war. "There was no air support on our side; anything in the air was hostile," he said. "The element of surprise, so necessary for small, fast and hard-hitting boats did not exist any more. Radar had seen to that."

In fact, 1944 was a dreadful year for the E-boats in the English Channel. Fifty-three were lost, and the trend continued. Another thirteen were destroyed in the first few months of 1945. Garmsen himself narrowly missed being killed on numerous occasions. Two boats of his 2. *Schnellbootflottille* went down on April 7, 1945, during a bitter fight with MTBs in the mouth of the Humber River. "I was lucky," recalled Garmsen. "I was not involved in that encounter because I was away. Maybe some of you will remember that scrap," he said in 1989, while standing in front of his former adversaries meeting in Toronto. There were no takers; nor, in all likelihood, was it expected there would be. Only a ripple of sorrowful understanding greeted his remark. They knew what he meant. Several of Garmsen's friends had perished. He himself would have been killed, if not by his hosts then by others just like them. It was their job.

Listening to Garmsen speak, whether movingly of lost comrades or the daily rituals of life aboard an E-boat, it is hard not to be struck by the similarities with that of Coastal Forces. Both had their share of eager young men enamoured with the prospect of "riding roaring boats at breakneck speed" to do the other side in. Both had their superstitions which, in the case of the E-boat crews, included never sailing on a Friday the thirteenth. They also refused to eat fish after receiving sailing orders so that "fish would not join fish," just as they would not go to sea wearing shirts with ties: it signified an intent to meet one's maker. "And we always left an unfinished card game on the table to create a serious need for returning," said Garmsen. Here were superstitions the Allied raiders could appreciate. They weren't that different from their own.

In one important respect, however, the E-boat service differed from Coastal Forces. It was considered an élite formation which, like the dreaded U-boats, was involved in offensive actions to the last, despite its frustrations. Indeed the atmosphere in which E-boat crews operated was so akin to that of their *untersee* cousins that to imagine a film called "Das E-boot" (a mild corruption of Rudolph Petersen's 1981 film masterpiece, *Das Boot*) would not be overly stretching the point.

The service was also a tightly knit family, Garmsen revealed. Many E-boat officers came from the same Naval College class, which bred a certain fraternal competitiveness. Some were well-to-do and had enjoyed the benefits of their class by indulging during the pre-war years in such pursuits as motor racing and yachting, which has a familiar ring to it. Numerous sources give examples of MGB and MTB skippers hailing their E-boat counterparts as they passed at night in the English Channel in search of each other's coastal convoys: such tales are difficult to accept, except metaphorically. The greatest of all the Allied small-boat raiders, Robert Peverell Hichens, certainly knew a few of the E-boat skippers from his racing days on the Continent. Yet he, especially, would not have hesitated in sight of any opportunity to engage the enemy, for that is what the E-boat skippers were in the final analysis—foe, not friend.

Respect was a different matter entirely. This was earned by both sides. There was chivalry, too, except when the Gestapo was rumoured to be aboard the E-boats, riding shotgun on the bridge, their Lugers tucked into glistening leather holsters and a menacing pout forewarning the skippers and ratings. Mac Knox was certainly one of those who believed the reports. "This was a development which really ruined the morale of those E-boat crews," he said ruefully. Daniel Lang concurred. The Gestapo had changed everything, although the Canadians were occasionally sympathetic towards their counterparts. "The funny part is we got to know what those men were like from some of the British sailors who had been captured by them," said Lang. "We'd get to know their names, and a sort of sketch of their personalities. I gather they had quite accurate information on us, too."

Lang also said that captured sailors generally got back to England within about three weeks. "The German captains would pick up our survivors and release them in France or Holland, just let our men go, and they'd work down from a chain in the underground, through France, into Spain. Golly! That was well known! As long as there were no Gestapo involved," he said. "As long as they were captured by the *Kriegsmarine* they were fine."

Such tales enliven the mythology of small-boat warfare, but it is difficult to judge their accuracy. How much either side knew about the other's personnel remains an open question. (According to naval historian Donald Graves, the war diaries of E-boats that fought in the English Channel as well as documents from the FdS do not reveal in-depth profiles of the Canadians.) Nor is there any hard evidence to support the claim that captured MTB or MGB crew members were sent back to England. Still, the anecdotal record cannot be ignored completely.

Of course both sides were eager to learn as much as they could about each other, particularly the details of their boats. The capture of an MGB in September 1942 gave the FdS a certain tactical advantage, as well as an opportunity to dissect the small high-speed craft designed specially to thwart E-boats in the English Channel. The British also captured one of their adversary's boats. Fittingly, it was Hichens who brought one back to be analyzed. But the episode was not without its twist of irony. One day while sitting in a secretary's office waiting to see the shore-based Staff Officer, Operations (otherwise known as SOO), Hichens was idly flipping through the pages of a 1938 edition of *Jane's Fighting Ships*. "Suddenly my attention was riveted," he said. "There before my incredulous eyes was an admirable photo of an E-boat exact in every detail like the one we had captured the year before. The raised foredeck, the bridge, the four torpedoes, two of them re-loads, the let-in torpedo tubes, the large after compass, the low side rails, the smoke apparatus. I collected my scattered wits and read the paragraph beneath."

It turned out to be an advertisement for Lürssen Werft, a shipbuilding yard in Bremen-Vegesack, Germany. "The whole thing seemed too fantastic," Hichens protested. "The reiterated instructions to bring one back alive at all costs; the intense interest in all the details we could guess at or find out; the continual bombardment of questions on every point, even as to whether the engines were diesels, carried on for weeks over Admiralty tele-phone lines; the tremendous discussions and controversies as to maximum speed....And here it was all laid out for us in *Jane's*. Come see, come buy!"

Hichens angrily suggested that prior to the outbreak of war the

Admiralty, had it been as curious then, could have bought all the E-boats it needed.

His bitterness might have been tempered by the fact that, like the British boats, E-boats evolved continually throughout the war to meet changing demands. Harro Garmsen said that when he joined the small-boat service in 1944, the E-boats were "faster, more heavily armed and better equipped than the models of the earlier war years." They had to be. British MGBs were forever in pursuit. But added Garmsen: "With a top speed of 45 knots we knew that we could outrun anything afloat."

It is curious, this interest in being able to outrun the enemy. The subject was raised during the First World War, too. Admiral Bacon, in his account recalling the exploits of the Dover Patrol, said, "The one marked characteristic of the enemy was his disinclination to lose a vessel." Such an overly cautious mentality differed from that of the army which he said "never hesitated to lose men." Thus, Bacon insisted the enemy's ideas were in fact predominantly military rather than naval. They reminded the Admiral of "saving the guns," an ancient *military* tradition.

It is interesting to apply Bacon's argument to the experience of the Second World War. In 1940 the German Navy found its ability to meet the British on the war's high seas severely limited. Not enough capital ships had been built owing to the limitations placed on Germany by the Treaty of Versailles. This partly explained the Third Reich's predilection for submarines and *Schnellboote*, which could be produced clandestinely. Of the ships that did exist at the outbreak of hostilities, too many were lost or put out of action during the Norwegian campaign in April 1940. Indeed, it is widely felt that an important factor in the success of evacuating so many Allied troops at Dunkirk was the Royal Navy's ability to operate without fear of retribution by enemy warships. There simply weren't enough to go around, given the Third Reich's wide area of interest, to risk losing any more in the English Channel. Interestingly, the only exception to this were the E-boats, which sank a number of British vessels and continued to enjoy certain advantages in the English Channel until, say, the middle of 1942.

So why, if they were successful, did E-boats purportedly exhibit a disinclination to fight?

There appears to be no simple explanation. By all accounts, the E-boat captains and their crews were heroic enough in their assigned roles. "They were bold, young—like fighter pilots," said Garmsen. Perhaps it was because they saw as their primary target Allied coastal convoys, not the MTBs or MGBs. Garmsen added that the heavy armament of MGBs especially "was considered a good reason by us to try to steer clear of them."

In all fairness to the E-boat crews, the British were critical of just about everyone else serving aboard small boats, accusing not only the Axis—particularly the Italians in their high-speed MAS boats—of faint-heartedness but also, occasionally, their American cousins aboard the PTs. The latter made their first appearance in the English Channel in April of 1944. Their primary task was to help defend the flanks of the attack on Normandy in June, and to guard the subsequent flow of cross-Channel shipping. They were used also for a number of "false nose jobs," landing secret agents employed by the OSS on the coast of France. Some undoubtedly deserved credit for their actions, among them, Lieutenant Commander John D. Bulkeley, USN. Bulkeley was famous for having rescued General MacArthur from the Philippines in 1941, an episode sensationally recorded in a book called *They Were Expendable* published the following year (even during the war, the Americans were not slow to capitalize on a good marketing opportunity). His reputation was such that Eisenhower personally had requested his services in the English Channel.*

On D-Day, Bulkeley led as many as sixty PTs into action off the

---

*MacArthur called his saviour "Buckaroo" Bulkeley, which if known to the British might have prompted a few raised eyebrows. It should be added that Eisenhower, as a major, had served as MacArthur's assistant in Manila and so would have had a vicarious if not keen interest in the man who rescued his former superior officer.

coast of Normandy. With him, briefly, was the film director John Ford, now a captain leading a photographic unit assigned to cover the invasion while also preparing to make a dramatic feature based on *They Were Expendable*. They had met previously. In fact, according to a Ford biographer, Bulkeley was invited by the director to visit him at his suite at Claridge's in London. Bulkeley and a fellow officer knocked on the door for several minutes until a gruff voice answered, ordering them inside. Ford was still in bed, but when introduced to Bulkeley "he insisted on getting up and saluting the Medal of Honor winner—even though he was stark naked."

Such was the effect that Bulkeley had on others. He was a larger-than-life hero, at least among many Yanks in Britain during the war.

But he was also about the only noteworthy PT skipper who fought in the English Channel. They had arrived too late to make much of a difference, for one thing. The open contempt sometimes reserved for the millions of American soldiers, sailors and airmen that had invaded England during the war, with their boorish manners and inability to say "leff-tenant" instead of "loo-tenant," also had a bearing on the way they were treated. How could anyone be gracious to this callow, wide-eyed lot who had only arrived but were prepared to reap the spoils of victory earned by others? That the colossal industrial might of the United States was also essential to this victory remained an indignity not too deeply hidden beneath such resentment.

But even this did not alter the fact that in four years of warfare, a bond had formed between the MTB crews and their adversaries. They had fought so often, knew each other by name and tactics, and adhered to a code of chivalry that had served them well (until the Gestapo arrived and spoiled it), they could not help but feel this was *their* war, however absurd, quixotic or outmoded such a sentiment might be viewed today. Harro Garmsen said that he and his fellow E-boat crew members admired the long tradition of the Royal Navy and were very aware of the lack of a similar inheritance, yet in battle they fought as equals, vying for supremacy. Both sides were raised in this Old World ethos.

So, too, were the Canadians, even if they insisted on a distinct identity and mixed their avowed patriotism to "King and Country" with a rough-hewn frontier mentality. They were stubborn, and fiercely independent all right, but unlike the Yanks they could sing "Britannia Rules the Waves," and were easily moved by it.

Perhaps, then, they would not have minded so much to learn that Garmsen and his mates lumped the Canadians together with the British, Australians and New Zealanders—as well as Norwegians and the few Poles serving with Coastal Forces—and called them by a single evocative nickname. "To us you were 'Tommies,' " said Garmsen. "Your boats were handled skilfully, boldly and with determination." That, evidently, said it all.

For their part, the E-boat crews had a cheekiness that was both refreshing and familiar to the British, and perhaps especially the Canadians, who had a maverick reputation of their own. Retiring to their concrete harbours along the coast of France, the E-boat captains grew weary of firing recognition signals that were not always acknowledged promptly except by gunfire, so instead they flashed by Aldis messages that began with "You assholes...," which usually did the trick. Garmsen said his flotilla commander tried this once and was called in by the trigger-happy commandant of the coast protection unit, "who had one stripe more on his sleeve and resented being addressed in such a disrespectful manner by someone not his equal."

Had they known more intimate details of their adversaries' everyday life the British might have also laughed, as Garmsen did, at the 3rd E-boat Flotilla's Supply Officer, who had barely managed to escape the advancing Allies in Sicily. "He crossed the Straits of Messina in a rowboat clutching the flotilla cashbox, which he brought back safely," Garmsen recalled mirthfully. Such a character could have been just as easily a creation of Evelyn Waugh.

But by the end of 1944, it was becoming increasingly difficult for the E-boat crews to find much amusement in their predicament. In the Mediterranean, too, ever since Italy's capitulation in fact, the E-boat crews were reduced to living as water gypsies, moving from port to port while never sure of the welcome they would receive. In July 1943, Oberleutnant Schmidt, commanding *S54*, entered Venice, moored his boat in the harbour and was immediately surrounded by *militaria* ordering him to surrender. Schmidt bluffed his way out of this stand-off, informing the Italians he was in the vanguard of a large invasion force that would destroy the city if he was harmed. This had a sobering effect on Schmidt's would-be captors. It is said five thousand of them surrendered to the E-boat skipper and his crew of twenty-six. Several days later, with propitious timing, a large German army unit just happened to stumble into Venice, to the relief of Schmidt and the crew of *S54*.

Such opportunities as Schmidt had enjoyed were soon a thing of the past. The Allied march up into the boot of Italy in 1943, and the landings at both Normandy and along the south coast of France in 1944 no longer threatened merely to hammer at the "anvil" to which Hitler's grand strategy had been reduced, but to break it entirely. In this desperate atmosphere a number of fantastic weapons were introduced to the conflict. In June 1944 the world's first jet fighter, the Messerschmidt 262, became operational. More worrisome that month was the use against England of the first *V1* rockets. Ten were launched in the initial salvo; only four crossed the English Channel, one landing in London, killing six civilians. Nevertheless, only a few days later Hitler raged in front of his generals that the *V1*s would force Britain out of the war. He was wrong, of course, although throughout the summer as more of the "buzz bombs" were launched—and an improved version, the *V2*, was introduced—thousands were killed in England. Hitler's scientists were also experimenting with another kind of bomb, the human torpedo, as well as explosives-laden small boats to be used against Allied shipping. The Italians had done this already in the Mediterranean; indeed, they were experts in the field. Not surprisingly, so too were the Japanese, whose one-man *shinyo* boats, the marine equivalent of *kamikaze* aircraft, were mass-produced during the latter stages of the war in the Pacific. In July 1944, on the west beach at Trouville just south of Le Havre, the Germans launched the first of their "secret weapons" into the Allied anchorages off the French coast. These were human torpedoes, or "Negroes," as the racist Nazis called them. They were really two torpedoes strapped to each other, the pilot in the upper portion hunched beneath a Perspex dome allowing him to see his target when he pressed the trigger mechanism that released a warhead below. In their first run at the enemy, the "Negroes" were only marginally successful. Most important: they lost the element of surprise. The slow-moving craft were easily spotted on the surface once the British had been alerted to their possible use, and as they were virtually defenceless they could be sunk easily by gunfire. Losses of these weapons soon outran their meagre successes. In a matter of weeks, they were no longer taken seriously by either side. Nor were the Allies alarmed by their adversary's use of small boats armed with explosive charges in the bows, which were aimed at a target and let go at full speed to do their worst, leaving the sole operator to jump clear at an opportune moment. British MTBs and MGBs had a field day picking these off before they were able to effect any damage. Of all the Jules Verne contraptions introduced by the enemy late in the war, only his fleet of one-man midget submarines, known as "Beavers," caused the Royal Navy much concern. These were introduced in November 1944, months behind their production schedule. Nevertheless, between December 1944 and April 1945 they sank some ninety thousand tons of Allied shipping in the Scheldt. One "Beaver" pilot, Senior Midshipman Langsdorff, succeeded in entering the harbour at Antwerp and firing both his torpedoes into the lock gates, which were put out of action for several weeks as a result. But Langsdorff never returned from his mission. Indeed, the majority of the "Beaver" skippers were killed off.

It is easy, with the benefit of hindsight, to mock such efforts, although it should be remembered that the British experimented with similar weapons. For their part, the E-boat crews might well have viewed "Negroes," "Beavers" and especially the suicide boats with more than disdain. They were gimmicks, desperately employed even if they succeeded in claiming a few enemy lives. And while precious resources were being squandered on their development or use, the E-boat crews in the English Channel continued to harass Allied movements, relying primarily on their courage and fortitude. In the minds of naval strategists, they represented a vain hope of regaining an advantage in the tonnage war if only to forestall the collapse of the Third Reich. But to the E-boat crews, it became a matter of survival while attempting to preserve their self-esteem—and professionalism.

Thus death, and its often arbitrary nature, became the last obvious link between the small-boat raiders on either side. Harro Garmsen saw enough of it. "We buried one young officer who, upon returning to port, used a machine gun to support himself as he vaulted to shore. The thing went off." Similarly, he once witnessed the destruction of an E-boat when it hit one of its own beach mines while returning to port. "It was a matter of pride for the young lieutenant commanding it not to ask for navigational aid," recalled Garmsen. Nor did the young officer's mistaken hubris permit him the use of lights for even a brief period as he motored towards the shore, which was one of his options. "So he and twelve of his crew lost their lives because he thought he knew where he was."

How men reacted to death was their own business. But like their counterparts with Coastal Forces, the E-boat crews were reminded daily that it was a distinct possibility, a fact revealed by an excerpt from Harro Garmsen's notebook, which he used to record impressions of *S 221*'s actions between January and March 1945:

Jan 23	*Got scare of a lifetime, when V2 was launched 400 yards away on Dutch coast. Attacked by planes.*
Jan 24	*Mine operation, Thames, uneventful.*
Jan 29	*Mine operation, Scheldt, gale force winds, in action with MGBs, one destroyer, attacked by planes.*
Feb 5	*Torpedo attempt against convoy, ran into thunderstorm, broken off, attacked by planes.*

Feb 18	*Mine operation in Thames, 17 hours, foggy conditions, surface action with MTBs, destroyers, S 177 hit, rudder damaged.*
Feb 20	*Torpedo operation within sight of British coast, surface action with MTB and destroyers, no targets found. Attacked by planes.*
Mar 6–10	*Instant readiness.*
Mar 11	*Mining attempt, ran into MTBs, broken off.*
Mar 14	*Mining attempt, attacked by planes, broken off.*
Mar 17	*Mining operation, Thames, attacked by planes, ran into destroyer, prolonged surface action.*
Mar 21	*Torpedo attempt against convoy, attacked by planes, S 181 sunk by rocket, rescued survivors... prolonged bombing.*

In two months of action off the English and Dutch coasts, Garmsen said only one operation had been carried out without interference from MTBs, MGBs, destroyers or aircraft. Two of his flotilla's boats were sunk, one damaged; a number of men were killed. The following month, two more E-boats were lost. Whenever this happened, said Garmsen, he and his mates tuned in to the BBC, which would broadcast the names of crew members that were rescued. Garmsen remembered the BBC invariably followed such broadcasts with the ominous assurance, "They belong to the few surviving E-boat men of the war."

They listened to the BBC for more than this. "We were great fans of Glenn Miller, the Andrews Sisters, Artie Shaw and the like," said Garmsen, who added that Miller's "In the Mood" became the unofficial signature tune of 2. *Schnellbootflottille*.

They were so alike, even as they tried to kill each other.

12

Disaster at Ostend

IN THE MIDDLE OF January 1945, the 29th Flotilla had occasion to celebrate. It was leaving Felixstowe to be based in Ostend full time as part of the Coastal Forces Mobile Unit No. 1. Moreover, as the flotilla roared across the Channel on this brilliant sunny day, the quiet Glen Creba used the occasion to announce by radio to the other speeding boats in the formation that he was now engaged to the young Canadian army nurse with the sparkling personality that all officers in the flotilla had come to know during their courtship the past few months. Bobby Moyse, intent on extending his congratulations, broke formation and slammed into Bones Burk's boat, putting a hole in the bow of his own craft. Well, what was one more hole? The boats had been so often riddled and splintered, if it had not been for the patches covering these scars called "tingles," they would have all resembled pieces of floating Swiss cheese.

The new location in the Belgian port town meant saving long hours pounding back to Felixstowe after their patrols. Besides, Ostend promised to offer pleasant diversions as the city tried to struggle back to pre-war comforts after five years under German occupation. Nightclubs were reopening and there was a proliferation of new restaurants scattered in the town centre around the beautiful old Gothic cathedral. The 29th's skippers found pleasant billets in a charming hotel named the Queen Mary whose staff not very many months before had tended other motor torpedo boat officers as guests, the German E-boat skippers who had used the same hotel.

Unfortunately, there were no suitable accommodations for the crews who had to make do once more with living aboard their tiny shorts. The truth was that the routine was much the same as it was in Felixstowe. Out on patrol at darkness, back at dawn. There was no relief from the tension of these nightly sorties. The anticipation of battle kept the level of adrenalin up and the winter seas demanded vigilance. As the officers settled in, they acquired a captured German Volkswagen, which was christened Adolph, to speed them back and forth from the Queen Mary to their berths in the harbour. Law's artist's eye absorbed the colour of this foreign landscape.

> Fishermen were a constant part of the scene at Ostend, as they clopped along in their sabots with salty caps at a jaunty angle. The jerseys of the young fishermen, like their owners, were a brilliant, sharp red, while those of the old fishermen, like their owners, were mellowed by age, sun and salt. Screaming seagulls hovered over the boats waiting for their bit as the fish were cleaned, and when anything was thrown overboard they would dive into the water after it fighting among themselves. The little armada of fishing boats, their warm red sails hanging loosely, drying in the hot sun, were gaily striped with brilliant colours, each in the individual colour scheme chosen by its owner.

This was the peaceful scene that met the departing and returning torpedo boats as they gurgled at low throttle through the crowded port jammed with the stained grey warships making their way to the end of the harbour. The flotilla was berthed in a basin of water called The Crique. From above, it resembled the thumb of a man; it was surrounded by a jumble of jetties, ramshackle warehouses and scurrying vehicles bringing supplies and men to the ships.

February 14 dawned bright and sunny. By noon, a force four wind had been clocked and whitecaps were visible at sea beyond the harbour. Seven of the 29th's nine boats were snugly rafted together in The Crique, most of their crews aboard sleeping or tending to the various needs the shorts constantly required. One of the boats, Bishop's MTB *464*, was scheduled for gunnery trials at sea. Bishop himself would not take her out. He was taking the day off and planned to take in a movie in town. Under the command of Sub-Lieutenant George Hobart, her first officer, MTB *464* inched out of the crowded harbour and into a growing sea that Hobart decided was too rough to effectively carry out the gunnery exercise. He steered back to Ostend. Besides, the centre engine of MTB *464* was running rough because of water contamination in the gas tanks and had to be shut down. The boat had been troubled with a mixture of fuel and water over the past week, a condition that worried Fred Walden, the same petty officer whose efforts in November in plugging a shell hole and getting back to Felixstowe had won him a Mention-in-Dispatches, an award he had only recently received. When the contaminated water was first discovered, Walden reported the fact to Hobart, who passed it on to the staff at the Coastal Forces Mobile Unit office across the harbour. Although Hobart was told someone would be detailed to pump out the tanks, still after a week no one had arrived to do the job. Walden again asked for help but was told by the chief motor mechanic of the Canadian Base Staff that there wasn't anyone available and he would have to do the job himself. This he had done a couple of days previously but after the aborted gunnery trial patrol, it was apparent to Walden the tanks were still contaminated. MTB *464* was scheduled for a patrol that night and the conscientious Walden knew if the tanks weren't pumped the patrol would be cancelled.

A little after 3 p.m., and assisted by only one rating, Walden connected the boat's bilge pump to a long length of rubber hose, snaked it through the boat and into the middle gas tank and began pumping. The water in the tank was sucked up the hose through the bilge pump in the engine room and out a discharge fitting about six inches from the water on the starboard quarter. The pumping went on for about twenty minutes and by Walden's estimate it had discharged about fifty gallons of fluid which he judged to be water by checking a dip-stick into the tank.

The 100 high-octane gas contained a green colouring substance to make it easier to recognize in the event of leaks or spills. But whatever was being pumped from the boat was already probably discoloured by the sludge in the tank. Trying to recognize it in the oily water of The Crique was impossible. About the time Walden was finishing his pumping operation, a Royal Navy MTB was returning to harbour. Her skipper, Lieutenant Commander W. B. G. Leith, detected a strong smell of gas and after tying up hustled over to the C.F.M.U. office to report the odour which he suspected was 100 octane. The gas was highly inflammable and the strong presence of it in the air was to Leith a potentially dangerous situation. Four other RN officers also remembered smelling gas but none thought it that important to alert anyone.

There were standing orders setting out procedures in practices of both fuelling and dumping gas, and in most cases these orders were observed. Yet, as the war ground on, crews sometimes ignored the safety procedures for any number of reasons, fatigue, haste and a false feeling of security because the fuelling operations had become so familiar. For instance, in the 65th Flotilla it was discovered after the sailor stole the grenade and committed suicide that he had gotten it from an ammunition locker that was left unlocked. Standing orders or not, taking shortcuts in both flotillas was commonplace.

Undoubtedly of more concern to Leith as he trundled to report the smell of gas was the fact that the numerous MTBs and minesweepers in the harbour were each ticking time bombs, packed with huge amounts of ammunition, torpedo warheads, depth charges and various calibre ammo from the six-pounder shells to .303s. The fact was every ship was a floating arsenal.

All the elements were present for disaster.

The seven Canadian MTBs were all tightly rafted together that afternoon of February 14. If the reader can imagine the "thumb" of water that was The Crique, picture four rows of boats tied side-by-side all facing towards the end of the thumb, three boats in the first row closest to the end and four boats in each of the three rows behind. The Canadian boats were mixed in with several Royal Navy shorts in the first three rows. The fourth row of four boats were all RN Dog boats.

Stoker Jack Johnson had spent most of the afternoon in the mess deck of MTB *466*, which was against the dock in the third row, being "bugged" by a mate, Tony Caruso, of Niagara Falls, Ontario, to go ashore with him to buy a suitcase. "I was trying to write letters," Johnson recalled, "but Caruso kept after me to go into town with him. Finally I said, 'Okay, let's go.'"

Everyone who was in Ostend that day had their own account of what happened at two minutes after four o'clock. John Howard, the First Lieutenant on Chaffey's boat, MTB *465*, was on dockside talking with Keith Scobie and John Cunningham when he heard someone shout, "Fire!" Howard, whose back was to the boats, turned and his heart skipped a beat. Flames were shooting up between his boat, MTB *462* and the three other boats in the second row. To his horror, event though it was mere seconds, he knew the boat was gone. Helplessly he watched as the fire engulfed the entire row of boats and leaped to the third row setting ablaze all the boats there. At the same time, the fire was licking its way across the water towards the first three boats at the head of The Crique. A stoker aboard one of these boats crash-started the engine of MTB *485* and gunned ahead to the end of The Crique carrying along two other boats rafted beside it. Already the stern of his boat was ablaze. As these three boats moved forward some of the crew began heaving ammunition overboard while others battled the flames on the burning stern.

Then at five minutes past four o'clock, just three minutes after the fire broke out, came the first explosion. To those who experienced it, the sound was borne on a shimmering wall of heat that rose out of the harbour sweeping in all directions, an ear-piercing blast so powerful it broke window-panes a mile from the epicentre, violently shaking the ground under the feet of people several miles away.

The explosion was so tremendous the blast was heard in England across the North Sea. The source of the explosion was the dreaded 100-octane gas. Thousands of gallons of the lethal liquid erupted in a blinding flash in the tanks of MTB 465. The boat disintegrated as did a Royal Navy torpedo boat beside it.

The first blast rained sheets of flames across the entire harbour. The four British Dog boats in the fourth row behind the Canadian boats, already set on fire from the original flames on the surface of the water, were now burning fiercely.

Their crews panicked. Those closest to shore jumped on to the jetty. Others leaped into the burning water to escape the flaming decks.

Then came a second explosion, just as powerful as the first. MTB 462 disappeared in a white fireball spewing tongues of fire hundreds of yards into the air that rained down and set more boats aflame. The blast of the second explosion parted mooring lines on two boats sending them adrift into the harbour like fire-ships. And worse, the ebbing tide carried other burning ships into the harbour.

As the fire spread there followed an almost continuous rumble of smaller explosions as ammunition, shells, depth charges and torpedoes began blowing up.

Bedlam was supreme.

Chuff-Chuff Chaffey, skipper of MTB 465, whose boat was the first to blow up, was a mile away watching a movie with Craig Bishop, Dick Paddon and John Shand. When they reached the town square, they saw the harbour was an inferno of heat, billowing black smoke and huge fireballs floating skyward like flaming balloons.

Joe Adam, skipper of MTB 466, the same boat that Jack Johnson had left shortly before the fire broke out, had himself gone ashore about the same time as Johnson. Adam had left his First

Lieutenant, Bill Hale of Toronto, on board to secure the boat and grant leave to the crew. It was Hale who let Johnson and Caruso go ashore to buy the suitcase. When the fire broke out, Hale was seen dashing below decks trying to put out flames in the forepeak with a hand extinguisher. He was never seen again. When Adam heard the first explosion, he was in the officers' quarters at the stately Queen Mary Hotel. Running back to the harbour, he was told his boat was gone. Assembling a collection of sailors and soldiers who were standing around in a state of shock, Adam led them to the three MTBs that had been moved en masse. They were now tied up at the very end of The Crique. Adam and his "volunteers" jumped aboard and helped to dump the remaining ammo.

Glen Creba was asleep at the Queen Mary (he was scheduled to go on patrol that night) and was so tired he slept through the explosions. When he was awakened and told of the disaster, he immediately went to the harbour. The scene that greeted him was one of utter devastation. Boats were burning, docks were ablaze and various buildings throughout the harbour had been set afire. He joined Adam aboard the three boats at the end of the harbour to help neutralize the torpedoes by removing the primers from the warheads.

Back at the Queen Mary, the officers began the grim accounting of survivors and victims. As night fell came the realization of the depth of the disaster. Beyond in the harbour, rescue craft picked their way through the burning debris retrieving bodies, and on shore a stream of vehicles and ambulances came and went, eerily silhouetted against a few fires still burning. As the night wore on, the officers went over their rosters of names disbelieving there were so many men still unaccounted for. Perhaps some were stranded in the harbour.

By morning the staggering loss was confirmed. Twenty-three Canadians were dead. The total number killed, including Belgian civilians, reached seventy-three. The fire also destroyed twelve motor torpedo boats, five of them of the 29th Flotilla.*

---

* A list of the dead is contained in the Appendix.

Tony Law and Bones Burk, two of the originals of the flotilla, were not in Ostend on the tragic day. Burk, who had fallen ill with jaundice and had just been discharged from hospital, was on his way back to Canada. Law left the very afternoon of the fire to take his boat back to Felixstowe to get a radar set repaired that had baffled the technicians in Ostend. He heard the shattering news the following day over a large gin presented by the man who brought the terrible news.

The navy called a Board of Inquiry, heard over one hundred witnesses and delivered its findings. In a carefully worded opinion, the Board found that the gas dumped from Walden's boat was responsible for the fire but added there was equally sufficient evidence that other short-boat crews pumped fuel overboard and in all likelihood contributed to the amount of gas in The Crique on the fateful day. Fred Walden was to say years later, "No one knows really what happened."

This was especially true as to what caused the spark. Some possible causes listed were defective leads from shore power to the boats, a spark from an auxiliary engine in one of the boats, even sun rays that became focused through masthead lights or reflected off the glass of a porthole. The most likely cause, the Board said, was that some sailor tossed a lighted cigarette butt into the water.

The commander of the Ostend base, M. A. Brind, RN, was relieved of duty, censored because he hadn't effectively enforced standing orders prohibiting the discharge of inflammable fluid into the harbour. Law, Chaffey and Bishop were criticized by the Board as well, Law for not issuing orders to ensure there were sufficient officers and ratings on board the MTBs during non-working hours. Even though Chaffey was acting as the Senior Officer in Law's absence for the one day, he too was expected to issue the same order, the Board said. Bishop received the Board's displeasure for not having been aboard MTB *464* when it went to sea earlier that day for gunnery trials. If he had been aboard, he would have known that the problem with the contaminated tank still had not been solved. There was an additional observation from the Board that was considered a most spurious remark by all who read it on the character of Craig Bishop. The Board said Bishop "appeared to take very little personal interest in the condition of his MTB." This was a cruel remark in the face of Bishop's courageous record and fighting spirit, someone who had the reputation of an aggressive, determined skipper, whose honours won in battle attested to his courage.

No mention was made anywhere in the findings that the officers and men of 29th Flotilla may well have reached the extreme limits of their physical and emotional endurance. For nearly a year the 29th, as was the case for the 65th, had performed brilliantly as a fighting unit, facing the enemy at close quarters patrol after patrol, engagement after engagement. In reading the flotilla's action reports, there is a feeling of astonishment that any of them survived at all the guns of battle at sea and the deprivation that came with service in the short boats. Ironically, it was not the enemy that destroyed the fighting flotilla. It was fate.

The fire at Ostend doomed the existence of the 29th Flotilla. It ceased to operate as a fighting unit. Shortly, the remaining boats were paid off, the crews reassigned to other ships and duties.

In the closing days of the Second World War, Angus L. Macdonald, the Minister of National Defence for Naval Services, the man who had led Canada's navy from the very beginning of the conflict, rose in the House of Commons to pay tribute to all who had served in the Royal Canadian Navy. Yet his words may well have been directed at Canada's small-boat warriors.

"Our men have fought on every sea of the world. They have brought honour and glory to this land. They have been actors in a great drama which now seems to be drawing steadily, inexorably, to its close. Soon they will come back—those who are left—back over the great oceans where their laurels and honours have been gathered.

"Yet I venture to say that so long as memory lasts, the recollection of these great days will be with them, and along with the consciousness of duty done, they will carry in their hearts forever the image of a gallant ship and the spell of the great sea."

As of February 14, 1945, His Majesty's Canadian Motor Torpedo Boats of the 29th Flotilla were no more.

Within two days, five Dog boats of Canada's 65th Flotilla

arrived at Ostend harbour, its crews sobered by the news of the disaster that had struck her sister flotilla. The 65th was now alone to carry the fight to the enemy.

13

Costly Victory

HE HORROR OF THE FIRE and explosion that killed so many
sailors daily haunted the crews of the 65th Flotilla for the
remainder of February. For weeks, bodies came to the
surface, were recovered and funeral services conducted. Some
men were buried in Ostend's Nouveau Cemetery, others taken to
sea to be piped to their final rest, all the corpses weighted down
and stitched in canvas shrouds, the dignified yet simple ceremony
that went back to the days of Nelson; a final prayer, the shrill of the
bo'sun's pipe and one by one the bodies were committed to the
deep to mingle with the bones of the enemy dead below. Sunday,
February 20, six days following the disaster, the formal mourning
ended. Officers and ratings were drawn up on the decks of a group
of motor torpedo boats in Ostend harbour for a quiet memorial
service.

Then, it was back to war.

Two days later the boats of the 65th Flotilla were back in action.
On February 22, Bert Morrow and a British MTB shot up a group
of E-boats and the next night Morrow, Knox, S. O. Greening,
Collins and a new skipper, G. D. Pattison, engaged six of the fast
enemy torpedo boats. Before the month was out, the 65th went to

235

sea thirty-eight times. There was to be no reprieve from the deadly routine, even for a few of the 29th's remaining crews.

Sailing with the 65th were five ratings and two officers from the decimated 29th. With a touch of gallows humour, the sailors joked they'd rather face the Germans again than be posted back to the hated manning pool that was HMCS *Niobe*. Kirkpatrick noted the volunteers were "welcomed with open arms." Their decision to return to battle surely exemplified the indomitable spirit that had so characterized the fighting 29th Flotilla.

The continuing spectre of death and injury in the small-boat war was not lost on the navy. With the war clearly in its final stages, the pressures and fears were even more intense.

"About this time, a lot of people were beginning to ask themselves, 'Am I going to get through this?' " recalled Norn Garriock. "Remember, we'd been going at it now for a year. The irony of not making it was a question I think we all asked ourselves. It put a few people over the deep end." One, a gunner, went berserk, spraying the harbour with machine-gun fire. "We talked some sense into him and he stopped," Garriock said. "Fortunately no one was hurt."

To alleviate the tension, the 29th's former flotilla surgeon, Lieutenant William Leslie, of Sault Ste. Marie, Ontario, recommended a "compulsory rest leave" for all remaining members of the 65th, a suggestion that was quickly endorsed by the navy, to go into effect beginning in March. Leslie had been commended for his "heroic" efforts in the aftermath of the explosion and fire. Leslie was entering Ostend when the first blast shook the city, as it happened, returning from a nearby military hospital with a truck-load of medical supplies. On seeing the fire, Leslie raced onto the jetty and "performed splendid services in attending to wounded men and worked gallantly under flying rockets and debris rescuing the injured." Recognizing the trauma brought on by the disastrous fire, and knowing intimately of the stress the small-boat sailors had been under for months on end, his compulsory rest leave was warmly endorsed. But the more pressing demands of the war deprived all of immediate relief. The boats were still faced with replacement shortages. "Unfortunately," Kirkpatrick noted, "it [the plan] has had to be abandoned for the moment." It was not until the following month that the first sailors were able to take advantage of the compulsory leave.

Throughout March the action continued unabated. A brief, explosive engagement in the early morning of March 18 only confirmed the fact that the war was still deadly, that victory was beyond the horizon. Malcolm Knox and A. M. Byers, who had taken over Greening's boat, were idling in the darkness off the approaches to the Scheldt Estuary, hoping to intercept four E-boats that radar-hunting aircraft above had discovered and plotted. Knox and Byers got within a thousand yards before the German torpedo boats spotted them and turned to escape with their greater speed. Nevertheless, they roared in, shot up the second and third boats in the enemy formation, and silenced the fourth in line. In the almost laconic style of the action reports, Knox reported on this occasion the plight of the fourth enemy boat. "A large cloud of smoke was seen to billow from amidships and his hitherto accurate fire ceased," Knox said. Four sailors, two on each of the Canadian boats, were wounded in the sharp exchange and both boats suffered numerous hits from the German fire.

A curious aspect of the final days of fighting was the fact that encounters with the enemy did not slacken. They were recurring and deadly to the end. Such was the case on the night of April 12–13 for John Collins (MTB *746*), Lieutenants R. C. Smith (MTB *797*) and G. D. Pattison (MTB *727*), Les McLernon's former boat. Collins's action report for that night is as tense and as dramatic now as it was forty-five years ago.

> At 0101 four enemy E-boats were sighted right ahead steering approximately due south. Due to the poor visibility, range on sighting was two hundred yards or less and, as the combined closing speed was something over sixty knots, there was not sufficient room to alter to starboard onto a parallel course. Course was therefore altered to port to a reciprocal of the enemy's course and fire was opened at a range of 50 to 20 yards. Inaccurate fire was returned almost

immediately. The engagement was very brief, but numerous hits were observed with 6-pdr. and 20-mm. on the second, third and fourth boats in line. The fourth boat received the biggest share and was seen to pull out of line to port and either stop or reduce to a very slow speed. All four enemy ships began to smoke. Course was altered 180 degrees and an attempt was made to close the damaged E-boat which was clearly visible under our starshell. However, before the range could be closed, the enemy became obscured in his own smoke screen and, when this was finally penetrated, it was seen that he got under way again and rejoined his unit. E-boats retired at high speed and, as no further contact was made, unit resumed patrol.

In the first burst of return fire, a 20-mm. shell pierced the armour plate of the bridge in MTB 797, wounding the Commanding Officer, Gunnery Control Officer and the Coxswain. The Commanding Officer remained at his post throughout the action and took his ship back to harbour before receiving first aid. Signalman B. Frederickson, who was on the bridge when the others were wounded, took over the Coxswain's position at the helm without orders and handled the ship throughout the engagement in a highly commendable manner. In view of the fact that MTB 797 had one engine out of action, she was ordered back to harbour when the balance of the unit returned to patrol.

MTB 746 had a fire under the starboard .5 turret and forward torpedo tube caused by a light-calibre shell cutting the low-power wiring. This was quickly extinguished, but unfortunately had put the compass lights and communications out of action, which was not very helpful.

The action was rather disappointing, even though damage was inflicted on the enemy. Had they been sighted even one hundred yards sooner, we could have altered to a parallel instead of a reciprocal course and, in spite of their superior speed, maintained contact for some time. At that range, much more satisfactory results would have been obtained.

Besides Smith, 797's skipper, Jack Beeman, his first officer, was wounded. The coxswain whom Frederickson replaced was C. Laviolette. The fourth wounded on the boat was A. George, the MTB's cook.

But the last battle of the war for the small-boat raiders was fittingly enough not against the enemy but the after-effects of a colossal piss-up and the attendant hangovers the celebration produced, remembered by one of the newer officers as "monumental." This was yet another Burke whom Canada had inflicted on the enemy. Stanley was Corny Burke's younger brother, and of course no relationship to Daddy Bones Burk. Less celebrated than Burke/Burk, Stanley's fame was to come in the post-war years as a dashing foreign correspondent and later as a television anchorman for the CBC, where he projected the same élan so characteristic of the small-boat warriors when he appeared before his nightly audience on the national news in impeccably tailored pin-stripe suits and gleaming black brogues. Stanley Burke's memory of the VE-Day party was the morning after. The 65th's officers and ratings were mustered on the parade square to hear a victory speech from some British admiral or commodore who informed the bleary-eyed Canucks that he would lead them in three cheers and reminded the sailors that the correct pronunciation for "hooray" was not "haw-rah." No sooner had the admiral uttered his last "hip," when a fog-horn voice blasted across the parade square, "HAW-RAH, you old bastard!"

It *was* a party to remember. Jim Kirkpatrick recalled that after drinking the kegs of beer that the navy had provided, the flotilla then went to the rum locker for headier grog. This indiscretion required some fanciful bookkeeping when everyone sobered up, said Kirkpatrick.

> We were sent the large sum of fifty pounds from London to buy something for the troops when we were celebrating VE-Day. About a month later I got the curtest telegram saying they had no record of our spending the fifty pounds and would I report forthwith, in writing, what happened to it. So, I looked it up (and I may have the details wrong) but it wasn't 50 pounds, it was 150 they'd sent. I wrote back and I told them that they'd sent us 150 and I went on elaborating what kind of a party we'd had because it was a very good one and the aftermath of this party. I didn't even get an acknowledge-

ment of this accounting I sent the Paymaster. But this curt
telegram, as if I'd embezzled the 50 pounds. What happened
to it? Well, we had the party and we went beyond our limits
because we'd broached the rum locker and we had to keep a
few boats in service for a number of days after the crews had
departed, so we could write off the tots every day until we got
it down to an acceptable limit. Why we worried about these
things after it was all over, I don't know.

There had been much to celebrate. When the officers and men
awakened on that day in May in 1945, it was the first dawn in
nearly six years that was not accompanied by a promise of death. It
was the first dawn in a year since the 65th Flotilla had assembled
for operations in Brixham that the crews knew that they would
most surely see other sunrises. It was the first time in a spectacular
year of warring that they knew they would not be called on to go to
sea to kill and destroy the enemy.

Victory meant, too, they could now go home, forever mindful of
those who had not survived this dreadful struggle that had been
played out in the Mediterranean, the Adriatic, the Aegean, in the
Channel, and the final campaign in the North Sea, the dangerous
seas of their youth where so many of their mates died young and
far from home.

The German capitulation of 2:41 a.m., May 7, 1945, at Reims,
France, was the end of the greatest story in history, an event of
such magnitude and complexity, it has created a vast body of
literature but surprisingly little about the work of the Coastal
Forces. There have been a number of personal memoirs (and more
are said to be in the works) by British MTB skippers and by Tony
Law, whose *White Plumes Astern* gives a commander's view of
the Channel war from the bridges of MTBs *459* and *486*. In more
formal histories, Coastal Forces rate mere pages, historical foot-
notes at best. Given the dashing image the Canadian flotillas

projected and the daring, reckless tactics they employed, it was curious the lack of attention they received.

"I often wondered about that," said Norn Garriock. "I don't know the answer."

In truth, Coastal Forces performed splendidly and the losses it inflicted on the Axis powers were significant. Of the 1,600 small-boat fleet, 223 were lost, a costly number by any measure. Although the German and Italian losses of 403 were nearly double those of Coastal Forces, more than half of the enemy's 714 boats were sunk. Bryan Cooper, the British expert on torpedo boat warfare, concluded that British and Commonwealth flotillas clearly won the overall hand when it came to small-boat battles. On the other hand, Cooper pointed out, while the Canadian and British skippers sank more merchant ships, a total of 140, the German and Italian small boats nearly doubled the tonnage even though their total of merchantmen was only 99 ships. Through-out the war Coastal Forces remained a menace to the enemy who was never really sure when and where these speedy little warships would appear. How many men and resources the enemy had to employ to meet the challenge of Coastal Forces, men and boats that might have been used elsewhere, is difficult to know.

There was no doubt whatever that both the 29th and 65th Flotillas were pushed to their very limits of endurance by the Royal Navy under whose command the Canadians served, a severe test in the memory of a few Canadians that bordered on ruthlessness, a memory too, after all these years that is tinged with some bitterness.

"The Canadians were invariably in the thick of everything," said Garriock.

More remarkable was the pounding these small boats took in repeated actions, but yet returned again and again. The pre-war planners certainly failed to recognize the exhausting demands that were imposed on the crews in this kind of hit-and-run warfare, especially in the smaller seventy-one-and-a-half-footers, which were never built to live aboard but which, given the operational character of the small-boat war, became necessary.

Not surprisingly, few of the boats have survived. The most notable of the survivors is perhaps the famous MTB *102* that was at Dunkirk. She has been kept in more or less running order by a group of Sea Scouts in Essex. Quite a few of the larger Dog boats remained in service as long-range rescue craft used by the RAF, but by the late 1950s most were gone, sold as scrap. In any case, they were never built to last. Hurriedly assembled, some often went to battle still wet with new paint. In constant use during the war, many were literally falling apart. John Lambert, the British author of the definitive book on the development of the D-boats, recalled going aboard one boat where he was "shown the area under the forward mess deck where large angle irons had been worked into the framing to give added strength." Alex Joy, who served in the Mediterranean, saw his first command sink beneath his feet. The boat simply broke in two pieces, "it just split down one side and across the bottom," Joy remembered with a chuckle. Jim Kirkpatrick's boat MTB *748* ended up as a target ship in 1946, and presumably some time later was sunk by Royal Navy practice gunners. Other boats were sold after the war to various Allied governments, probably to the only kind of organization that could afford to operate and maintain them. This factor alone certainly was a significant reason why so few ended up in private hands. The boats were such enormous gas-guzzlers that even a millionaire's resources would be sorely tested.

To their list of achievements at war's end, the 29th and 65th could add this distinction: unwittingly, they had outlasted the other Canadian-led unit, "Wimpy" Maitland's 56th MGB/MTB Flotilla, which was formally disbanded in the spring of 1945 following the loss of *655*, the result of yet another mine explosion. This left only two of the original six Dogs in the Adriatic. Burke's *658*, now Reynolds's boat, finished the war as a "glorified lamp, directing convoys to Trieste" and a liberty ship for cruisers lying off the port. She was paid off in a solemn ceremony in August 1945.

Despite Jim Kirkpatrick's ruse to keep the 65th Flotilla's boats on the books to square up the rum account, they were in fact decommissioned at a rapid rate. Barely a week after VE-Day, Ollie Mabee's MTB *745* bore little resemblance to a fighting ship. Her guns wore canvas coverings, the ammo lockers were emptied, and the running and masthead lights, darkened since the day she was launched, now shone underway as she steered for Great Yarmouth for the last time.

Gunner Tom Jones recorded the end simply, stoically:

> May 18. Ship is decommissioned by 12:00 hours and all men are sent to *Niobe* with leave enroute.

One by one, the remaining ships were paid off. Crews departed, only a harbour watch left on each boat to bid the last farewell.

14

Here They Come Now

FOR ALL THE PUBLICITY the small-boat sailors received and the hoopla they endured during the Second World War, it seems odd that when they returned to Canada in 1945 they were soon as anonymous as when they had left their native soil. Many of them slipped quietly into their well-to-do lives again; others merely went about finding a job and keeping it. In the postwar boom, competition was tough.

In October 1989, several hundred members of the Canadian Coastal Forces Veterans Association met at the Royal York Hotel in Toronto. It was so unlike them, in a way. But there they were, mingling noisily, happily. Behind a podium at the front of the room was a tattered and somewhat faded white ensign, retrieved for the occasion. And spread out on tables to one side were photo albums some of the members had put together. These drew the biggest crowds.

But even the photographs—to an outsider—seem misleading. In one well-known picture of "The Three Musketeers," standing on a London sidewalk in 1945 (judging by the rank insignia on their sleeves), Maitland looks like a detective in a Hollywood movie, or a quarterback in that era when even professional athletes

244

wore leather helmets and very little padding. Ladner, he's your friendly neighbourhood milkman, if you can believe it, or possibly an accountant. So much for the visual record, except that Burke probably *always* looked the part, as he does in this particular snapshot. He had just the right amount of cockiness, his cheeky grin perfectly set on his angular Sinatra-like mug. Maitland and Ladner stand with hands curled at the bottom of their jackets; Burke made sure he had at least one of his hands thrust halfway into a pocket, as though concealing a revolver. He seems an agreeable sort, and likely amusing even if you haven't heard the stories about his exploits.

Yet, all of them were ruthless in battle, Ladner, as much as Maitland; Maitland as much as Burke; and so on. How this came to be was largely a combination of circumstances, although you have to wonder what such individuals would have done without the war.

There remains only to attempt to solve the riddle of what motivated these extraordinary young men. Patriotism? That was always part of it. Three square meals a day? That turned out to be a joke. So what was it?

Gordon Stead, whose mine-sweeping off Malta was lauded by many of the small-boat raiders, has tried to put it into words. In his memoirs, published in 1988, Stead wrote: "Men seem to need to put themselves at hazard now and then. In peacetime the means to do so must be sought, and not all of them are socially acceptable. My generation had a suitable occasion thrust upon it."

But is that enough? How was this ragtag fleet of small high-speed boats transformed into a "Champagne Navy," by men who not only "put themselves at hazard now and then" but sought it nightly on the war's high seas, closed to impossibly short distances with the enemy's small boats and carried out the most devastating attacks in the face of extreme risk of personal injury, or death?

Ironically, it was Harro Garmsen, who saw the war from the other side, who may have best captured the essence of why they did it, when he spoke to his former adversaries in Toronto in 1989.

"You have experienced the heady feeling, as I have, of six or eight boats running side by side at over 40 knots, with a bright moon behind and a target in front, white water rushing by, stern tucked deep and bows high, engines roaring.

"It was a young man's world."

APPENDIX

The following is a list of Dead or Missing, Presumed Dead in the fire that swept the 29th Canadian Flotilla in Ostend Harbour, Belgium, February 14, 1945.

Bahleda, Stephen H. Telegraphist. Mr. A. Bahleda (father), 2103 St. Urbain Street, Montreal, Quebec.

Bond, Neil A. Able Seaman. Mrs. E. Bond (mother), 3 Douglas Street, Glace Bay, Cape Breton, Nova Scotia.

Brown, Wilfrid L. Able Seaman. Mrs. Martha Brown (mother), 48 Duke Street West, Guelph, Ontario.

Brush, John C. Ordinary Telegraphist. Mr. John Brush (father), 1777 Moy Avenue, Windsor, Ontario.

Byrne, John E. Able Seaman. Mrs. N. Byrne (wife), 768 Markham Street, Toronto, Ontario.

Cathcart, Norman. Able Seaman. Mrs. M. Cathcart (mother), 5 Rose Avenue, Toronto, Ontario.

Crang, William R. Able Seaman. Mrs. Ethel Crang (mother), Outlook, Saskatchewan.

Cross, Albert J. Able Seaman. Mr. W. H. Cross (father), Post Office Building, Yorkton, Saskatchewan.

Dick, Benson G. Able Seaman. Mrs. L. Dick (mother), Hensall P.O., Ontario.

Gauthier, Joseph A. R. R. Able Seaman. Mr. H. Gauthier (father), 846 Flora Avenue, Winnipeg, Manitoba.

Hale, William Frederick. Lieutenant RCNVR. Mr. Samuel C. Hale (father), 187 Ash Street, Winnipeg, Manitoba.

Harper, M. Telegraphist. Mr. Frank Harper (father), 10710 107th Street, Edmonton, Alberta.

Hunter, Ian W. Motor Mechanic. Mrs. Verdun Hunter (wife), 508 Eighteenth Avenue West, Calgary, Alberta.

Kenny, James. Able Seaman. Mrs. Josephine Bond (mother), 554 Mary Street, Woodstock, Ontario.

Long, Charles W. Stoker First Class. Mrs. C. Long (mother), 170 Canon Street, Hamilton, Ontario.

Long, Gordon. Ordinary Seaman. Mrs. Emma Long (mother), 32 Sydenham Street, Woodstock, Ontario.

MacRae, Ralph. Able Seaman. Mrs. Sarah MacRae (mother), 41 Lansdown Street, Campbelltown, New Brunswick.

Motley, David C. Able Seaman. Mrs. Kathleen Motley (wife), 1046 Mason Street, Victoria, British Columbia.

Naydo, Michael. Able Seaman. Mrs. P. Naydo (mother), 450 North Avenue, Fort William, Ontario.

Newbigging, W. Able Seaman. Mrs. O. Newbigging (mother), 144 Winnett Avenue, Toronto, Ontario.

Park, William R. Able Seaman. Mrs. Gladys Park (mother), 159 Stanley Avenue, Hamilton, Ontario.

Purdy, Gordon F. Stoker First Class. Mrs. A. Purdy (mother), 4 Jones Street, St. Catharines, Ontario.

Routh, John M. Motor Mechanic. Mrs. Edith Routh (wife), Canoe, British Columbia.

Watt, John A. Motor Mechanic. Mrs. K. A. Watt (wife), Villa Coldicutt, 5-B, 1525 Marine Drive, White Rock, B.C.

Wellington, William E. Motor Mechanic. Mr. W. Wellington (father) 13 Bridge Road, Llandaff North, Cardiff, Wales.

Wright, D. S. M., James B. Able Seaman. Mrs. W. H. Wright (mother), 448 Stewart Street, New Glasgow, Nova Scotia.

BIBLIOGRAPHY

Bacon, Admiral Sir Reginald. *The Dover Patrol 1915–1917*. Vol I. London: Hutchison & Co, 1919.

Bekker, C. D. *Swastika at Sea*. London: Kimber Pocket Editions, 1956.

Bradford, Ernle. *Siege: Malta 1940–1943*. London: Hamish Hamilton, 1985.

Bryden, John. *Deadly Allies: Canada's Secret War 1937–1947*. Toronto: McClelland & Stewart, 1990.

Butcher, Harry C., Captain, USNR. *My Three Years with Eisenhower*. New York: Simon and Schuster, 1946.

Calder, Nigel. *The English Channel*. New York: Penguin Books, 1986.

Collier, Richard. *The Sands of Dunkirk*. London: Collins, 1961.

———. *1940: The World in Flames*. London: Hamish Hamilton, 1979.

Cook, Graeme. *Small Boat Raiders*. London: Hart-Davis, MacGibbon, 1977.

Cooper, Bryan. *PT Boats*. New York: Ballantine Books, 1970.

———. *The Battle of the Torpedo Boats*. London: Pan Books, 1972.

Dickens, Peter. *Night Action: MTB Flotilla at War*. London: P. Davies, 1974.

Donovan, Robert J. *PT 109: John F. Kennedy in World War II*. New York: Fawcett World Library, 1962.

Frank, Hans. "Schnellboote in Einsatz vor der englischen Küste 1943/44" (translated: "E-boats in Action off the Coast of England, 1943–44). Marine-Rundschan, 4/87.

Granville, Wilfred (with Robert A. Kelly). *Inshore Heroes: The Story of HM Motor Launches in Two World Wars*. London: Allen, 1961.

Hichens, Robert. *We Fought Them in Gunboats*. London: Michael Joseph, 1944.

Holman, Gordon. *The Little Ships*. London: Hodder & Stoughton, 1943.

Kemp, Peter (editor). *History of the Royal Navy*. London: Arthur Barker Limited, 1969.

Lambert, John. *The Fairmile "D" Motor Torpedo Boat*. London: Conway Maritime Press, 1985.

Law, C. Anthony. *White Plumes Astern*. Halifax: Nimbus Publishing, 1989.

Lawrence, Hal. *Victory at Sea: Tales of His Majesty's Coastal Forces*. Toronto: McClelland & Stewart, 1990.

Lower, Arthur. *My First Seventy-Five Years*. Toronto: Macmillan, 1967.

Lynch, Mack. *Salty Dips* (vol 1). Ottawa: The Naval Officers' Association, 1983.

Pope, Dudley. *Flag 4: The Battle of Coastal Forces in the Mediterranean*. London: William Kimber, 1954.

Pugsley, William Howard. *Saints, Devils and Ordinary Seamen: Life on the Royal Canadian Navy's Lower Decks*. Toronto: Collins, 1945.

Reynolds, Lloyd C. *Gunboat 658*. London: William Kimber, 1955.

Schull, Joseph. *The Far Distant Ships: An Official Account of Canadian Naval Operations in the Second World War*. Toronto: Stoddart, 1987.

Scott, Peter. *The Battle of the Narrow Seas: A History of the Light Coastal Forces in the Channel and North Sea, 1939–1945*. London: Country Life, 1945.

Stead, Gordon W. *A Leaf Upon the Sea: A Small Ship in the Mediterranean, 1941–1943*. Vancouver: University of British Columbia Press, 1989.

Tucker, Gilbert Norman. *The Naval Service of Canada, Vol II*. Ottawa: King's Printer, 1952.

Von der Porten, Edward P. *The German Navy in World War Two*. New York: Ballantine Books, 1974.

White, W. L. *They Were Expendable*. New York: Harcourt, Brace and Company, 1942.

Index

253

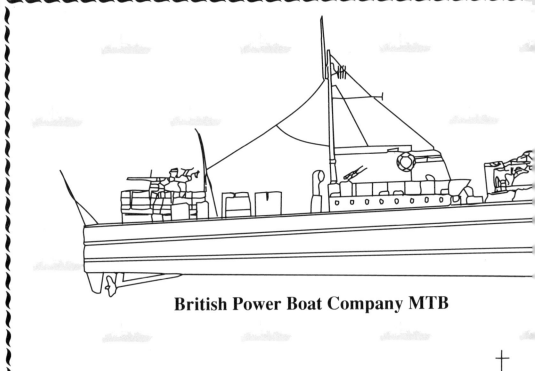

British Power Boat Company MTB

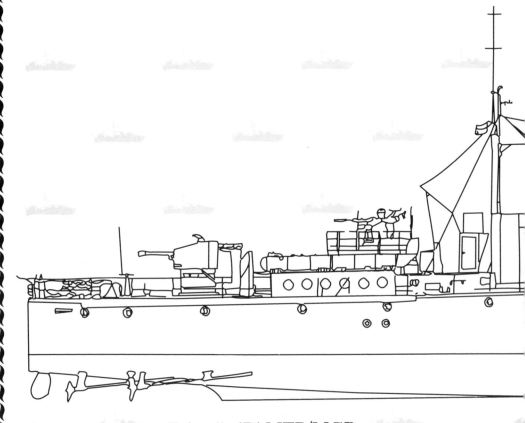

Fairmile 'D' MTB/MGB